BULLDOZED

BULLDOZED

"KELO," EMINENT DOMAIN, AND THE AMERICAN LUST FOR LAND

CARLA T. MAIN

ENCOUNTER BOOKS
NEW YORK · LONDON

Copyright © 2007 by Carla T. Main

All rights reserved. No part of this publication may be reproduced, stored in a retrieval system, or transmitted, in any form or by any means, electronic, mechanical, photocopying, recording, or otherwise, without the prior written permission of Encounter Books, 900 Broadway, Suite 400, New York, New York 10003.

Published by Encounter Books, an activity of Encounter for Culture and Education, Inc., a nonprofit tax exempt corporation.

Encounter Books website address: www.encounterbooks.com

Manufactured in the United States and printed on acid-free paper.

The paper used in this publication meets the minimum requirements of ANSI/NISO Z39.48-1992 (R 1997) (Permanence of Paper).

Library of Congress Cataloging-in-Publication Data

Main, Carla T.
Bulldozed : Kelo, eminent domain, and the American lust for land / Carla T. Main.
p. cm.
Includes bibliographical references and index.
ISBN-13: 978-1-59403-193-9 (hardcover : alk. paper)
ISBN-10: 1-59403-193-2 (hardcover : alk. paper)
1. Eminent domain—United States. 2. Kelo, Susette—Trials, litigation, etc. I. Title.
KF5599.M35 2007
343.73'0252—dc22 2007010622

10 9 8 7 6 5 4 3 2 1 / 2010 2009 2008 2007

CONTENTS

Author's Note

Quotations of spoken and written material from East Texas are true to local speech patterns. The use of *sic* has been avoided as an unnecessary distraction.

INTRODUCTION

At night, the tall spires of the Dow Chemical plant glitter for mile after mile on Highway 288, flickering in the dark as if they were part of some weird futuristic city. They are not really buildings, for there are no interiors—just looming, fantastic tangles of pipes that jut out in all directions. Still, they are easily the highest structures on this part of the Gulf Coast until you hit Houston. Their lights blink on and off against the Texas night sky, which stretches out like an endless roll of black velvet unfurled across the heavens. It would be lovely if it weren't for the occasional skunk-like stink that hits a driver in his face like a wet rag. Oh, it doesn't happen often, and you have to be downwind of it at just the right moment. But heaven help you if you are.

Welcome to Freeport, a place where reality has a rude way of blasting illusions to smithereens.

Freeport is an old industrial town on the Gulf Coast of Texas, dominated physically and financially by a hulking 5,000-acre Dow Chemical plant. The town itself is not much more than a small, bell-shaped curve jutting out near the mouth of the Old Brazos River, a skinny channel just a stone's throw from where the main artery of the mighty Brazos River finishes its journey from the arid heights of Texas hill country to the languid bayous near the coast. To the east, the land stretches out wide and flat against the Gulf horizon, with acre upon acre lying vacant near Port Freeport. The port was built a hundred years ago as a place for oceangoing vessels to offload goods bound for the vast Texas interior. Industry, fast-food joints, empty lots and motionless green water make up a large part of the vista in Freeport. It's not a pretty place, but then, a town founded and built up by a sulfur company doesn't need to be pretty. At least no one ever thought so during the twentieth century.

But lately things have changed in Freeport. There is an agitated sense in the air that things should be better than they are; it hangs over Freeport's many abandoned lots and its lonely, boarded-up downtown. The economic underpinning of the town's past—its sulfur mines and oil storage tanks and great fleets of shrimping boats—has buckled. The city council sees other towns prosper with tourists all along the strips of land that stretch down the rim of the Gulf from Galveston to Corpus Christi, and they wonder: What magic bullet does Freeport lack? The town's website tries to paint a picture of a tourist mecca with sunny beaches and a golf course. Only fleeting mention is made of the Dow plant that looms like a Colossus over Freeport, employing 5,000 people in this town of 13,500. Indeed, one has to hunt for any mention of Dow on the website, even though, truth be told, after the September 11 attacks the town worried that the chemical plant was a likely target for terrorists because of its size.

And then in 2003 the magic bullet appeared. One of Freeport's richest sons descended like a savior. True, he is not really one of them. He does not live among Freeport's working class in one of the tiny clapboard houses. It's not likely he would ever be spotted socializing at one of the city's riverside festivals. He is a son only in the sense that his family made a lot of money there many years ago and then left for greener pastures. But who can really blame them for leaving? A family with money moves on when it must. What matters is that he has returned. He was called to duty, in a sense, and he answered the call. After all, that is what the upper class is taught to do. What's more, he has been taught the ways of finance, and even has a degree in it. He knows what needs to be done downtown. Business is business—that's how rich people think, and maybe that's the sort of thinking Freeport needs right now.

The young man, thirty-four years old, has a name that befits his lineage: Hiram Walker Royall. He is the descendant of two of the greatest oil families in Texas history: the Blaffers (of Humble Oil, now Exxon) and the Campbells (of Texas Company, later Texaco). The Blaffers have been good to Freeport, donating the City

Hall building not long ago. They own a bank that used to occupy a large building on the main street downtown. When commerce dried up in Freeport, there wasn't much point in keeping the whole building for the bank, so they gave the building to the city. Now the bank occupies just half of it. Well, the city practically fell over itself in paroxysms of gratitude. The building is large and square and modern. It is three stories high. It is the tallest building in Freeport.

Walker has agreed to the proposition put to him by the town—at least that's how people on the city council tell it. That is to say, Walker did not seek out this deal. No, no, no. His family used to have a factory that sat on ten acres along the Old Brazos River. What a shame to see the land go to waste—and right across the street from the City Hall that the Blaffers were nice enough to donate. Now the young man, who has inherited that land along with ten of his cousins, will build a great marina, a tourist attraction. It will turn the town around, no doubt about it. He has generously agreed to use the old factory land to jump-start it all.

There is just one problem: the marina will require his neighbors' land, too, downstream and upstream.

At present, the land upstream is occupied by a family named Gore. They are an old-fashioned lot, persisting in a shrimp processing business called Western Seafood when nearly all such businesses on the Texas Gulf folded decades ago. It was founded by their grandfather, Wright Gore Sr., who came to the Gulf Coast as a young man and put everything he had into the business for fifty-five years. It will not be easy to get rid of these people who would expect to be paid market price for their land, if not a premium; they have a business they have no intention of giving up on anytime soon, a going concern where they are making a profit.

But there is more than one way to acquire a piece of land. The young man has a limited partnership. A deal is negotiated between his limited partnership and the city; copies circulate of a development agreement for a marina in Freeport. The city works hard to make the agreement happen. According to its terms, Walker will offer the old factory land, or at least part of it, in a complicated deal. He will provide no personal guarantees, nor will his partnership. The city will make a loan of $6 million of taxpayer money to the city's economic development corporation—a princely sum in a city where the annual budget is $13 million, the median income is $30,000, and 22 percent of the residents live below the poverty line. The economic development corporation, in turn, will loan the money to the limited partnership, which gets a nice, long tax abatement. The partnership has more than twenty years to pay the money back, assuming it is around that long—for this is a non-recourse loan. That means if the partnership goes out of business, the city is out of luck.

In exchange for its $6 million, the partnership is to construct the marina and give the city a lien on the profits it makes, if there ever are any profits, and a mortgage on the marina. As for the old factory land, which now stands vacant, it's hard to say if the dreamed-of hotel and condominiums will ever be built there; perhaps nothing will. The city council assures the citizens of Freeport that the town is protected if the deal is a flop and the developer bolts, since Freeport then gets to keep the marina and all the improvements. In other words, the town would inherit a failing business as its security.

And what of the Gores' land? Here is where the city must grit its teeth and make good on its promise if this deal is to happen: It must choose among its sons. The Gores have been in business in this thirteen-square-mile town for half a century. They employ fifty-six people, not counting the dozens of shrimp trawlers who sell their catch to them. The Gores' fate is closely tied to Trico Inc., a shrimp boat operator on the Old Brazos River. Trico will also be affected by the marine plan. If one falls, so will the other.

But a deal is a deal, and a bright gleaming future lies ahead. In addition to coughing up $6 million, the town must make the Gores' land available, as well as the land of all the other businesses on the Old Brazos River. So the city council takes a good look around. Why not use eminent domain? Hell, everyone else is doing it. They call them "economic development takings." Here's how it works: If a town has a distressed waterfront, or a dismal downtown, or a dingy outpost, or even a fear of sprawl, economic development can be a viable ground for a city government to use the power of eminent domain. The land is taken by the city and it pays "fair compensation" to the owner. (What's fair is a matter of some debate, especially when one party holds the cards, the legal power.) Then the city turns the property over to *another* private owner, usually a developer, who will build something new. The town reaps the benefits from an improved economy. A rising tide lifts all boats. Well, not *all* boats; a few of them have to be sunk first to make way for the developer. But Freeport is optimistic. The city council and its economic development corporation figure it's worth taking a shot.

So the town sets the legal machinery of a "taking" in motion. Then rumors start to fly. People talk about a marina. Then they stop. Then they start again. An item appears in the local newspaper. The Gores get some calls. "What's it gonna take to buy that property?" "It's not for sale." The Gores seek an injunction. And then another. Over the course of three years, they spend more than $450,000 in legal fees to save their business. Their son, Wright III, becomes locked in a battle with the city council, bringing one citizen ballot initiative after another in an effort to undo the marina agreement. The Gores sue the city. The city sues the Gores. Mud starts flying. The local media start covering the marina controversy on a regular basis. Council meetings turn into bimonthly brouhahas. Walker Royall sues Western Seafood. Walker Royall sues the Gores. By the end, Wright Gore Sr.—the bright and spirited eighty-six-year-old man who devoted himself heart and soul to his business, who ate and slept in the original "fish house" of Western Seafood back in the early days, right after he and his wife bought it with their life savings in 1950—has had a series of strokes, and the family debates how much to tell him about the case with its endless appeals and permutations.

Then history intervenes and everyone holds his breath. A momentous case winds its way up to the U.S. Supreme Court: *Kelo v. New London, Connecticut*. The modest houses of some working-class homeowners sit on suddenly desirable land overlooking Long Island Sound. These homeowners have challenged a project that is very similar to the one in Freeport. Here too there is a depressed waterfront, plans for a marina, talk of economic development, and intense attachment to the property. The judge in the Gore case stays (or freezes) their legal action until the *Kelo* case is decided. Like thousands of other individuals around the country who are the subject of takings, the Gores watch and wait during the winter and spring of 2004–2005 for the decision in *Kelo* that will likely seal their fate.

In the meantime, folks in Freeport take sides: the public officials, the ordinary voters, the downtown business owners, the Gores, the employees of Western Seafood, and a group of activists called Citizens for Freeport who believe their city council has run amok. Winter comes and the Vietnamese shrimp trawlers who have done business with the Gores for a generation sail home for the winter, as is their custom. The justices on the Supreme Court have no idea that their decision in *Kelo* could determine whether those Vietnamese shrimp trawlers will find Western Seafood still there when they come back to the Old Brazos River next year. But that's the funny thing about landmark cases at the Supreme Court: they trickle down into countless lives in myriad unexpected ways.

Western Seafood is the last shrimping business left on the Old Brazos River; there were nine back when Wright Gore Sr. founded the business. The Gores believe that the free market should decide whether they stay in business or fold. They say they are fighting for their constitutional rights. Many in the town see the family as a stubborn impediment to the rejuvenation that lies just around the corner for Freeport—a city ready to rise from its industrial, sulfuric past.

▪ ▪ ▪

On a chilly day in November 2004, a small group of people gathered in an auditorium at the University of Chicago Law School for a panel discussion on eminent domain. The panel included Professor Richard Epstein, a leading scholar in the field of law and economics who has written often on eminent domain, as well as a former Chicago municipal bureaucrat who oversaw eminent domain projects in that city. Dana Berliner was on the panel too. She is a public-interest law advocate with the Institute for Justice, who was representing the homeowners in the *Kelo* case. The panel's topic was the growing phenomenon of economic development takings, which represent an expansion of the traditional understanding of government power under the Fifth Amendment of the Constitution to "take" private property. In particular, the panel was there to talk about *Kelo v. New London, Connecticut,* which the U.S. Supreme Court had just agreed to hear in the coming term. The case would test how far communities may go in taking the land of their fellow citizens in order to shore up their sagging economies.

The power of the government to take private property is limited by the language that comes at the tail end of the Fifth Amendment: "nor shall private property be taken for public use without just compensation." The homeowners in *Kelo* were taking their case to the Supreme Court to argue that the words "public use" didn't mean that people's homes or businesses could be condemned and given to another private owner for the lone purpose of raising tax revenues or generating jobs. To allow "public use" to include this, they would argue, meant there would be no limit to the circumstances under which the government could swoop in and take private property. No property owner in America would be safe. The meaning of private property would fundamentally change. A homeowner or business owner would own his land or building only by the good graces of his local government.

I was moderating the panel as part my work as an editor at a national legal newspaper. Before the discussion began, I circulated among the audience, introducing myself to the guests, trying to gauge who had shown up. It was tough in those days to generate interest in eminent domain among the general public and the non-legal press. I noticed a tall young man with dark hair, who caught my eye because he was wearing a suit and tie. He obviously wasn't a University of Chicago student. He was unpacking a silver attaché case filled with rather elaborate recording equipment. That worried me; I had jumped through a lot of hoops with the protocol people at the University of Chicago for this event. Now here was someone taking out all sorts of high-tech gear. I introduced myself and asked what he was doing.

"Ma'am," he said politely, in a drawl I couldn't quite place, "I hope it's all right if I record this event. My town is trying to take my family's shrimping business. They want to build a marina. And the worst thing is, they want to give the land to our next-door neighbor. I'm trying to learn all I can about eminent domain. I've come here from Freeport, Texas."

"You came all the way to Chicago just for this event?"

"Yes, Ma'am."

"What's your name?"

"Wright Gore III."

I got clearance for him to record the event and gave him my business card.

"Stay in touch with me, Wright. Let me know what happens in your case."

Wright was not the only person who had traveled far to hear a discussion about the *Kelo* case that day. The audience included a couple from New Jersey whose house was caught in limbo while an eminent domain project dragged on, and there was a woman from California who stood to lose a farm. The phenomenon of economic development takings was well known at that time chiefly among a small circle of legal practitioners and academics, real estate developers and municipal bureaucrats. Beyond that, in the wider American public, takings were akin to grave diseases that had become intimately familiar to the families of the afflicted few, but were unknown to most people.

By the end of the afternoon, I began to appreciate the intensity of the feelings that those living through such takings had for those rare scholars and advocates who were speaking out against economic development takings back in 2004. When the panel discussion was over, some people in the audience had stayed around to speak with the panelists. The young man from Freeport handed me his camera.

"Would you take my picture with Dana Berliner?" he asked. "She's my hero!"

He stood next to her and smiled as broadly as if he were having his picture snapped with a rock star. A moment later there was a bit of a commotion a few feet away. The woman from California had joined a small circle of people who were chatting with Professor Epstein. Suddenly she blurted out quite loudly, "Richard Epstein is a god!" Professor Epstein, usually unflappable, took a quick step backward. There was a tense moment when we all stood looking at each other in silence. I considered calling security. But the woman got hold of herself and then decided to buttonhole me. "You have no idea what they are doing to farms in California," she said in a low, urgent whisper.

The small circle of *Kelo* watchers was keeping a close eye on the case because the eminent domain world had already been rocked by another watershed event just a few months earlier, in the summer of 2004: The Michigan Supreme Court reversed itself, admitting it had been wrong a quarter-century ago in the infamous Poletown case. It was Poletown, Michigan, that started the ball rolling in earnest on economic development takings. Back in 1981, the Michigan Supreme Court decided that it was a legitimate use of eminent domain for the City of Detroit to clear five hundred acres and hand it all over to General Motors. The people who lived there had tried to stop the onslaught. There was a legal challenge, widespread protests (some led by Catholic priests disobeying their own dioceses), and sit-ins at churches. Men sat with rifles on their front porches, daring the bulldozers to do their jobs. In general, chaos reigned for six months.

In the end, a living, breathing community was leveled and some 3,400 people were relocated. The GM factory was built, but never operated at capacity; it sputtered along, providing only a fraction of the jobs promised. The cost to the city, state and federal governments exceeded $300 million, a fortune in rust-belt times. The social cost of Poletown was incalculable.

Despite the mess it left in its wake, Poletown served only to embolden cities around the country. It proved that with enough political will, the little man could be moved out of the way for all sorts of projects intended to jumpstart local economies. Federal and state money could be made to flow and private money could be raised by bringing in local developers and businesses. "Public use" could mean something as vague as better times or that ultimate elixir: jobs. Poletown laid out the enticing prospect of a new kind of public-private partnership, and set the stage for two decades of economic development takings. The Poletown model was copied again and again, usually on a smaller scale; the pattern was repeated in New London, Connecticut, scene of the *Kelo* drama, and in the marina project in Freeport.

In truth, the erosion of property rights began long ago in America, but the public wasn't paying close attention. Early warning signs emerged in the nineteenth century, but social and political forces aligned to keep the use of eminent domain in check. The modern expansion of government's use of eminent domain began piecemeal in the twentieth century and took off with the passage of the Federal Housing Act of 1949. It catapulted into a national phenomenon after *Berman v. Parker* (1954), which gave the constitutional stamp of approval to the use of eminent domain for slum removal.

The U.S. Supreme Court in *Berman* said that if a legislature determines it to be in the public interest to improve a community by removing an entire neighborhood, lock, stock and barrel, it is not the place of the court to second-guess the legislature. There followed a tidal wave in the use of eminent domain during the heyday of urban renewal, mostly hitting minority communities. This cleared the way for the relocation of thousands of Poletown residents to make room for a factory. Subsequently, people were booted out of homes and businesses around the country to make way for big-box retail stores and luxury boat marinas, in far less dire economic circumstances than those facing Detroit in 1980.

▪ ▪ ▪

The question at the heart of economic development takings is not whether they always hurt those forced out. Some owners sell willingly, and some among the very poor may reap windfalls. This happened even amidst the general calamity of Poletown. And of course, there are also those who come in afterward to garner the benefits—the developers who make a profit, the towns that fill their coffers with taxes, the shoppers at the big-box stores, the buyers of the condominiums, the tourists. They all figure into the equation. The question this book sets out to answer is what price American society pays for economic development takings.

America has always aspired to be a society of equality before the law. When we allow such takings, we risk becoming a society with two sets of rules—one for those who have political or social or financial power, and another for a small group within the community who must make an unfair sacrifice so the rest may prosper. (The same holds true when we allow "blight" takings in poor neighborhoods, where blight is an excuse for an economic development project, a way to force poor people out of a neighborhood so as to bring in richer people.) When we set up such divisions at the local level, we corrode the fabric of American culture, our sense of how we are supposed to live with each other.

What happens when we take a group of people in a small town who have known each other for decades and endow them, if they serve on the city council or the local economic development corporation, with the power to take away each others' homes and businesses and destroy each others' lives? Urban planners, municipal officials and economic development corporation officers defend the practice as a way of assembling land. "Just compensation," they say, takes care of the "unfair burden" part of it. They call it sound economic planning. At a town hall meeting in Freeport about the marina controversy, a woman in the audience had another name for it: "coveting thy neighbor's house."

PART 1

A GLEAM IN FREEPORT'S EYE

CHAPTER 1

THE FISH HOUSE

American Dream stories aren't supposed to end this way. An old man lies in bed surrounded by the proof of a lifetime of hard work and ingenuity: a beautiful house in a lovely subdivision, birds chirping in the garden, two gleaming white luxury cars in the garage. Yet he cannot rest. Death approaches, but he cannot die in peace. Day after day, he fretfully asks his firstborn and favorite grandson, "Did you get a judgment yet?" There are lawsuits pending; his life's work hangs in the balance. His devoted grandson, Wright III, has no choice but to answer, "Not yet, Pappy, not yet, but we will." The old man tells him, "Don't let them take it from me." It wasn't the way Pappy Gore's life was supposed to end. Not given how far he had come.

Wright Winston (Pappy) Gore was born in 1919 in Trinity, Texas. He was about as poor as a little boy can be. His daddy worked a number of jobs: in the oilfields, as an engineer on the railroad, in the cotton fields. Pappy spent most of his youth in the spare, unforgiving part of Texas known as the Highlands. He had two pairs of overalls when he was very young, one that he wore during the week and one that he kept for church on Sundays. It was a childhood filled with hard labor and the knowledge that you worked for the necessities of life. "He tells stories of the great American Depression," said Beth Gore, Pappy's daughter-in-law, the wife of his eldest son, Wright Jr. "He would have to go shoot a squirrel if he wanted some dinner."

Pappy Gore worked with his family in the cotton fields, where his parents would find him out of breath in the blazing Texas sun. They thought they had a very lazy boy because he kept "pretending" to faint or going off to lie down. "Don't be lazy," they admonished him, fearing he would amount to nothing. Their child actually had a hole in his heart, a condition that was not corrected until he had open-heart surgery when he was forty years old.

"They didn't know," Pappy said, waving his arm, forgiving his parents as he listened to relatives recount this story. He was eighty-six, and speaking was difficult after a series of strokes. "They didn't know," he insisted.

Pappy loved to learn, but hated the schoolmarm, a strict disciplinarian who had no patience with a cut-up like him disrupting her classroom with his antics. Fortunately, at this point in his childhood he had lucked upon a pair of wide-wale corduroy pants, thick enough to soften the blows of the fierce whippings administered by the schoolmarm, after which he was banished to the schoolroom closet. But fear not; this turned out to be a great boon to his education. For there the schoolmarm, great enemy of fun and learning, had stored the treasure of all treasures: the *World Book Encyclopedia*. Pappy would keep the closet door open just a crack to allow in enough light so he could read the encyclopedia all day long, drinking in A to Z of famous men and women, exotic places, foreign wars and civilizations and all manner of diseases and animals. It was glorious and well worth the whipping.

A poor boy became a man quickly in the Highlands in those days. A visitor asked Pappy, "How old were you when you were responsible for taking care of yourself?"

"Fourteen," Pappy answered, forcing the words out through his dysphasia.

"What kind of work did you do?"

"Anything. I would do any work."

The year was 1933. Tall for his age but still a child, Pappy had to earn his keep. "He started working in service stations when he was just a kid," said Isabel Gore, his wife of sixty years. He pumped gas and later drove a laundry truck. Graduating from high school with dreams of a better life, he enrolled at Lee College in Baytown, Texas, and began studying chemistry. He was going to put himself through school. But his education was cut short when Tillman Falgout asked Pappy to go to Galveston Island and run a Gulf Oil service station for him and deliver fish to the Falgout and

Godfrey fish markets. Falgout was a partner of Walter Godfrey. The Falgouts and the Godfreys were among the most powerful Texas business families of their era. So Pappy went where Tillman Falgout sent him. He started working on Galveston Island in the early 1940s. At that time, Galveston Island was considered a high point of civilization along the Gulf Coast of East Texas. There were grand hotels, bathing beauties, casinos and dance halls and even some legendary racketeers. There was money to be made in a place like Galveston Island. There was the pulse of life.

But Pappy never stopped longing for an education. Later on, when he was working from dawn to the wee hours of the night as his own boss at Western Seafood, in rare moments of leisure he loved to sit at the kitchen table and read the dictionary. He would search out the perfect word for every nuance of human emotion or thought; Merriam-Webster never had a bigger fan. "My grandfather had a vocabulary like William F. Buckley," said Wright III.

In the mid-1940s, the Falgouts had the idea of setting up their own "fish house." A fish house is a place where shrimp boats offload their catch and sell it to a processor, who prepares the shrimp for sale to a wholesaler, who in turn supplies it to retailers all over the country. In this way, the Falgouts could sell the shrimp to retail outlets of their own on Galveston and along the Gulf Coast. Around 1945 they bought a small tract of land about 200 feet wide in a little town in East Texas called Freeport, right on the banks of the Old Brazos River, which empties into the Gulf of Mexico. They decided that Pappy should go down there and establish the shrimp business for them. Once again, Pappy pulled up stakes. Leaving Galveston Island for Freeport was not a step up in terms of locale, but Pappy had little choice in the matter. He set out for Freeport to run a little company called Western Shellfish.

One day a young woman named Isabel Maier came to Freeport to visit her sister, whose husband worked with Pappy at Western Shellfish. Her sister introduced her to Wright (Pappy) Gore.

"Six weeks later we were married," said Isabel Gore. Pappy was twenty-six; Isabel, still a teenager, had just graduated from high school. "Wright had a friend who was the judge up in Alvin, so we got married up there."

Isabel and Pappy Gore worked side by side at Western Shellfish. It was hard work. Some would say it was a man's work, but Isabel didn't mind. She was no stranger to hard work or to shrimp. Isabel Maier Gore was one of eight children—"the fourth in line"—from Ocean Springs, a small town on the Mississippi Gulf Coast near Biloxi. Her father was an itinerant canning plant supervisor. "We went where the work was." When she was a young child, her father supervised a shrimp canning plant. She and her brothers and sisters started helping their daddy at the plant at the age of five or six. "There weren't any laws back then at the time. We worked when we had to." Isabel's family moved around the Gulf Coast, going next to Franklinton, Louisiana. "My daddy ran a vegetable canning plant there," said Isabel. Later they settled in Bayou La Batre, a tiny Gulf outpost that would become famous in the movie *Forrest Gump* as the setting of the Bubba-Gump Shrimp Company.

When Isabel and Pappy settled into Freeport in 1946, there was little in the town that a Hollywood director would have found picturesque. Freeport was just beginning to shake off its reputation as little more than a Gulf Coast pesthole.[1] But Isabel and Pappy didn't intend to work for Tillman Falgout forever. They had dreams and ambitions for the future.

Not all young married couples in the eastern part of Texas were living such hard lives in those years. Houston and its environs had a high society, and for its stars the world was a glistening oyster. The unquestioned queen of that society was a woman named Sarah Campbell Blaffer. "According to many of Houston's old guard, Sarah Campbell Blaffer was the nearest equivalent of Texas royalty," says *Debrett's Texas Peerage*. "Her husband was Robert E. Lee Blaffer, a founder of Humble Oil [later Exxon]. Her father, William Thomas Campbell, signed the original charter of the Texas Company, which became Texaco. The Blaffer-Campbell marriage combined two of the world's great oil fortunes. Governor James Hogg, a partner of Campbell's, later called it, 'the conglomerate of the century.'"[2]

Sarah Campbell Blaffer's great-grandson H. Walker Royall was slated to be the developer of the Freeport marina project, for which the City of Freeport wanted to take Pappy Gore's property.

Around the same time that the newlywed Gores were pulling themselves up by sheer force of will from the grimy oilfields of

Texas and the sticky poverty of Mississippi bayous, Sarah Campbell Blaffer's children were coming up in Houston society. John, Jane, Cecil Amelia (Titi) and Joyce had been raised by "a French governess and spent every summer on her farm in the wine district of Charente in order for them to perfect their French, and their mother to visit the studios and galleries of Paris."[3] Mrs. Blaffer's children and grandchildren received their secondary education in the Northeast, an uncommon thing in many Texan circles, and her home became a literary salon. She developed a keen eye for paintings and became an enthusiastic art collector until her death in 1973; she shared her paintings with all of Texas by making donations to public collections, a fact that endeared the Blaffer name for generations. To honor her husband, who died in 1942, she founded the Robert Lee Blaffer Memorial Collection at the Museum of Fine Arts, Houston, in 1947, through which a large and generous collection was given to the museum.[4] She insisted that there be traveling exhibits of valuable masterpieces she donated, at a time when such a notion was unheard of. "Mother wanted a museum without walls," said Titi Blaffer von Furstenberg, "because she herself lived in a small town once and never forgot the hunger of intelligent people in such places for excellent things." (Titi was married to Tassilo von Furstenberg, whose son Egon was married to Diane von Furstenberg.) *Town & Country* magazine, known for chronicling the nation's wealthiest and most powerful families, did a profile on "Blaffer Women" in December 1981.

Sarah's son John Hepburn married a young woman named Camilla Davis, whom he met at her debut party, which was covered by *Life* magazine.[5] Camilla was no slouch in the lineage department; she was the daughter of the Texas real estate tycoon and banker Wirt Davis.[6] The couple followed in the tradition of John's mother. If there was a fundraising ball for the Museum of Fine Arts, Houston that needed organizing, Camilla pitched in along with her sister-in-law Jane Blaffer Owen. Through Houston's new Allied Arts Association they were involved in creating the first museum ball, called the Beaux Arts Ball of 1952. The ball was given intermittently until 1960, and then it became a yearly event under the steady hand of the Blaffer sisters. Camilla and John donated a wing to the Kincaid School, a prestigious private school in

Houston founded by Robert Lee Blaffer. The couple also funded the construction of a wing at the Museum of Fine Arts, Houston, dedicated to the memory of Robert Lee Blaffer.[7]

Jane Blaffer had made an interesting match too. She was married to Kenneth Dale Owen, a descendant of the British industrialist and philosopher Robert Owen, who helped found New Harmony, a utopian society in Indiana established in the first half of the nineteenth century. Jane later undertook the enormous project of restoring the town of New Harmony, which had gone to ruin over the past century. She also donated many new structures, including the "Roofless Church" designed by Philip Johnson, "a dazzling-white library" designed by Richard Meier, an inn built by an Indianapolis architect named Evans Woolen, and ceremonial gates for the town sculpted by Jacques Lipchitz.[8] Clearly, this was a family that had an eye for beauty and wasn't shy about combining its love of art with civic causes.

Sarah Blaffer's four children gave her numerous grandchildren. John and Camilla had five children. Their oldest child, Camilla (Coco), married a man named John Royall. Coco has enjoyed society life, although her last name caused a bit of confusion in England, where the word "royal" has a literal meaning. According to Richard Kay, observer of British blue bloods for the *Daily Mail,*

> Multi-Millionaire oil heiress Coco Blaffer (her grandfather founded what became Exxon Oil) can dine out for years on what happened to her when she attended the glittering 50th anniversary ball for the Guards Polo Club. Coco—who has homes in London, New York, Monaco, Rhode Island and Houston—thought the £1,175-a-ticket for the Windsor Castle event was worth it, not least because it was hosted by the Queen. She tells me: "Mostly I am 'Coco Blaffer.' Coco is short for Camilla and Blaffer is my maiden name. But I went to the ball under my married name of 'Camilla Royall.' When I told the equerry who I was, he just stared at me and asked: 'are you an imposter?' Then, when I met the Queen, she exclaimed, 'We have had trouble with that name before.'"[9]

Hiram Walker Royall, who goes by "Walker," is Coco and John Royall's son. His name alludes to a family connection to the famous Scottish liquor business. Walker tends to stay out of the limelight. He runs an investment company in Dallas and serves on the advisory board of a company called Sun Resorts, which operates commercial marinas in the Texas Gulf region and in the Caribbean. His Sun Resorts bio describes his company, Briarwood Capital Corporation, as a "real estate investment vehicle with an emphasis on Texas retail properties." The company "currently oversees a portfolio valued at more than $100 million," the website says.

Though some Blaffer women went to school in the Northeast (Coco went to Bryn Mawr; a first cousin, the noted anthropologist Sarah Blaffer Hrdy, attended Radcliffe and Harvard), Walker stayed closer to home and attended a traditional Texas school, Southern Methodist University, where he got a BBA in finance and real estate. At thirty-four, Walker is a nice-looking young man, tall and fair with broad shoulders and a rather patrician appearance. On a website for Maverick PAC, a loosely organized fundraising group of young Texas Republicans, there is a picture of Walker at an event. He is wearing a pinstriped suit with an understated tie, the very picture of upper-class elegance. He looks perfectly at home in the mahogany-paneled room lined with bookcases as he chats casually with George P. Bush, the nephew of the president. George P., being much shorter than Walker, looks up at him with an inscrutable expression, a mixture of seriousness and what can best be described as puzzlement. To the left stands Bryan Pickens, heir to the Dallas Wildcatters. We will never know what Walker, George P. and Bryan Pickens were talking about that night, but whatever it was, that mahogany room was a world away from the troubles of a small industrial town like Freeport.

▪ ▪ ▪

Freeport wasn't much to look at in 1945. The official story of Freeport's founding is that a sulfur company came to town in 1912, and that's true. But it was a few hundred Cajuns who had paved the way, laying out the town in a grid pattern. They numbered the streets from one to twelve, skipping from Second Street to Fourth Street because they couldn't pronounce the "th" sound in "third." They figured the town was rightfully theirs and would seldom see outsiders. Why suffer a lifetime of embarrassment mispronouncing an awful word like third? Better simply to leave it out. After all, the Gulf Coast in those days was no place to stand on ceremony. Life was rough, the work was dirty, and there was little or no escape from the heat and humidity and mosquitoes. So there was something slightly off-kilter about Freeport from the very start—an insistence on pretending something is there, when everyone knows perfectly well that it isn't.

The Freeport Sulphur Company turned the town into the world's largest sulfur mine, discovering great reserves of the resource at Bryan Mound and filling the city's Cajun nostrils with its rotten-egg odor. Soon Freeport was rollicking with industrial action as sulfur was loaded onto the cars of the Houston and Brazos Railroads to be shipped inland. By 1929, the population had zoomed to 3,500, enough to justify building some schools. In 1937, the town was so respectable it had two schools: one for whites and one for blacks. But eventually the sulfur mounds petered out. Today the red-brick processing plant is a crumbling relic on the banks of the Old Brazos River, sitting alongside the detritus of other failed business ventures.

The real action that would sustain Freeport for the long term began when the Dow Chemical Company, which showed up in the late 1930s, stepped up its activity in Freeport during World War II. It's impossible to overstate the importance of Dow's presence there. To imagine Freeport without Dow is similar to picturing Washington, D.C., without the federal government. Approximately 13,500 people live in Freeport. Dow employs 5,000 of them—4,000 in blue-collar manufacturing jobs. Although people casually refer to the "Dow plant," these words might create the wrong impression for out-of-towners. What Dow laid down around Freeport is a sprawling complex that stretches across 5,000 acres in three different locations, on both sides of the Old Brazos River, complete with a canal system for transportation among the plants and direct access to the Union Pacific Railroad, whose rail line sweeps across the north end of Freeport and makes a loop-de-loop through miles of Dow industrial land. It is the largest chemical facility in the United States. And it is not the only chemical plant in Freeport. Just west of Dow Plant B is the BASF plant; there are also Synthetec and Rohm plants in town.

As early as 1940, Dow had major industry contracts to fulfill and essentially had to create a town where its workers could live.

The Dow Hotel was built on East Broad Street in 1940, slapped together in three weeks' time. For many years, the only hospital in town was on the Dow industrial grounds. Soon the Dow Hotel was filled to bursting, so Dow brought in a building crew to put up bungalow-style houses in record time, and also dug the sewer lines. These houses would become the permanent homes of Dow employees involved in construction of a new magnesium plant. Eventually, Dow built hundreds of residences like these. Many of them are still standing, and given Freeport's demographics, it's likely that many are still occupied by Dow employees. They are the same houses that the city now scrutinizes, cruising up and down the streets to check for peeling paint, torn screens, cracked windowpanes or tall weeds, and citing the occupants for violations in a program of strict code enforcement, lest the city appear to have fallen on hard times—which it has.

Dow wasn't the only business that wanted to be on the Old Brazos River in the 1940s; the Falgouts considered this a good place to build a fish house. In fact, it was perfect for shrimping boats to come in from the Gulf and offload their catch, protected from the strong tides and hurricane winds. And the location made transporting the shrimp inland a breeze.

Pappy Gore worked hard managing the fish house in Freeport for the Falgouts and the Godfreys, displaying shrewdness as a businessman. Western Shellfish and the Gores survived the war years, since Pappy realized that shrimp could always be bartered for other goods, and he made sure that the local military officers always had enough shrimp. He was firm but fair with the shrimp trawlers who brought in their catch from the Gulf, and held on to his best worker by paying him twenty-five cents an hour more than anyone else on the river. He and Isabel lived frugally and saved enough money to buy their own little house on Sixth Street in Freeport. It was the first solid thing either one of them had ever owned. Two of their three sons were born there: Wright Jr. and Raymond. It looked to Pappy like the years of itinerant work, of being dirt poor, of worrying about where his next job was coming from, were finally over.

Then in 1950, Tillman Falgout told the Gores he was thinking about closing down Western Shellfish and selling the property. He didn't see a future in the shrimping industry.

Pappy was thirty-one years old. He'd been working for other men for seventeen years, since he was a boy. Just like his father. That was what all the men he'd grown up around in the Highlands had done—never having something they could call their own, working themselves to death for other people's balance sheets. Pappy had known hunger as a child. He was still hungry, but in a different way: hungry for something better. And he knew how to work. When you come right down to it, he figured, isn't that what it takes to make it in America: hunger, work, self-reliance?

"It was do or die," said Pappy Gore.

He and Isabel sold the house on Sixth Street and everything else they had to scrape together $6,000 for the down payment. Isabel took the boys, Wright Jr. and Raymond, who was still a baby, and they got on a train to Bayou La Batre, Alabama, where Isabel's mother lived. Conditions were very bad. "You don't have to be more than four or five years old to know that Alabama is not the place to be living with your relatives," said Wright Jr. Meanwhile Pappy moved into the fish house, a wooden structure that abutted the pier and wasn't meant to be lived in. It was a 1,000-square-foot shed, filled with wooden crates, large tables for sorting and heading shrimp, ice buckets, ice-crushing tools and a cold-storage room for crushed ice and shrimp. But Pappy was there, twenty-four hours a day, seven days a week for six months. Then, after what seemed like an interminable separation, the young couple was reunited. Pappy got a trailer and they parked it on the property near the fish house. Eventually they changed the name of the business to Western Seafood. For the next sixty years, Pappy and Isabel were inseparable, working side by side at Western Seafood. Isabel did any work "a woman her size can do," Pappy said. "Hell, she wanted my job!"

"We lived in a little ole trailer down here, just a little trailer," recalled Isabel. "And of course, they didn't pay any attention. They'd just knock on yer door and say, 'Hey! We need some *ice*!'"

By "they," Isabel was referring to the shrimp trawlers of the Texas Gulf, who would start knocking at the little trailer door at five o'clock in the morning. "Shrimpers, their hours were five o'clock in the morning 'til twelve o'clock at night. The shrimpers would say 'We need ice. We need to put ice on our boat.' We'd have to get up and do it!" said Isabel. "We worked twelve, fourteen hours a day. My mama came and she took care of my boys when they were small. Later, we got a nanny to take care of them. We got to prosper a little bit and we could afford more and more." Isabel soon had a third boy, Gary.

In the early days of the shrimping industry in America, shrimp boats were small and wooden, typically 35 to 40 feet long and 15 feet wide. The shrimp trawlers would leave port before dawn and fish until late afternoon in the shallow waters of the Gulf. They had to come back daily because they had no refrigeration on board; they could store only a day's catch of shrimp in the ice they had loaded that morning. The shrimp had to be offloaded that day at a packing house—a "fish house" like the one run by Pappy and Isabel.

Once the shrimp boats got their ice and were out to sea for the day, then the real work began. "We'd have to clean off the docks, get the ice ready to ice the shrimp," Isabel explained. "We'd have to crush the ice. They'd throw a 300-pound block down and we would crush it. There was a machine, it was electric, but we had to operate it ourselves. The kids really don't know what it's like to have to work the way we did. Of course Wright Jr. works hard. But it was different then.

"During the day, we had to head the shrimp that came in from the night before. They came in with heads. Everything was by hand. We had eight employees." The workers, Pappy among them, would heave the tubs of shrimp, pouring out the glistening loads onto the heading tables. Thousands could be headed in a single day. "We had these headers [employees], who took the heads off the shrimp, and they'd help us. We'd never sell 'em with the heads on 'em. They'd come in with the heads on 'em and we'd take 'em off. That would be done in the fish house.

"That would go on into the morning [after midnight]. Then we'd ice 'em down and then the next morning we'd start again." Whatever shrimp had not been headed the night before would have to be finished before the current day's load came in. This work would go on throughout the day until the shrimp boats returned, around four or five o'clock in the evening. Then it would begin again with that day's catch.

The white shrimp season takes place during the height of the Texas summer heat in July and August, and the old fish house was not air-conditioned. "It got pretty warm in there," Isabel recalled. "But not to the extent that it was intolerable. Wright set up a system of fans. And we had all the open windows so we had enough fresh air too."

Somewhere between the heading and the ice-crushing, Pappy and Isabel would keep the books, negotiate with the wholesalers and the ice sellers, oversee the unloading of ice, maintain the plant. The shrimp had to be sorted into boxes and weighed. Counting shrimp is an art and a science. Merely weighing the shrimp doesn't tell you how many are in a box; only years of experience enable a man to do that. Pappy would negotiate payment with the shrimp trawlers, who lived or died by what they made on a day's catch. Pappy had to give them a fair enough deal to keep them coming back to him. After all, the Gulf Coast back in the late 1940s and early 1950s was littered with fish houses competing with Western Seafood, not to mention those along the Old Brazos River. "All up and down the river," Pappy recalled, "nine fish houses when we were getting started. Now there's one." But Pappy still had to figure in a margin for profit when he sold to wholesalers from inland. What price would the wholesale market bear? Every purchase he made from a shrimp trawler was a calculated risk.

They worked seven days a week, month in and month out. "In those days, there was no off season," said Isabel. Today, the shrimp season is from July to September. Back then, the shrimp trawlers fished for brown shrimp, too, from January to April.

"I worked from can till cain't" said Pappy.

"That means you work, until you *cain't* work no more," said Isabel.

They worked hard enough to earn the respect of the Falgouts. After making the down payment, Pappy and Isabel had been making monthly payments to Till Falgout on the balance they owed him for the property. "They gave us an opportunity to lease-purchase the property, because they wanted to move out of Freeport. So we did. Every month we made our little lease payment. I think there was still $5,000 that we still owed on the property, and Till Falgout said to us, 'You kids have worked so hard, I'm just gonna forsake that last $5,000. I'm gonna give you the deed to that property.'"

Five thousand dollars was a fortune in the early 1950s. Pappy Gore would not forget Till Falgout's generosity. Over the course of his life, Pappy helped other people start their own businesses. He never said no when private charities or the town of Freeport called at the door of Western Seafood for help or donations, nor would his sons. And so the American Dream began for Pappy and Isabel: sweat, daring and a little luck had placed them on the humid banks of the Old Brazos River in East Texas, where the shrimp trawlers were numerous and their catches were abundant. Year after year, the business grew. They bought more land. They expanded into related businesses. They paid more taxes to the city, the navigation district, the county. For fifty-six years, Freeport was very glad to have them there.

▪ ▪ ▪

The shrimping industry in the Texas Gulf has changed since the old days. Now it is dominated by Vietnamese shrimp trawlers in their single-owner boats; they like to trawl only for white shrimp during the summer and then sail home to Vietnam for the winter. Since their boats have refrigerated cargo hulls, they can stay out in the Gulf for weeks at a time, and shrimpers like the Gores don't have to pack the shrimp on ice every single night, the way Pappy and Isabel did. Back when they started the business, there were trawlers of many more nationalities and they took brown and white shrimp, during both seasons, and without refrigerated cargo hulls. They'd go out early and return late each day. The Gores would keep the business open on Sunday, when other shrimp processors along the river were closed. That kept the trawlers coming back to them one extra day and hopefully more days during the week. Over the years, the other shrimpers on the Old Brazos River went out of business, one by one, but the Gores stayed. Pappy still believed in the future of the American shrimping industry. He was not only expanding, but going into related enterprises.

"One day, my grandfather had to buy a shovel," explained Wright III. "So he went to the local hardware store in town and it cost eight dollars. And he knew that was too much and he figured he could get it for less at another place.

"So he drove around and sure enough he found the same shovel for two dollars. Now, he knew that when the shrimp trawlers came in and docked on the Old Brazos River, they picked up all kinds of supplies to fix their boats. They all went to that hardware store because it was nearby. My grandfather figured they were getting ripped off there. So he got the idea to sell the trawlers what they needed right there at Western Seafood. And sell it cheaper and better."

That was the beginning of Marine and Industrial Specialties Inc., a maritime supply business. Not far from the Western Seafood fish house was an old, unused schoolhouse, and next to it a decaying building that had served as a "bus barn." Pappy bought the bus barn from the city and turned it into a store, making the front look like an old western trading post adorned with a decidedly unsexy sign that says "Marine Industrial." "My father had the idea that if you make it look too good, the shrimp trawlers will figure you're not giving them enough for their shrimp, so he decided to fix up this old school bus garage as a store," explained Wright Jr. The inside of Marine Industrial is a cavernous space, like a Home Depot, filled with every imaginable item one could need to stock or repair a boat. It is not a place for dabblers or sportsmen, but it is heaven to a man who knows what he needs and how to use it. The Gores eventually bought the old schoolhouse too, boarding up the windows and using it as a warehouse for the marine supply business.

Marine Industrial became a variation on the old coal mining "company store" system: the Gores extend credit to the shrimp trawlers at the beginning or end of the shrimping season so they can repair their boats and buy supplies. The trawlers pay back the debts with shrimp. Isabel became an expert at balancing these accounts, which she calls "settlements." The Vietnamese trawlers have grown especially fond of her, calling her "Mama." She has been balancing the accounts and keeping everyone honest for fifty years now.

The system set up by the Gores with Marine and Industrial Specialties is an extraordinary example of what Francis Fukuyama, in *Trust: The Social Virtues and the Creation of Prosperity,* calls a high-trust relationship. Shrimpers walk into Marine Industrial and walk out with goods without paying for them. The Gores take no security for the goods. "We hope they catch enough shrimp the next season to pay for them," said Wright Jr. There is no guarantee that they will do so, nor can the Gores even be certain they will return; it is simply hoped that they will. These are shrimpers, bear in mind, who sail back to Vietnam every winter. The shrimpers, for their part, are trusting the Gores to give them a fair price both on the Marine Industrial goods and on the shrimp catches that will serve as barter. It is an arm's-length transaction that is completely consensual and based on mutual trust. It makes a striking contrast to the eminent domain warfare that would go on between the Gores and the town over a period of several years, marked by extreme mutual distrust from the get-go. That in turn resulted in what economists call "high transaction costs." Ordinary humans call it big legal fees, stress, lost business opportunities, bad karma.

Until 1999, Western Seafood still operated out of the original fish house. Then the Gores moved the operation downriver into a modern processing plant that was formerly used by ConAgra. Built to access the docks, it's a 30,000-square-foot concrete structure, easily the largest on the south bank of the Old Brazos. Wright Jr. purchased state-of-the-art shrimp processing equipment from Iceland, which required custom installation. Moving into the new facility was a $1.7 million investment for Western Seafood, begun in 1993 and completed in 1999. The investment was made with the assumption that the Gores would be in business there for many years to come. During a good year, Western Seafood grosses $40 million. The company has steadily employed fifty-six people. The big central room with the Icelandic equipment is immaculate and barely smells of shrimp. During the height of white shrimp season, the room is kept as cold as a refrigerator. As much as 4 million pounds of shrimp is processed through that room in a good season, 2.5 million in a poor year. The company used to operate some of its own shrimping boats and still sells shrimp under its own labels: Western Waters and TexSeaCo. "Most of the shrimp wind up on the East Coast," said Wright Jr., "in places like the Chesapeake Bay area, Philly and New York." Though there have been difficult years, the company has continued to be profitable.

The last few years have been very hard in the American shrimp industry. Pick up a bag of shrimp at the local supermarket and you'll see that it says, in small print, "Farm Raised." That means it comes from Thailand, India, China or another country that farm-raises its shrimp, using chemicals to ward off disease, rather than catching them in fresh waters as American trawlers do. But the Gores were standing up to the competition. After fifty-six years in business, the family was used to ups and downs. "Shrimping is like farming," said Beth Gore, who is Wright Jr.'s wife. "There were Christmases where we could buy a lot. One year we bought a pinball machine for the boys. And then there were Christmases when we had to tell the boys, 'Not this year.'"

Wright Jr., having worked alongside his father since childhood, joined the business on a formal basis after he graduated from college—the first in the Gore family to do so. He has been running the business since the 1980s, when Pappy began to slow down. His younger brothers, Raymond and Gary, have worked in the family business since the mid-1970s. All three brothers bought homes, raised their families, planned their children's future and their own retirement on the assumption that Western Seafood would continue as a family business as long as the market held out. Despite recent spikes in fuel costs and the dumping of farm-raised shrimp on the U.S. market, Western Seafood was holding its own. But odd things were starting to happen.

"I remember the first time that we realized that they wanted to put the marina right on our property," Beth recalled. "It comes out on the front page.... Big picture: this is where the marina is gonna be. And Wright looks at it and says, 'I don't think so. That's our property!' And that was the first time, that we kind of had an inkling, aware, that they were gonna put the marina on our property. There was the big picture, you know, what they were projectin'. Where the marina was gonna be and there was our property, right over there."

Yet it hardly seemed a reality to the Gores. The plans appeared to ebb and flow. The city made informal assurances that something could be worked out.

In the summer of 2002, the strange phone calls began. Lee Cameron, the head of the Freeport Economic Development Corporation, started calling Wright Jr. He seemed to be calling on behalf of H. Walker Royall, which was odd, because Lee worked for the city and Walker was a private citizen. "Walker wants to buy this property," he said. It seemed that Walker was going to develop the old Intermedics site and wanted to buy Western Seafood's property. Intermedics was the business that the Blaffer family used to own next to Western Seafood; the plant had been shut down years ago. It seemed these calls had to do with a marina on the Old Brazos River. Wright Jr. told Lee that he wasn't interested; the Western Seafood property wasn't for sale. The Gores had heard something about a marina, but Wright Jr. "kinda thought that was kind of pie in the sky," said his wife, Beth. Wright Jr. couldn't understand why someone from the city was calling if this was going to be a private marina. Some things just weren't making sense.

Lee Cameron was persistent. He arranged a meeting in Houston in early fall 2002 and asked Wright Jr. to attend so they could discuss the marina project, on the premise that it was an important change to the river where his business was located. The marina would abut Western Seafood land, and there were navigation issues. "My father had no experience in real estate, and I did," said Wright III. "So he asked me to come to the meeting." Wright III had an MBA from Rice University and had worked in commercial real estate. Before the meeting, he did some poking around and found that the City of Freeport had commissioned a master plan by the Maritime Trust Company, an urban planning firm that specializes in waterfront developments. He got hold of a copy. Hardly light reading at nearly eighty pages, the master plan recommended the development of a marina on the Old Brazos River. It also zeroed in on the neighborhood near the waterfront known as the East End, which had many older homes, and identified *every* residential property there as "blighted." To reach this conclusion, Maritime Trust had relied partly on appraisal figures supplied by the City of Freeport, which the city had gathered in its own blight study exactly one year earlier.

The Gores were under the misapprehension that they were being asked for their input on an important civic undertaking, and Wright Jr. did have grave concerns about safety on the river if a marina were built there, not to mention the fact that the drawings in the master plan showed docks very close to Western Seafood. These docks could cause serious navigation hazards for both the yachts and the shrimp boats. But what particularly worried Wright Jr. was Lee's entreaties to buy the Western Seafood property for Walker, despite his refusals.

The meeting was filled with government people: Lee Cameron; Ron Bottoms, the city manager; and John Smith III, a city council member. Also present was Charles Leyendecker, a member of the legendary Houston real estate family. H. Walker Royall, the marina developer, was supposed to be there too, but he was running late.

In the meantime, the men pored over the aerial shots of the river in the big foldout map that was part of the Maritime Trust study. Wright Jr. was concerned about the way the marina plans as they had been explained to him, and the master plan illustrating them, called for long docks running out into the center of the channel, eliminating the deepest navigation waters. Shrimp boats don't navigate well in shallow water; if they had to sail upstream past the docks in shallow water to get to Western Seafood, it would create an obvious hazard. Wright Jr. talked about how the smaller boats on the river would be tossed about like flotsam, competing for space with the larger boats.

"My father explained to them that it would be better to build the marina upriver, past the businesses that are on the Old Brazos," Wright III said. That way, the shrimp boats would never have to sail their way around the docks. Instead, the much nimbler yachts would be passing the shrimp boats and the businesses on their way upriver. It would be better for everyone. But Wright Jr. was thinking like a shrimper, not a marina builder. The businesses along the Old Brazos were ugly—a sight to see and not in a good way. Who wants yachts and sport-fishing boats sailing past all that? If the shrimping operations and the pile-driving service and the other commercial enterprises were going to clash with a marina, then *they* would have to be the ones to go.

"It was at that meeting that they started talking about condemning Trico and Wanda Jones's property," said Wright III. Trico is a shrimp boat operator on the Old Brazos, run by Dennis Henderson. The catch from Trico's boats accounts for 20 percent of Western Seafood's business. Wanda Jones owns a commercial storefront building near the river. Lee Cameron told Wright Jr. that he would probably have to get rid of Baron's shipyard, just upstream from Western Seafood. Baron's does sandblasting and painting. Lee's rationale was that Baron's line of work with its noise and dirt would conflict with the marina. The reality of the situation was beginning to dawn on Wright Jr.

Then Walker arrived. "He was wearing an expensive suit," said Wright III. "He looked like a Texas oil man."

Actually, Walker was the descendant of two legendary Texas families, but that didn't quite register with the Gores at first. Right off the bat, Wright III recalled, Walker "started talking about us moving the large blue packing house" upriver. "Walker was saying, 'we could do a no-cost swap. Your property for another property.' It was as if the packing house were nothing," said Wright III.

The packing house Walker referred to is the center of Western Seafood's operations, the 30,000-square-foot concrete building with its state-of-the-art Icelandic equipment. The packing house works in conjunction with Western Seafood's adjoining docks, the Marine and Industrial Specialties depot, the old brick schoolhouse that serves as the marine supply warehouse, the Western Seafood office and related buildings that together constitute the small corporate village of Western Seafood, occupying several acres along the Old Brazos River. Walker made no suggestions as to who would pay to "move" the packing house upriver, assuming such a thing could even be done.

It became clear that this was a meeting to discuss a marina that would be downriver of Western Seafood—no matter what was in the way. It seemed there wasn't much more to talk about. The meeting broke up. That was the last the Gores ever saw of Charles Leyendecker, as his involvement in the marina project ended. Later, the name of Sun Resorts became associated with the project. Walker sits on the advisory board of Sun Resorts, a well-known marina management company on the Gulf Coast. The managing director of Sun Resorts is Johnny Powers, who attended the BBA real estate program at Southern Methodist when Walker did in the early 1990s.

At first, Walker's comments about "swapping land" and "moving" the packing house struck the Gores as so far out of left field that they didn't sink in, said Wright III. "It was only later, when we walked outside and got into our truck, that it hit us. 'Did Walker really say that?'" As they drove home, they thought again about the comments Lee Cameron had made about Wanda Jones's storefront property and about Dennis Henderson's Trico shrimp boat operation right down the road. *I can't guarantee we won't use eminent domain.*

But even at this point, the Gores had not put all the pieces of the puzzle together. They knew that H. Walker Royall was somehow connected to the Blaffer family. Earlier in 2002, Wright Jr. had entered into a lease arrangement with Walker for a warehouse that sat on the old Intermedics site, which people in Freeport called the Blaffer land. They knew that Walker was associated with a limited liability partnership called Freeport Waterfront Properties LP. But they still didn't realize that Walker *was* a Blaffer. "We just didn't click to any of that until later," said Wright III.

What the Gores would eventually "click to" was this: That H. Walker Royall had inherited an interest in ten acres of waterfront property next to Western Seafood's land on the Old Brazos River—specifically, the Blaffer land. That Walker and the City of Freeport had big plans to put a private yacht marina on the choicest part of the Old Brazos River, where boats are sheltered from storms, with possible hotels and condominiums on the Blaffer land. That the whole point of the project was to develop the part of the river where the Blaffer land sat, and to make a happy marriage of that parcel and everything else that Freeport, a willing bride, could give away as its dowry. That there would be no talk of a marina upriver, away from the shrimping operations like Western Seafood and Trico, because this was to be a private marina, developed by Walker and run by Sun Resorts. That to Walker, this deal would be one of many in his busy financial portfolio. But to the city, it would become a focus of political warfare, a matter of civic life or death.

■ ■ ■

The winter of 2002 and the spring of 2003 came and went, and little was said to the Gores about their property. That strange meeting in Houston faded into the background. Oh, people around town talked about the marina from time to time, but "we couldn't believe they were really gonna pursue that," said Beth Gore. It seemed that the storm had passed—until late August 2003.

On an ordinary Wednesday, as the summer was drawing to a sticky end in Freeport, the Gores opened up a copy of the *Facts*, a newspaper for Brazoria County, and read this headline: "Freeport Puts up $6 Million for Marina." This time, it seemed very much for real, the details very much pinned down. The article said that the city was going to loan $6 million to H. Walker Royall so he could build the marina, taking $3 million out of reserves and raising $3 million with certificates of obligation. The marina would be built by a "partnership" made up of "heirs of the Blaffer family," which would put up Blaffer-owned land in town plus cash as collateral. "If they default, the city gets the land," said Ron Bottoms, the city manager.[10] The city was pretty far along in the planning. They even knew exactly where this marina would go: between Cherry Street (where Western Seafood's property began) and the Pine Street Bridge.

Now the city was pestering Wright Jr. in earnest about 330 linear feet of Western Seafood property directly east of the packing house. If the city were actually to take this waterfront land by eminent domain, as they were threatening to do with some of the properties downriver, the docks and the packing house would be unusable. The Gores repeatedly offered to negotiate a compromise: Take 100 feet. Hell, take 150. Leave us the rest, the upriver portion, they said, so we can still access the river and offload the shrimp.

"I felt like we'd able to come up with some sort of thing just to be able to let 'em, give us, let 'em—" said Wright Jr. He was almost stuttering when he talked about the possibility of losing the business his father founded and to which he has devoted his life. "Let 'em buy half of our property that they wanted. Make it a three thousand, uh, a three thousand one hundred and fifty foot project instead of a thirty-three hundred foot project. What could it matter? And not steal it from us."

Wright Jr. soon learned it was not meant to be that simple. "Lee Cameron liked to say "eminent domain" since the first time he ever showed up," said Wright Jr., recalling the negotiations between the Gores and the city that summer. "At the time," added Wright III, "we did have the regular eminent domain gun to our heads. It was right up front, from the very beginning, something that was threatened, not part of this 'last resort' sort of thing that people talk about."

The Gores were about to embark on a three-year, half-million-dollar odyssey that would take them through the state courts, the federal courts, the seamy underside of municipal politics, and the state legislature in Austin. It would include fighting off not only a federal administrative proceeding and eminent domain suits by the city government, but also a defamation suit brought by H. Walker

Royall, as well as a breach-of-lease suit for $40,000 or so brought against them by Royall's limited partnership—the very same limited partnership that was going to develop the Freeport marina. Yet the strangest land they would visit was the compensation side of eminent domain, a weird netherworld where the property owner negotiates with no leverage, sitting at a table with people who are not the decision makers, for a goal he does not even desire.

Freud once said that biology is destiny. Had he lived on the Gulf Coast, where access to natural resources is the key to survival, he might have said that geography is destiny. Dow Chemical knew it, so they built a sprawling plant around a town that had been only a Cajun spit on the map, and started churning out magnesium and chlorine, moving it easily around thousands of acres on their own barge system, near a river, near the Gulf, near railroads. The Falgouts and the Godfreys knew it, which is why they sent Pappy Gore to Freeport to establish a shrimping operation for them on the Old Brazos River. Pappy Gore knew it, so when the Falgouts were ready to give up on shrimping, he reached for that waterfront property near the Gulf and established his own business there. And the Blaffers knew it. When they invested in a medical business, they bought waterfront property on the Old Brazos River. It happened to be right next door to Pappy Gore's land.

The only thing that Freeport had going for it after coughing up the last of the stinking mounds of sulfur that had given rise to the city in the first place was its nearness to the Gulf and the way it sat astride the Old Brazos River. Everything that made Freeport livable was on the south side of the river: the numbered streets that the Cajuns laid out long ago, the little square houses that Dow built in the 1940s, waterfront businesses, the downtown shops and the City Hall. The north bank of the river was industrial corporate land, chemical land. In the 1970s and 1980s, Freeport expanded beyond the East End, its original downtown, but the farther the town moved away from its riverside origins, the lower its fortunes seemed to sink.

Strictly speaking, the Old Brazos River, which winds its way around like a snake from the west end of town to the east and then empties into the Gulf of Mexico, isn't a river at all. People just call it that for old times' sake, and to make it sound grander than it really is. It's actually a channel, and the distinction matters.

The Old Brazos River used to be a tributary of the "mighty Brazos," which trickles from mountains in New Mexico to form a river in the great central expanse of Texas and empties into the Gulf of Mexico in a town not far south of Freeport. Many years ago, that small tributary was cut off from the main river with landfill at the western end of Freeport. This created an independent channel that runs through Freeport and empties into the Gulf. At about 500 feet wide, the Old Brazos is too narrow and too shallow for oceangoing barges or container ships to navigate, but the shrimping boats do just fine.

And so would yachts, if they could be enticed to come there. The city is convinced that people would clamor to dock their yachts in a commercial marina in Freeport. Then investors would build restaurants and hotels on the waterfront, and Freeport would become a destination, just as Ron Bottoms has been saying all along. "One of the keys to our economic vitality is tourism, creating ourselves as a destination," he wrote in a memorandum to the city council accompanying the 2005–2006 budget. *Build it and they will come.* But why would a yacht or a sport-fishing boat take the trouble to sail up the Old Brazos River, which is a good half-hour from the mouth of the Gulf? There is nothing beautiful about the Old Brazos, especially the stretch near Freeport. At the moment, in fact, it's one of the ugliest places anyone can imagine and there's not much likelihood of its becoming suddenly a lot more scenic in the foreseeable future. The north bank is littered with the detritus of Dow's industrial past and hums with the company's present commercial activities. There is nothing romantic about a chemical plant.

Dow's history in the area can be read along the north bank of the Old Brazos River. Slightly upriver from where the marina will be built sits an abandoned railroad trestle bridge that juts halfway out across the river, every inch a rusted relic. Nearby is another structure that used to connect to it: a huge section of the railroad bridge with high arches and crossed beams of rusted steel, sitting on a round perch. The whole contraption looks as if it once turned on a spigot like a lazy Susan, but now it is frozen in place. Near the railroad bridge is a building that must have been its operations tower; the roof is now completely rusted through. Just downstream from it, gargantuan storage drums lie around on their sides as though they had been tossed hither and yon by bored teenage Titans. Downstream, opposite to where the marina is planned, sits the concrete plant; this is not a relic but a lively operation. A large storage building with yet another rusty roof looms in the background. The real eye-catcher, though, is the concrete works itself: a system of dredging and gravel pouring that involves huge, bright yellow towers and sifters resembling giant-size Tonka Toys. Finally, if you are there on the right day you can catch sight of the Dow barge lumbering through the Dow canal with its cargo, or the trains making their loop-de-loop, carrying their loads to market. It will give the sport fishermen on their yachts plenty to see as they sip their beers or martinis. That's for sure.

The 2003 development agreement for the marina project called for the city to "exercise best efforts" to "request Dow Chemical to beautify areas across the Old Brazos River from the Project Site." Translation? The city has to ask Dow, pretty please, clean it up. But as generations of street-smart New Yorkers know, askin' ain't gettin'. After all, what's in it for Dow? And even if Dow did sweep up a bit, there is nothing Dow could do to alter the fact that beyond its immediate shoreline lie miles of industrial land, huffing and puffing through the daily chemical manufacturing routines. This would be the delightful view from any hotel windows—in the event the hotels are ever built.

But that is the ultimate goal of the marina development in the minds of the city fathers. *Build it and they will come ... to Freeport!* And "they" will want to build hotels here and restaurants and shops. All these projects will be built in the only place they can be built, which is on the south bank of the Old Brazos River. At the moment, the vacant land available for such projects is the Blaffer land, which Walker Royall was to contribute to the deal as equity. At least that was how things stood at the beginning.

Anxiety was running high in Freeport over whether the city council and the economic development corporation would eventually get the notion in their heads to begin condemning people's homes to make way for all those hotels and restaurants and businesses that would miraculously revive the city. It wasn't hard to observe certain realities, what with the Blaffer land and the Gore land being right next to each other and the Blaffers getting to keep their land and the Gores having theirs condemned. People who were poor couldn't help but feel vulnerable. What's more, it doesn't seem to have occurred to the City of Freeport to condemn any land belonging to Dow, the better to clean things up and build a scenic view. The plans are for the other side of the river, where there are smaller fry the city can push around, like the Gores and Dennis Henderson and Wanda Jones.

No, Dow is there to stay. The thing that has everyone clamoring over the Old Brazos River is not its beauty. Rather, it is a rare body of water that can actually be closed off on *both* ends, and then reopened on one end. There is landfill at the western end and a guillotine gate on the river near the eastern end of town. True to its name, the gate looks and functions like a giant guillotine. It is a looming steel structure that sits above the middle of the river, supported by long masonry walls that form a low-lying dam spanning the river from bank to bank. Ships pass underneath the lifted gate. In the event of a tidal storm, the enormous steel gate slices downward, setting a wall in the middle of the channel and closing off all possibility of rising water flooding into the Old Brazos River from the Gulf of Mexico. If you own a small boat and there is a storm coming, the ideal place to be is inside that guillotine gate, safe from the waves crashing up against the other side. But when the city first installed the gate about twenty years ago, it wasn't built high enough to accommodate ships with tall masts. At first the city tried dredging the river so taller ships could get through, but eventually the guillotine gate was becoming a hindrance. Something had to be done. The engineering solution was to raise the gate, reworking the masonry so the bottom edge of the steel sheet stood higher above the river and passing masts would not hit it. That would cost the city $300,000, a huge expenditure at a time when the town could ill afford it.

So Wright Gore Jr. paid half the expense, $150,000, out of his own pocket and Western Seafood's coffers. It made good business sense to fix the guillotine gate for Western Seafood and all the other enterprises on the river. What was good for the town was good for business. And it was his way of giving back to the city where he had grown up, the city that had given his father a shot at the American Dream, where he was now raising his own children. There was civic recognition, a handshake with the mayor, a ribbon-cutting ceremony, a picture in the local paper.

Many years later, that improved guillotine gate would become the big draw for a Freeport marina. *This will be the safest harbor in East Texas!* But Western Seafood—with its river traffic of lumbering shrimp boats and an industrial-looking packing house—was standing in the way of progress. Never mind that there was far uglier stuff on the north side of the river. The guillotine that Wright Jr. made possible was about to come down on his head.

Freeport has fallen on hard times. One by one, the downtown stores have closed up. Now when a stranger arrives, the downtown is an eerie place. Most of the windows are boarded up. The streets are deserted. The white lines painted on the streets perpendicular to the curb are gleaming and bright in the sunlight. It takes a moment to remember what the lines are for: so people would know where to park their cars. The downtown waits, frozen as if it had been dipped in amber. Freeport's population is roughly the same as it was twenty years ago, hovering below 14,000. To make matters worse, the downtown sits across from the Freeport City Hall, a constant rebuke to the town officials. The boarded-up windows mutely protest their fate, prodding the city to do something—anything—to revive them.

So the City of Freeport looks to the Old Brazos River to save it. Come to Freeport and the first thing people show you is a map. Not because you are lost, but because *they* are lost. "Let me explain the geography," they will say with tremendous excitement. In geography lies salvation. There is only so much land along the Old Brazos that is inside the guillotine gate on the south bank of the river. The city is prepared to elbow out anyone it has to from the land inside the guillotine gate in order to do this deal—to put an end to those silent rebukes once and for all.

CHAPTER 2

THE MYSTERY FAX

Talk of the marina in Freeport came, and talk of the marina went. Truth to tell, people had been talking about a marina in Freeport since the 1960s, so at first it was hard to know whether this was serious or just a lot of hot air. Then city officials started calling the Gores, leaning on them to sell. Wright Jr. explained to them that the 330 linear feet of property directly to the east of the blue packing house meant life or death for Western Seafood. But he did understand that the marina was important to the city. There was another 100 feet owned by a Gore company called Western Shellfish, a little farther downriver, and he was willing to negotiate on that. And maybe he could accommodate the city on part—just a part—of the 330 feet adjacent to the Western Seafood packing house. This was the crucial waterfront land used for offloading shrimp from the boats into the processing plant. The 330 feet constituted the "packing line," where boats lined up and a complex system of cranes and conveyors brought millions of pounds of shrimp out of the ships' hulls and hauled it into the plant. Without that land, the packing house would be like an airport without a runway.

As surreal as it seemed at moments, there was reason to believe it would all go away, like a bad dream, or at least end tolerably. After all, Pappy Gore had been a well-known businessman in Freeport since the 1940s. And when one looked at the devastated downtown area, the Gores were one of the largest taxpaying businesses left, with a payroll of fifty-six people and a sizable piece of land. It would be insanity to put them out of business. At least that's what they kept telling themselves. Beth Gore recalls a man who used to be on the city council: "That's when this was first developing and he said, 'Well, of course we expect Western Seafood to . . . protect your interests, we don't wanna—you wanna make sure your business is there and everything. I know you have lots of questions.'" And so the Gores went on with their lives.

A week after the August 27 article in the *Facts* with a banner headline announcing the launch of the marina project and the $6 million loan to H. Walker Royall, the plan was met with mixed enthusiasm by a *Facts* editorial. "There are plenty of skeptics," the newspaper said. "One noted that if the project were a sure bet the city wouldn't have to make the loan. The banks would have been lining up." The *Facts* observed that the city had been discussing the marina project with the Blaffers—and apparently *only* with the Blaffers—as early as 2000. This disturbed the newspaper's editorial board. "[T]he city seemed to be putting a tremendous amount of faith in a single developer. . . . [It] would have been wise to open the door to other offers just to see what else might be out there."[1]

The newspaper had another wild idea: competitive bidding, at least for some of the project. "We also questioned whether it might not have been a good idea to open various phases of the project to competition rather than handing the whole thing to one firm, and we expressed concern that it was the city and not private developers that seemed to be taking much of the risk. Now, with the city dipping into its rainy day fund to finance this project, those doubts haven't waned." Nonetheless, the *Facts* editors were "pulling for" the city.[2]

As the news settled on the city, the residents tried to figure out what to make of it. Was this a Blaffer land grab, or a brilliant stroke on the part of city officials, or some combination of the two? Could it be the bold step forward that would finally turn Freeport around, or was it just the latest dumb idea to come out of City Hall? Right away, there was concern about that $6 million coming out of city coffers. Meanwhile, city officials were coming around Western Seafood and talking about the two parcels of waterfront property. The city was making plans to move forward, and the words "eminent domain" were coming up in negotiations. But the parties were trying to stay civil, trying to talk.

Then in early September 2003, just as the shrimping season was winding down and the Gores thought perhaps they could work things out with the city over the winter, something very mysterious happened. Someone sent a fax, with no cover sheet, to the offices of Western Seafood. It was a copy of a document issued by the Army Corps of Engineers, Galveston District. It said "Public Notice" in one-inch, bold letters at the top.

It almost escaped notice. Wright Jr. reviews the mail in the Western Seafood office. "I'll tell you. You're not going to believe this. I usually, in our company, I go through the mail . . . not every day, depending on the time of year, and a lot of these things, as you can imagine, just end up going in the trash," he said. "But, uh, it caught my eye, from the U.S. Army Corps of Engineers, a bundle in there, and I set it aside and I said, literally, I'm curious about this, and looked and looked and I thought, this looks so familiar, and it's *our property* and it's an application by the City of Freeport to replace our docks with their docks."

The fax had a lot of legal mumbo-jumbo about a permit application, but in the midst of all that there was something about a marina and a dock platform and the Old Brazos River and the City of Freeport, with a map and some nautical terms. Now Wright Jr. has never been much for legal documents, but the map and the schematic drawing showing a marina with piers and the description of the coordinates spoke to him. It was very clear: *This is about us. These docks are going up right over our part of the river. They'll cut off our access.* He looked at the dates. The notice said: "Date Issued: 27 August 2003" and "Comments Due: 12 September 2003."

The day he got the fax was September 8.

"For whatever reason, and I'll never understand it, you ordinarily are notified of these things thirty days ahead of time and you have thirty days to respond and so forth, and we literally, we were *four days,*" Wright Jr. said, holding up four fingers in the air, his face flushing a deep crimson. He is a kindly-looking man in his late fifties with not much hair left after three years of worrying, and when the blood rises up to his face, it continues all the way up to his scalp. "Why I'll never know. I have no explanation as to why we had four days instead of thirty days. I'll never know, but there it was."

Though Wright Jr. is normally a quiet man who prefers to leave the talking to his eldest son, when he relives the experience of how he stumbled on the public notice, the words come pouring out, as if from a spigot. "Now the court takes this position and most people think, and rightly so, that here's a stretch of waterfront property, and you own this and I own that and he owns this, and by and large I have access to that water adjacent to my property and you have access to the water adjacent to yours and that's the tack the court takes, *unless, unless* someone comes along and applies for a permit to do otherwise," Wright Jr. said. "If I come along and quietly apply to the court to put my docks in front of your property, now my docks are not touching your property, I wouldn't be allowed to take my docks and run parallel to your property or touch your property. But I could run them back to my property if you raise no objection to it. If you raised no objection, then the court would say, well, she doesn't care, let the city do it. Well, we were within four days of that happening."

To run a dock adjoining or actually touching property requires additional approvals from the Texas Government Land Office. The city clearly would have to obtain such approvals for the docks it intended to build for the Freeport marina, as well as negotiate a lease with the GLO for an easement (the right to use the waterway itself). But the Army Corps permit application put the Gores' rights of navigation on the river at risk. If the Army Corps approved the plans, "they would have had everything of value associated with that 330 feet of waterfront property in front of Western Seafood," Wright Jr. explained. Imagine an airplane terminal that lacks clearance for planes to take off. Without river access, there could be no Western Seafood. Without Western Seafood, there is no need for Marine and Industrial Specialties, as the shrimp trawlers would have no reason to moor their boats on the Old Brazos River and buy supplies there. The Gores would go out of business.

"And, and the unlikely—and this kept striking me—the unlikely scenario, almost unbelievable scenario," said Wright Jr., "is what we have here is a threat of eminent domain or condemnation situation and the way we're responding to it is with our admiralty attorney who we've used for personal injury situations and defenses on our boats and things of that nature, because I had *four days* and who could I think of who would be familiar with federal maritime permits with the Corps of Engineers and that's who I thought of. And so to this day, our 330 feet is in federal court before the Fifth Circuit, right?"

He looked at his son for confirmation. The case had been pending in federal court for about three years. But there were also corresponding condemnation cases in state court—and the constant legal Ping-Pong game between the cases, as well as the appeals and the injunctions that lifted up and down like a drawbridge, had confounded Wright Jr., as they would anyone who has spent a lifetime in business, not law.

"Correct," said Wright III gently.

The Gores never learned who sent the fax. If Wright Jr. had not happened to glance at the pile of mail on his desk that day, or had not understood the fax's importance, Western Seafood would have waived its right to challenge the permit application. Without opposition, it's far likelier that the right to build the docks would have been granted. The fish house would have been cut off from the river permanently. The Gores would have had a hard time obtaining compensation, because strictly speaking no act of eminent domain would have occurred under state law (since their land was not taken), and because they would, in effect, have waived objection to the public notice. No matter what actions the city took later (for example, starting an eminent domain action against them to acquire their waterfront land), the Gores would have been crippled financially and legally by having lost their access to the Old Brazos River and hence their ability to operate Western Seafood. Had they lost water access, the value of their riverfront property would have been practically nil. They certainly would have lost all leverage. It would have been over before the Gores ever had a fighting chance.

Not knowing whom to call, Wright, Jr. figured that since the permit application related to the river, his admiralty lawyer might know something helpful. He called Randall A. Kocurek, a Houston lawyer who had handled ship-related matters for the Gores for many years. He had successfully defeated a frivolous personal injury suit brought by a seaman who claimed to have been injured on a boat. At trial, Randy showed videos of the man playing volleyball and helping to move heavy furniture. The judge came back with a verdict entirely in the Gores' favor. Randy had been their hero. But this was a different kind of case entirely.

Randy Kocurek had never handled anything related to eminent domain; the sea, not terra firma, was his domain. Over the next three years, the Gores would approach a number of high-profile firms in Texas with condemnation practices, asking them to take the case. They would all decline. Some said they had conflicts. Others simply said it was impossible to challenge a takings case on its merits in Texas. "They're looking at the political influence of the City of Freeport as opposed to our little operation down here, and who wants to get capped up in all that?" asked Wright Jr. And taking a position opposite to the interests of the Blaffer family may well have been an unattractive option for many firms. As a result, Randy, who has his own solo practice with a few associates, gamely remained with them on the case for three years, arguing all manner of constitutional and state statutory issues up to the Fifth Circuit Court of Appeals.

Randy had to formulate just what sort of lawsuit this would be. His aim was to convince a federal judge to issue a permanent injunction against the United States of America (since the U.S. Army Corps of Engineers is a federal agency). To make matters even more hairy, the central claim that Randy was bringing was a very unusual and complex wrinkle on an eminent domain claim: stopping what amounted to an inverse condemnation—or a "regulatory taking"—by the construction of docks. The clock was ticking. The first goal was to stop the Army Corps from giving anyone permission to build docks on that river before the Gores had a chance to weigh in. Randy could either go into court directly or seek relief first from the federal agency.

For four gut-wrenching days, Randy, Wright III and Wright Jr. marshaled their resources to figure out what the hell had happened in Freeport and to get either an extension from the federal agency or an injunction from the federal court, or both. Either way, something had to be done before the official comment period ran out on September 12. Federal regulatory comment periods are *not* fluid and federal agencies are generally not lax about extending them. Randy had a tall order ahead of him. The key point he wanted to get across to the Army Corps in his initial contacts with them was that someone had tried to pull a fast one on them, and a family business was at stake.

Randy contacted Chris Wrbas, the district engineer with the Regulatory Branch of the Army Corps of Engineers in Galveston, to obtain an emergency extension on the time to respond to the permit application. The reasons he alleged for requesting the extension were grave: lack of notice, misrepresentations in the permit application process itself, and serious safety concerns about the marina plans. Calls were traded back and forth, and Randy was granted a brief extension to file an initial comment. He filed his preliminary comment with Chris Wrbas on September 11, 2003. Randy would need to convince Wrbas both to extend the time for a final comment and, more importantly, to deny the permit application.

The key misconception of which Randy wanted to disabuse Wrbas concerned the ownership of the Western Seafood waterfront property and the littoral (or navigation rights) of the waterway adjoining it. By filing for the marina permit, he argued for Western Seafood, the City of Freeport had given the Army Corps the impression that the *city* owned all the property that the marina was designed to include along the Old Brazos River, and that it had unencumbered rights of navigation on the river. Randy explained that, to the contrary, the 330 feet in front of Western Seafood was privately owned. The city had not even *commenced* eminent domain proceedings against the Gores yet, much less obtained a judgment. In fact, the Gores had their *own* permit from the Army Corps to operate their own docks for their 330 feet of waterfront property! In addition, by filing the permit application, the city gave the Army Corps the impression that the marina was a public project, not a private one to be built and operated by a private developer.

The Gores hired a professional surveying company to establish the boundaries of their 330 feet of Western Seafood waterfront property, in order to demonstrate to the Army Corps that it fell within the boundaries of the permit application being submitted by the city. They also scrutinized the "Overall Dock Survey" that the city had filed with the Army Corps. They disagreed with its most basic finding: how wide—or rather how narrow—the Old Brazos River actually is. The discrepancy, the Gores believed, was suspect.

Things were moving at a dizzying clip. Randy filed Freedom of Information Act requests with the Army Corps, the Coast Guard and the Texas Department of Transportation—the latter two because of their jurisdiction over the Pine Street Bridge, spanning the Old Brazos. It appeared from the drawings that the docks in the marina plans were supposed to come very close to the bridge. He raised numerous issues in his preliminary comment filing to the Army Corps on September 11, including the concerns about navigation safety, whether the city had been completely forthcoming in filing a permit application, an allegation that trespass had occurred on the Gores' property when the city made its survey, and whether incorrect information had been provided to the Army Corps about such fundamental facts as the width of the river. This last factor was crucial, because the Old Brazos is a very narrow channel and the piers planned for the marina were long. Randy's letter stated that the Overall Dock Survey showed the channel as being 550 feet, when Western Seafood's measurements showed it to be 498 feet.

The marina plans called for docks to be built within 30 or 40 feet of the Pine Street Bridge. If the channel was actually narrower than the plans showed and ships had much less room to navigate than it appeared, then this was "an accident waiting to happen" when ships passed under the bridge, Randy wrote. The piers would restrict visibility near the bridge for ships passing beneath. And they would eliminate the deepest, central channel of the river for navigation by larger boats—namely, the shrimp trawlers. The result would be that shrimp trawlers would have to avoid the docks by passing under the bridge at the far end, a much more dangerous and restricted kind of navigation in shallower waters.[3]

Randy also made clear the relationship of the Blaffer family to the marina project. In his preliminary comment he sketched out what he saw as a behind-the-scenes drama playing out in Freeport, and how the Gores believed the Army Corps was being used in that scenario. The marina plan was for the "ultra protected waters" behind the guillotine gate. Randy alleged that the overall design was aimed at pushing out the shrimping industry. "Also, the gulf shrimp trawlers that have historically crowded the river behind the flood gate in storms would not be allowed entry due to lack of available space. This is what the permit application is really all about.... [I]t is obviously a plan to squeeze out the shrimp trawlers, Western Seafood and other similarly situated businesses. The 'applicant' plans to so constrain and confine navigation of the channel downstream from Western Seafood that the vessels that the business has served for years will elect to go elsewhere."[4]

All this would be enough to perk up anyone's ears. A conference call was convened with the district engineer and the chief of the Evaluation Section of the Army Corps of Engineers for the Galveston District. The Gores were granted until October 17 to respond formally to the public notice. They took a deep breath and wondered how this could have happened without their knowing about it. Even as the engineers were drawing up the marina plans and filing the necessary papers, city representatives had been engaged in negotiations with the Gores about Western Seafood's 330 feet of waterfront property without dropping any hint about the noose tightening around their necks—without mentioning the application to the Army Corps for permission to build docks that would choke off their river access and render their shrimp-packing plant a useless hulk.

"The thing that gets me is that we were negotiating in good faith. They say we are against the marina. We're not against the marina. Wright was working with 'em. *Helping* 'em. Thought they even had a deal a couple of times," said Beth. "Then they go behind our backs and do this. And this is when it got ugly. They were meeting with the city in good faith and everyone was in agreement and ... " Beth trailed off, shaking her head. This pattern of the Gores reaching an agreement in principle with the city, only to have it yanked out from under them—without explanation—would be repeated in the years to come.

Randy requested an Army Corps hearing in order to expand on the many thorny issues he had touched upon in his September 11 preliminary comment. On September 25, he filed the federal lawsuit, naming the United States and the City of Freeport as defendants. On the same day, he filed motion papers asking the federal court for an injunction to stop the city and the federal government temporarily from going forward with the permit application. The Gores' complaint alleged some rather unseemly actions on the part of the city. In particular, the motion attached as an exhibit a copy of the preliminary comment letter that Randy had just filed with the Army Corps. By commencing a lawsuit, the Gores created a public record of what was happening with the

Army Corps permit application. Up until that point, these unpleasantries were being exchanged in the relative privacy of an administrative proceeding. Now they were on file where the press or anyone else could have access to them. It wasn't difficult for the city to envision that the Gores and their counsel would be adopting a take-no-prisoners approach to keep the city from shutting down Western Seafood, and that if necessary they would lay out for public viewing anything they considered to be foul play on the part of the city.

The city knew just what to do.

The late comedienne Gilda Radner used to have a hilarious routine on *Saturday Night Live* in which she played Roseanne Roseannadana. She would appear on a news program raising holy hell over a subject, only to be quietly told by the somber, responsible news anchor that there was no basis for her bellyaching. Confronted with the facts, she would meekly murmur, "Never mind." In a similar vein, after turning the lives of the Gores upside down and giving Wright Jr. the scare of his life by instigating the filing of that permit application to the Army Corps of Engineers without so much as giving the Gores a howdy-do, leaving them to plead with a federal agency on fours days' notice and go rushing into court based upon an anonymous fax, the city in essence said, "Never mind."

On October 10, 2003, a month after the mystery fax, yet another fax was received. This time it came to the Gores' attorney, Randy Kocurek. It was a copy of a letter from an engineering firm, dated October 8. The letter was not addressed to Randy; it was addressed to Chris Wrbas, of the U.S. Army Corps of Engineers. It stated simply: "On behalf of the city we are withdrawing our permit application for the Freeport Marina (permit application No. 23112) pending new information. Once we receive new information we will resubmit a new permit application." The letter was copied to Lee Cameron, the director of the Freeport Economic Development Corporation, and to H. Walker Royall. The Gores learned about it through Randy, not the city. It was the Civil Division of the U.S. Attorney's Office—which was representing the United States in the suit the Gores had brought—that had immediately sent a copy of the letter by fax to Randy.

With the permit application withdrawn, there was no need to keep suing the federal government, so Randy asked the court to dismiss the suit as against the United States, but to keep the City of Freeport in court. The Gores, as they say on *Dr. Phil,* had some "issues" to resolve with the city. For one thing, there had been trespass on their land. It was only after they were all in court that Wright Jr. found the stakes that had been driven into his land by the surveyors sent there on behalf of the city. The city maintained that the Gores had known about it and had given them permission to enter the land for surveying. Wright Jr. will swear until his dying day that he would never allow someone to come onto his land and measure it so as to take it away from him.

The city decided to fight. It claimed that the entire suit should be dismissed now that the city had withdrawn the permit application. "City sought and obtained Western Seafood's permission to enter the tract for the purpose of performing the surveys," the city wrote in opposition to the Gores' papers. In any event, the motion papers said, the city didn't need the Gores' permission to drive in stakes under Texas law.[5]

There was another reason why Randy wanted to stay put and the city wanted to get out of Dodge. It was clear that there would be eminent domain coming down the pike at any moment; the Gores intended to raise constitutional challenges and wanted to do so in federal court, where they believed such arguments would fall upon more sympathetic ears. In the game of litigation, no one likes to let the other team pick the playing field, and it had to be dawning on the city that the Gores were intent on opening up quite a can of worms at the federal court in Galveston, what with their attorney running off at the mouth about the city trying to pull a fast one on the Army Corps of Engineers, and about the marina creating safety issues. If nothing else, it was clear that the Gores intended to fight this thing like the dickens. The city no doubt would have preferred to be the plaintiff, which is always a better position to be in than that of defendant in a lawsuit. Better to play offense than defense, see? For the city, that meant pursuing the state condemnation actions in state court. If they stuck around in federal court, things could get complicated. Who wants a federal judge sticking his nose into things? There was no telling what he might order.

So the city kept trying to get out of federal court and the Gores kept trying to stay there, until about three years went by.

Then in the fall of 2006, after the Gores had been soundly knocked down and pummeled by the federal courts, they would find themselves trying to get *out* of federal court and into state court. Such is the nature of litigation dramas that drag on for years.

Lawsuits in America are like chess games. Lawyers and their clients try to anticipate their opponent's next move. Part of this game is sizing up the opponent's war chest. In the case of a municipality, in theory at least, the war chest is bottomless, since tax dollars can always be a source of more revenue, balance sheets and budgets can always be rearranged, debt can always be taken on. That is, if the city is determined to see an opponent ground into the legal dust. The Gores were unusual as a family whose property was targeted for an economic development taking, because they had some means to fight the city. In the vast majority of cases, small businesses and owners of single-family homes cannot even conceive of fighting a municipality on their own. Public interest law firms like the Institute for Justice and the Pacific Legal Foundation take on a limited number of headline cases around the nation, acting as pro bono counsel. The cases are handpicked for maximum political and legal impact, which is the standard strategy employed by advocacy organizations.

Eminent domain right-to-take cases are complex and expensive to fight. It is costly to hire legal counsel even for the valuation trial phase of an ordinary eminent domain case (when the judge or jury decides on the "just compensation" for the home or business that is being taken). Advocacy organizations typically don't get involved in valuation trials; the Institute for Justice steers clear of them entirely, because public policy is not shaped through valuation trials. Many lawyers handle valuation trials on a contingency basis, often taking as much as one-third of the recovery, the way personal injury lawyers do. This happens because their clients frequently are poor or working-class people who cannot pay fees up front. Unlike other types of social and political issues that have arisen over the last several decades, there is no network of grassroots legal organizations like NYPIRG or NARAL or NAACP that is specifically set up to litigate eminent domain. The private bar is still the primary resource for home and business owners caught up in takings. Those rare targets who have money, fight. Those who don't are largely left to negotiate on their own or turn to whatever resources they can afford in the private bar. Clearly, the City of Freeport had not bargained on the Gores putting up a fierce fight. Over the next several years, the city would find out just how much of their assets the Gores were prepared to spend down in order to save their family business.

In the fall of 2003, with the permit application gone—the very thing that had brought everyone rushing into court in the first place—the federal court issued an order that "stayed" or froze the case and closed it "administratively." That is to say, the court kept it from moving forward to trial. In the meantime, over the winter months, the court wanted the parties to do some talking. They went for unsupervised mediation. That means the court figured this was a bunch of grownups who could handle talking to each other on their own. (Courts quite often reach the opposite conclusion about litigants who come before them.)

The Gores were now deeply distrustful of the city. It was a marked departure from the way they had felt a few months earlier. After all, this was the town that Wright Jr. and Wright III had both been raised in. It was the town to which Pappy and Isabel had given their life's labor, where they had become pillars of the community. People turned to them for business advice, for loans, for charity. No cause was ever too big or too little; the Gores could always be relied on. The betrayal on the permit application was something that Wright Jr. could not fathom and would not forget. His father had done business on a handshake; Pappy Gore had been known around Freeport as the sort of person whose word was his bond. Wright Jr.'s experience of having only four days to save his business—and getting those days only through sheer luck or the act of a faxing guardian angel—had flipped a switch inside him. This was not the town he knew, or thought he knew, all these many years. He would never again trust the government officials of Freeport.

"The one thing that happened since day one that is most descriptive of why we—the reason we fear these people," said Wright Jr., "is that while we're all around here trying to do a compromise to work this thing out, and they're giving us a pat on the back, they went behind our backs to the U.S. Army Corps of Engineers and applied for a permit that would literally remove our docks and our access to our waterfront property.

"All of this was ongoing," Wright Jr. said of the negotiations. "We were all still ... now I'm not gonna tell you that we met that day ... but it was a work in progress so to speak.... I'll tell you I was trying to talk them out of half of that property. I wanted them to deal with 180 or 200 feet, not 330 feet. I felt like if we could get that done, we could *save* our free and easy access and our traditional access to our offloading docks and get out of this burdensome legal expense that we still face today."

The hope was that the city would agree to take less than the full 330 feet of waterfront property. The Gores believed that if the city took 150 feet and left them with the remainder for access to the shrimp boats—cramped and inconvenient as it might be—then Western Seafood could continue to be a going concern. They were convinced that the amount of land was negotiable because the size of the marina itself had been a fluid subject from the beginning.

There were meetings, and at first they didn't go so badly.

On December 11, 2003, Mayor Jim Barnett and Lee Cameron walked around the Western Seafood grounds with Wright Jr. and Randy. Wright Jr. explained his concerns about the project and how much land he would need to keep Western Seafood in business. It seemed to make sense for everyone not to have a commercial marina practically sitting on the lap of a shrimp processing plant. Wright Jr. had a surveyor draw up plans, and together he and the city officials did a rough sketch of where the new boundary could be. It was all so civilized. They met again later in December, but things hadn't moved. The Gores suggested that the project developer be brought into the process so plans could be finalized.

Western Seafood has two unloading-packing lines that feed into the packing house. Each begins on an 80-foot pier that extends out into the river, perpendicular to the shore. These piers are used for a system of heavy conveyor belts, pumps, wash tanks, cranes and other equipment that move the shrimp from the cargo holds of the boats right into the packing house. If the marina were built too close to the packing house, as the drawings originally showed it, said Wright Jr., "it would have made navigation into and out of the most downstream parts of these piers a nightmare, if not a practical impossibility."

This was thoroughly explained to the city officials. "We had those city guys walk out on the pier with us and showed them what our concerns consisted of. I said, 'You can see that it is in our best interest and in the best interest of the marina to have a little more breathing room so as to avert conflicts and collisions between these awkward steel shrimp boats and those million-dollar plastic yachts.' They seemed to understand."

Then in early January the mood suddenly shifted. Another meeting was held and the city officials showed up with Xerox copies of conceptual plans for where the land boundaries would be. None of the concerns that Wright Jr. had so carefully expressed were reflected in those plans. It was as if everything he'd said had fallen on deaf ears. What had happened since early December to change everything? The city officials explained that they had to take more of the Gores' land because the marina was already a "marginal development deal." In order for it to be profitable, they simply had to have the land. This didn't sound like the same people who were being so reasonable out on the pier a month ago. It wasn't clear who was running the show anymore.

The little Xerox map showed a 50-foot "buffer zone," in the water and on land—not enough room to back up a tractor-trailer onto the loading dock of the packing house, or for shrimping boats to maneuver and offload their shrimp on the packing line. Later that would change to a ludicrous 30-foot buffer zone, not even half the length of the packing-line pier. *Buffer, my ass!*

It became increasingly clear to the Gores that the city officials—the mayor, the city council, the director of the economic development corporation—the very people who had the power to condemn the land—ultimately were not the ones making the business decisions. In the topsy-turvy world of economic development takings, the municipality dances to the developer's tune, no matter how the city might feel about it. Unless it's a city with a lot of options, which Freeport didn't seem to think it had. And cities with loads of options tend not to be the ones that enter into economic development takings.

Wright Jr. and his son sat down together to figure out what to do. If the worst happens and they take all that land and leave us with that little "buffer zone," we'll have to reconfigure the whole packing house. We'll have to move the netting house, our docks, reconfigure half of our packing lines, they figured. Father and son crunched the numbers: it could easily cost $1,360,000 to reconfigure the 30,000-square-foot packing house and set up a new packing line to the west of the packing house (upriver), assuming such a thing could be done. That would be the only way to save the business if the marina were pressed up close to it, cheek to jowl, as that little Xerox picture showed.

Meanwhile, the city was quietly moving forward with its plans for condemnation. They obtained an appraisal of the Western Seafood land; the appraiser said it was worth $260,000. Now here's the nifty thing about cities and eminent domain: they take only what they want. That is to say, the ordinary laws of decency don't require them to take more, or less, for the sake of fairly compensating the property owner. So in the case of Western Seafood, the city planned to take a long, skinny strip of waterfront property just to the east of the packing house. It wasn't going to take the land that the packing house sat on. Heavens, no. If the city took that land, it would have to compensate the Gores with millions of dollars for the building and its fixtures; get the case before the right jury and who knows what the Gores might walk away with in a valuation trial? It was much better to ask an appraiser to value just the skinny strip of land by itself—like valuing a runway at an airport. How much is a piece of tarmac, all by itself, really worth? From the city's point of view, the spin value was incalculable: We're not condemning the Gores' business or taking away their packing house. We're even leaving them a buffer zone. *They're* the ones who are being hogs. You know the old saying: pigs get fed and hogs get slaughtered.

The winter was dragging on and it didn't seem that the City of Freeport and the Gores were any closer to seeing eye to eye. The Gores insisted on having a conference call with Walker Royall. He was the developer, the one who signed the development agreement. As businessmen, Wright Jr. and Wright III felt instinctively that he must be the one making the fundamental business decisions about how large or small the marina would be.

On February 19 they got their wish. Wright Jr. and Wright III gathered with Randy Kocurek for a conference call with Ron Bottoms, the city manager, and John J. Hightower, an attorney for the city. Walker was on the phone. According to a chronology of mediation talks prepared for the court, there was a discussion of the Gores' cost projection for reconfiguring the packing house and other moving expenses. The report detailed: "Royall stat[ed] that Western's terms for property are too expensive given the current rates for boat slips at nearby Bridge Harbor Yacht Club." In other words, fully compensating the Gores would cut too deeply into the developer's profit margin. The report went on: "Western questioned the seriousness of the project developer." A letter report to the court about the progress of the settlement discussions stated that "the call ended abruptly after Mr. Royall appeared to have either hung up or become disconnected." Whether he hung up or got disconnected, we will never know. He didn't call back.

■ ■ ■

Wright III started digging up what he could about the marina project. With all the talk of a marina in town, it wasn't long before he found a draft of the development agreement—the proposed contract between the City of Freeport and a limited liability company called Freeport Waterfront Properties LP. The company had been formed in March 2002, six months *before* the consultants retained by the city issued the master plan suggesting that Freeport build a marina on the Old Brazos River. Freeport Waterfront Properties had a general partner called Briarwood Capital Corporation, the principal of which was H. Walker Royall. The only apparent asset of Freeport Waterfront Properties was a parcel of land along the waterfront in Freeport, inside the guillotine gate, and next to Western Seafood. It's where the Intermedics factory used to stand. Walker inherited a one-eighth interest in this parcel, while ten of his Blaffer relations inherited the balance.

Wright III, who used to review contracts for a commercial leasing company, pored over the draft development agreement, trying to parse its complex terms and clauses. What he found shocked him. Here is what the city agreed to do:

- The City of Freeport loans the Freeport Economic Development Corporation (EDC) $6 million.
- The EDC then loans the $6 million to Freeport Marina LP, a business entity related to Freeport Waterfront Properties LP, the developer of the marina. H. Walker Royall signs the

agreement as a principal of these business entities. (He shares his ownership interest in Freeport Waterfront Properties LP with other members of the Blaffer family.)

- If the developer runs through the $6 million and needs more money to finish the project, the city/EDC ponies up half of the first $800,000 he needs. The developer need not look far for his half of the $800,000—the city/EDC will loan him that $400,000, separate and apart from the $6 million loan.
- The city will put additional money (amount unspecified) into a pre-development fund, and that money will be used to reimburse the developer for money he spends on the project before the deal closes, including $50,000 shelled out here and there to acquire small parcels of city- and district-owned land.
- The city will give the developer a tax abatement. That means the developer will not pay city taxes, in this case, for a period that is open-ended. The city will also help the developer, Freeport Waterfront Properties, get "similar tax abatements" from as many other government entities as possible (e.g. the county, the school district). The tax abatement is a deal breaker; if the tax abatements offered are not "satisfactory," the developer can walk away in his "sole and absolute discretion" before the project begins.
- It is a "condition precedent" —lawyerspeak for deal breaker—that when the time comes to start building, the developer will have acquired all the property he needs along the river, and the city will do what it takes to make this happen. If necessary.
    - The city will condemn the Jones land.
    - The city will condemn the Henderson land.
    - The city will condemn the Glick land.
    - The city will condemn the Gore land (i.e., 330 linear feet in front of Western Seafood that the Gores are trying to negotiate with the city to keep).

Here is what H. Walker Royall, as signer of the agreement, would do:

- Freeport Waterfront Properties contributes $1 million of equity to the project. That's *not* $1 million in cash. The parties agree that the Blaffer land on the Old Brazos River "is a contribution of approximately $750,000."
- That $1 million contribution kicks in only when—and if—the developer runs through the $6 million loan he will be getting from the city and still needs money to build the marina. If he uses up the $6 million, he is supposed to fund the costs of development himself, "but not to exceed $1,000,000." However, the cash is not coughed up all at once. First, the developer gets what is essentially an equity "credit" of $750,000 (the value of the Blaffer land). Then, keep in mind that the city funds the first $400,000 of cost overruns and then loans the developer his share of the first $400,000 cost-overrun burden. In short, the city bears nearly the entire cost of development until the marina is up and running for costs over $6 million, on top of loaning the developer that first $6 million.
- The $6 million loan is non-recourse. That's lawyerspeak for: no guarantees—from the corporate borrower, or the principal of its general partner (Briarwood Capital), H. Walker Royall. In the event of a default, the city cannot seek repayment of the loan from anyone.
- Freeport Marina LP (the borrower) has twenty years to repay the loan at a rate no higher than 5.25 percent.
- For any payments made while construction is ongoing, the developer can use some of the $6 million to pay the accrued interest that he owes. (Since the $6 million will be held in an EDC construction fund account, which presumably bears interest, the developer would be using interest—from an EDC account—to pay interest that he owes the EDC.)
- As security for the $6 million loan, Freeport Marina gives a lien on the revenues (assuming there ever are any) from the marina and a mortgage on the Blaffer land, which at present is vacant.
- In its letter of intent for the deal, the developer states that it will contemplate developing the Blaffer land with things like

hotels, retail and multifamily residential buildings. Only time will tell whether that will ever happen; there is no hard and fast obligation to do so. (The development agreement refers to a plan for developing the Blaffer land, which may be "changed from time to time," to be prepared by the developer and approved by the city. The city is not to withhold or condition such approval "unreasonably." That's lawyerspeak for: the developer gets to do pretty much whatever he wants.)

- Freeport Marina will begin to repay the loan five years after it begins *or* when the marina "reaches a break-even point," whichever occurs first.
- Past-due principal and interest bear a punishing interest rate of 6.84 percent. No penalties.

In a nutshell, the taxpayers loan $6 million to H. Walker Royall's limited partnership, in which his relatives are the other investors, at a rate that magically remains untethered to the prime rate. According to a draft of the loan agreement for the marina deal that was attached to an internal Freeport memorandum dated May 18, 2005, the contemplated loan would be at an interest rate of 4.84 percent for twenty years and would allow for penalty-free late payments at a rate of 6.84 percent. If Walker walked away (presumably this would happen if the marina was not showing a profit), the city would be secured by a failing marina and the vacant Blaffer waterfront land. No copy or draft of the mortgage document ever surfaced during my research, and the development agreement and the loan agreement are ambiguous as to exactly what land the developer is putting up as collateral. The common understanding around town in Freeport was that the Blaffer land would be mortgaged. That meant the big chunk of land that used to have the Intermedics factory. But a careful reading of the development agreement showed that the contemplated priority lien was for the "Project Site," which was defined as the waterfront property used for the marina itself—that would be a narrow strip of land owned by the Blaffers along the river. The entire Project Site comes to about four acres. The larger chunk of Blaffer land, 8.82 acres, was defined in the development agreement as the "Adjacent Land," which might someday be developed. Walker's partnership was obligated to supply mortgage title insurance (to protect the EDC and the City of Freeport) only covering the Project Site. This suggests that the city and Walker were never contemplating that he would risk the larger parcel of Blaffer land as collateral for the loan.

The salvage value of the completed marina would not be very great. If Sun Resorts—the marina operator that everyone planned on for the deal—can't make a go of it, the city would not be likely to do much better on its own. If the entire $6 million were disbursed from the construction fund and the marina were not completely built, the city would be left with an uncompleted marina as its security—and four acres of empty Blaffer land, worth about $750,000 by the city's own admission. They couldn't go after the corporate entities involved or H. Walker Royall personally. He could walk away. So long, suckers.

In return, the city will condemn four businesses and pony up taxpayer money for the loan. The city has considered floating a bond to pay for half of the loan, in which case it would incur the cost of paying interest on the municipal debt, further burdening the taxpayers. If the marina development ends up costing more than $6 million—and it's worth noting that in the local press, City Hall officials have recently been referring to an $8 million marina—the city will have to kick in more money. And that's not to mention the more than $1 million in compensation to property owners who have settled. To rub salt in this sweetheart wound, the city will not see a dime in taxes from Freeport Waterfront Properties for many years to come; but it will immediately feel the sting of lost tax revenue from the businesses it has condemned.

One thing is clear: a city in dire straits dreamed of a beauteous awakening on a grimy old industrial river, where the largest chemical plant in the world still huffs and puffs alongside the shrimping industry and related businesses. So the city went knocking on the door of a legendary Texas family. A young man from that family, while managing to stay above the fray of municipal political warfare, parlayed a one-eighth interest in a few abandoned acres into a $6 million, low-interest loan to develop a marina. Nice work if you can get it.

By his own admission to the *Sentinel,* a Freeport newspaper, Walker had "never participated in a publicly financed deal like this before."[6] His statements to the *Sentinel* were provided by fax; he declined to be interviewed live. Nonetheless, the interview, published on May 6, 2005, got a breathless billing as an "exclusive" due to Walker's general unwillingness to talk to the press in Freeport.[7] "I have been involved in more than a dozen privately financed real estate deals including a Best Buy store that is currently under construction in Baytown, Texas and will be open in July," Walker stated in his fax.[8]

The Freeport deal had landed in his lap. He didn't come up with the marina idea, nor did he pursue it at its genesis, according to the city manager, Ron Bottoms. The director of the Freeport Economic Development Corporation, Lee Cameron, happened to be an acquaintance of Ken Clayton, the lawyer for the estate of Robert Lee Blaffer II, who owned the Blaffer land in Freeport until his death in the early 1990s. Lee asked Ken about the land and possibly doing a marina deal. Ken made inquiries with the Blaffer family. Eventually, according to Ron, the family decided that Walker would be the point person on this business. There is nothing in the public record to suggest that the city ever considered any other builder, much less opening up the process to competitive bidding.

For Walker, it was a chance to work with Sun Resorts, on whose advisory board he sits. About a year or so after the deal took shape, he brought Sun Resorts in as the prospective marina operator. In the business world they call that "synergy." The Freeport marina story reminds us that the upper class is alive and well in America. In an article about Wright Jr. and Wright III in the men's lifestyle magazine *Best Life,* called "A Property Owner's Nightmare," Ron Bottoms, reflecting on the development agreement after the passage of some time, "concedes that Royall got a sweetheart deal. 'If we'd negotiated it today, we might have done it differently,' he says, 'but we had to agree to some favorable terms to get the project done.'"[9]

At centrist organizations like the American Planning Association, eminent domain for economic development is not seen as inherently bad, but rather its overzealous use is considered dangerous. The APA advocates a responsible, limited use of eminent domain to revive economies, as well as reform of compensation in eminent domain. But this position assumes that people always behave well. It also assumes that government officials have the autonomy to act as they should, or as they really would like to, rather than at the behest of developers they are desperately trying to woo. It assumes, rather unrealistically, that even in small cities, government managers will behave as if they had just stepped off the pages of a Kennedy School of Government case study, as if no one had any personal scores to settle or political interests at stake. It ignores a recurring phenomenon in economic development takings that I like to call the ugly duckling syndrome.

Here's how the ugly duckling syndrome works: A city with bad self-esteem and in financial doldrums starts keeping company with a handsome corporate suitor who doesn't treat her with the respect she deserves. It's an invitation to caddish behavior. When General Motors came knocking at Detroit's door in 1980, they asked the city to bulldoze five hundred acres, pulverizing all the homes and businesses of the Poletown neighborhood. Detroit had to deliver the land clean as a whistle and construction-ready, plus relocate and compensate more than three thousand residents. So it got cracking and raised hundreds of millions of dollars from the federal and state governments. The Department of Housing and Urban Development kicked in $138 million. A very small percentage of the money came from the City of Detroit. GM did chip in $8 million—which is the equivalent of tipping the coat-check girl at a fancy French restaurant and letting the lady pay the tab. In the Freeport marina deal, the gentleman wasn't even paying the tip.

For twenty-six years, Poletown stood as a textbook example of a sweetheart deal between a private business and a municipality. The term "sweetheart contract" was coined in the 1940s to describe a deal between labor and management that is favorable to the employer and is entered into without the approval of the workers. Today people talk about sweetheart contracts or agreements in other contexts, often to describe deals that benefit outfits doing business with municipalities.

While Freeport's deal is small in comparison with the one that Detroit made with General Motors, Freeport could nonetheless put Detroit to shame in the sweetheart-deal department. With a city so in awe of its own developer, fighting the marina project politically was a daunting task. The old guard on the Freeport City

Council were not going to change their minds easily—if ever. There would have to be a public uprising, a tidal wave of protest. Wright III was convinced that if enough people in Freeport knew the truth about the marina project, they would rise up in opposition to it. The two points he most wanted to communicate were: that it was being funded with taxpayer money, and that the master plan on which it was based had described every home in Freeport's East End as blighted. And blight, in eminent domain, means bulldozers on the horizon. Maybe not now, but in the future. He would have to educate the public, and he would need help.

▪ ▪ ▪

As the City of Freeport picked up steam with its condemnation of small businesses along the Old Brazos River, individual citizens were growing restless. People who had not previously attended city council meetings began showing up and keeping an eye on what the council was doing. Some didn't like the idea of tax money going to a private marina when poor people were have difficulty getting basic services. Others were deeply distrustful of the whole concept of eminent domain. Some didn't like being bossed around by folks who had been sitting on the council for years and considered themselves big shots. Still others, like Clan Cameron, believed that the city needed to pay attention to fundamental infrastructure issues, like the levees along the Old Brazos River and the sewer pumps, and keeping the city from flooding when it rained. The council needed to cut the bureaucratic rigmarole that made setting up a business in Freeport such a headache that many small businesses gave up and left. That was the way to pull Freeport out of the hole it had sunk into—not go chasing some scheme and loaning money to a man from out of town in a deal that even the banks wouldn't get involved in.

While the grand plans for the marina were proceeding, ordinary small businesses were having a devil of a time opening up in downtown Freeport. "I invested $20,000 in renovating my building," said Angel Edge-Kant, who used to own a gift shop in nearby Oyster Creek. Her sister had persuaded her to move to Freeport. Angel figured that with all the abandoned buildings downtown, she could pick up a property easily and would be welcomed by the city administration. "I had professional electricians and plumbers in here," she said. She and her husband put a lot of time and money into the renovation. "I tried for seven months and I couldn't get it approved by city inspectors. They kept making it impossible for me to open." Finally, Angel just gave up.

She spoke of another entrepreneur who was met with similar frustrations. "A lady I know wanted to open a little shop across from City Hall. Not a big thing. Just to sell muffins and coffee to the people who work there. They told her she had to put in a ten-thousand-dollar exhaust system. She said she was only going to make some muffins. They gave her such a hard time, she finally said forget it."

Clan Cameron, who ran unsuccessfully for mayor and now serves as the councilman for Ward A, has heard many such stories. "Contractors are hassled all the time," he said, and there are a lot of complaints from landlords. Just a simple transfer to a new tenant requires a house safety inspection and a five-dollar fee. "Freeport is the only city in the county with that rule." In fact, he has heard so many complaints from small businessmen that he came to believe that making life difficult for people who want to open businesses is what passes for normal behavior in a municipality. He learned otherwise when he and his wife inherited a mobile home in Danbury, near the town of Angleton, which is about twenty minutes away from Freeport. They decided to use it as a rental property. "I went up there to get it set up and registered and all, and I just couldn't believe how easy it was. I was ready for it to take a long time and be terrible. I was shocked."

Wright III started attending city council meetings too. He couldn't understand why the citizens of Freeport were not getting more information about the deal. It was their money that was being risked—$6 million of it. That's a fortune in a town with an annual budget of $13 million. The council pushed the marina project with a kind of religious zeal; this was the Holy Grail that was going to save Freeport. They decided to make the loan without putting it to a vote of the people. What was the big rush?

Wright III knew that Western Seafood couldn't fight the Freeport City Council, the EDC and the mystique of the Blaffer family alone. He soon found a group of Freeport citizens who shared his growing anger toward the city government, and together they began a fight that would dominate municipal politics for three years.

CHAPTER 3

APRIL FOOLS

T. S. Eliot wrote that "April is the cruellest month, breeding / Lilacs out of the dead rain, mixing / Memory and desire. . . ." April 2004 would mark the beginning of a new chapter in the history of Freeport, and it would be cruel indeed. The fight over the marina project would be taken to the streets, and the once cordial social fabric of the town would begin to unravel. The winter hiatus in the litigation would come to a close and the case would go back onto the court's active calendar, where the judge would expect the parties to put up or shut up: either declare themselves in agreement on a settlement or prepare for trial.

The winter of 2003–2004 had dragged on with the legal process offering no respite to the Gores. The negotiations were unlike any normal business dealings. First, the parties negotiated a deal to save a family business without the developer of the marina being in the room. But toward what end? The Gores sensed the futility of the sessions. Wright III demanded that they take the "gun away from our temples." That is, take eminent domain off the table. The city deemed this unreasonable. It was their only leverage, and it was powerful leverage. They had a legal right to condemn, they argued, and they would not take it off the table. The parties were more than a million dollars apart. The Gores put their foot down and demanded the participation of the developer, Walker Royall. That disastrous conference call ended in a disconnect, literal and metaphoric. With no resolution in sight, Wright III looked ahead and saw the specter of the litigation opening up once more, with eminent domain poised to swallow up the family business just as a new shrimping season was about to get under way. Wright III—always controlled, always cool, always calm—began to lose it.

By late March, their time for mediation was almost up. They were headed back onto the litigation track. Wright III had deep doubts about all this legal wrangling. Increasingly, his thoughts turned to the political process. He had loved that sort of thing as a teenager. He used to attend weekend training sessions at the Morton Blackwell School for Republican Leadership, where they bring in politicians who talk to young people about grassroots politics. Wright could see that continued litigation was going to bleed them. Every letter, every phone call, every fax, every brief, every affidavit resulted in more billable time. Tens of thousands of dollars were slipping through their fingers with each passing month. His parents weren't sure how long the business could withstand this kind of cash drain.

Meanwhile, talk went around Freeport about the Gores' $1,360,000 cost estimate for reconfiguring their packing house. *Those greedy Gores! We made them an offer of $260,000 and they counter-offered for $1,360,000. Just how much do they think land is worth in Freeport? Obviously, this is all about the money to them.* The $1,360,000 began to pop up in odd places. Two years later, Walker Royall would mention it to a reporter from the *Dallas Business Journal,* saying that the Gores were trying to "extort" that money from the city.[1] The truth was that the Gores had never offered to sell their land at any price. They wanted to be compensated for the cost of the adjustments needed to stay in business.

After a particularly bad mediation session in federal court, Wright III returned to his apartment in Houston. Always a techie, he already had a computer back in the 1980s, when only geeks knew what the Internet was. He started noodling around and a website took shape.* He wanted to describe what was happening in Freeport. Pappy always knew the perfect word for everything, though lately the strokes had disabled him, dysphasia cruelly cutting him off from the deep well of his enormous vocabulary. What

*The website, scandalinfreeport.com, is currently the subject of a defamation and libel suit brought by H.Walker Royall against Wright Gore Jr., Wright Gore III, Western Seafood and Dennis Henderson. In the suit, H. Walker Royall denies the truth of the statements made about him on that website. Mr. Royall declined to be interviewed for this book.

would Pappy have called it? Wright could think of only one word: scandal.

The city was taking away his grandfather's business, ripping the land out from under them—the irreplaceable 330-foot chunk of America that proved what Pappy had believed all along: Where you are born doesn't determine where you end up in America. A boy whose daddy labored in the oilfields has just as much right to dream as a boy whose daddy owned those oilfields. But now it wasn't working out that way. For all they knew, Walker could have been descended from the owner of the very oilfields in which Pappy's daddy had worked long ago. And who were the other owners of Freeport Waterfront Properties LP? Why, other relations of Walker's. Now this thing called eminent domain was being used to pluck the fruit of Pappy's labor, simply because four people on the city council voted in favor of it.

Pappy was in his eighties and sickly, but he was aware of what was happening. Nothing could be hidden from him, and the family had too much respect for Pappy to lie to him. He had built Western Seafood with his own two hands, with the sweat of his back, with his own brilliant mind. Over the course of his life, he had pulled himself back from the brink of death—from open-heart surgery, from debilitating strokes—but he didn't complain. Life was a gift. A wondrous mystery set before us by a generous God who asks much but also blesses greatly. Pappy never had much book learning, but he knew more about business than anyone could ever learn in school. And now the city was insisting that his land was worth only $260,000—leaving him with an absurd "buffer zone" that meant the end of Western Seafood—and turning it over to a partnership owned by heirs of the Blaffer family, who didn't even have to pay hard cash for it. The city was going to loan *them* money to build a private marina. Saying it out loud made it sound unreal.

And the Gores weren't the only ones who stood to lose. When the City of Freeport first began seriously to consider reviving the downtown with a marina and other beautification and "destination" projects, they commissioned a study by the Maritime Trust Company. The consultants took a gander at Freeport and realized it was a candidate for the urban planning equivalent of a Hollywood-style *Extreme Makeover*—which is what it would need to match Ron Bottoms' dream of a place that people would drive or sail to in order to have fun, a place to invest in. Studying the downtown area, which included 655 homes, they determined that 97 percent of those homes were "either severely or moderately blighted," a figure based partly on an earlier blight study done by the city itself. As for the section called the East End, known as the poorest part of town, the master plan declared that "*every* home in this section of the Study Area is blighted." So many houses in such a poor neighborhood, so close to where people were talking about building all these fancy things—a yacht marina, hotels, condominiums. Given the history of eminent domain, it was easy to figure out who might be next in line for condemnation.

All of Wright III's rage and frustration burst onto the flat little screen. The flickering cursor beckoned him to say more and more: about the master plan, the development agreement, the taxpayer funding of the $6 million loan to Freeport Waterfront Properties, the absurd coincidence that the Gore property was being condemned and handed over to the landowner next door—a partnership headed by a descendent of the man who founded Humble Oil. He wrote about eminent domain and what it means for a property to be described as "blighted" in a city's master plan—how that is the first brick in the foundation of an urban renewal plan, the first step toward the bulldozing of your modest little home, your little piece of the American Dream.

Those weekend sessions at the Morton Blackwell School were kicking in. Wright III realized he would have to put his interpretation of all those indecipherable documents into plain English. With a flair for Texan slang, Wright III summed up the marina development for Freeport residents as he saw it, warning that they would "get the boot" and "the bill." The homepage of the website shows a silver attaché case wide open, stacked with documents. In bold letters, it entices the visitor: "Let's Peek Inside Walker's Briefcase.... What's in here? Things Walker doesn't want you to see ..." Arrows point to an enormous pile of cash—"Your $6 million"—as well as a copy of the master plan and an unsigned copy of the development agreement. Final signed copies of the development agreement and the corresponding draft loan agreement (for which public funds were to be used) were never made readily available to the general public of Freeport. Residents had to go to

City Hall and submit a letter in the proper format, specifically requesting the documents pursuant to the Open Records Law of Texas and stating the reason they wanted them. Such requests are reviewed by the city secretary and the city attorney.

The website went on to say that the documents were supposed to be available at the Freeport Public Library but they weren't. It wasn't clear how that would be the fault of Walker Royall, who lived in Dallas. But the website nonetheless painted a picture of a small town very much in cahoots with its marina developer. It's hard to say how much of this was small-town paranoia and how much of it was realistic. Freeport residents working in opposition to the marina project had made repeated, unsuccessful attempts for three years to obtain a copy of the signed development agreement. I was able to get a copy only after making a formal request pursuant to the Open Records Law. "Who are you with?" the city secretary asked me. At first she said she didn't think she could give me a copy of the original 2003 development agreement because the city was making changes to it (that is, entering into a new agreement). I made it clear that legally this had nothing to do with a request for the 2003 agreement. After a formal letter stating my bona fides, which included the name of my publisher and the existence of a book contract, I received a copy of the 2003 agreement. I also requested a copy of the exhibits to the agreement, which included the loan agreement, but the city did not provide this. I was able to obtain only an unsigned copy through other channels.

Signed final copies of these documents were important to the residents of Freeport because, like many complex business contracts, the development agreement was some forty pages and referred to several related contracts, namely a mortgage and a loan agreement. Without the final, signed copy, it was hard to know exactly what the city had agreed to. The grassroots group that grew in opposition to the marina, Citizens for Freeport, hankered to see these documents. They wanted to understand what was going to happen in their small town and where their tax dollars would be going. At one point Angel Kant made a request for the development agreement and was told she couldn't obtain it because of "pending litigation."

The virtual briefcase on Wright III's website held the master plan, with its repeated references to blighted homes and vacant lots, in a conveniently downloadable format, making it accessible to everyone in Freeport who had a computer, or a friend with a computer. Wright III even added electronic yellow "sticky notes," putting unfamiliar terms like "blight" into plain English. He did the same with the development agreement, explaining legalisms like "tax abatement" and "non-recourse loan." The website had plenty of links about eminent domain and recent news articles about the marina controversy and how to "take action."

But here's where it went a tad haywire: It also had personal information about Walker Royall, about his home in Dallas, his cars, and allusions to the grandness of his wealth. Was it over the top? Probably. But Freeport is a poor town. Even Judge Samuel B. Kent, who presided over the federal lawsuit, accepted the description of Freeport as "economically depressed."[2] The median income is around $30,000. Most people work in blue-collar jobs. The very idea that someone of another class so remote from theirs could benefit from an economic development taking, supplied with property seized from Freeport businesses and funded with sales taxes, could be a matter of some public interest.

The development agreement and the master plan were enormously long, complex documents. So Wright boiled the situation down to its simplest elements in sound bites that would make Karl Rove envious: Walker is rich, Freeport is poor. He's up in Dallas, we're down here in Freeport. We want to talk to him, he won't come down here. He'll make money on the marina, but *we* are loaning him *our* money to build it. You'll stay poor. He'll get richer.

There was no doubt that Walker had become the object of Wright III's deepest anger, the personification of the calamity that had befallen his family. The idea that someone born into the upper echelons of America's class structure should benefit from an eminent domain deal involving the taking of Pappy's business was too much for him. And for Wright, it was always *Pappy's* business.

"He was the first grandchild," said Beth Gore. "There was such a special bond between Wright and his grandfather."

Wright III, who looks younger than his thirty-three years, typically wears chinos and a preppy shirt, which make him appear still more boyish. He is painfully thin; since the lawsuits started three years ago, his colitis has kicked up, making it hard for him to eat and often causing him hours of pain in the morning. Wire-rimmed glasses frame his dark eyes, drawing attention to his delicate features and jet-black hair. Wright III is a quiet person; his normal tone of voice is just above a whisper. Upon first meeting him, one might get the impression that he is fragile. He is not.

"When he was starting junior high school, we had just moved to Lake Jackson," recalled Beth. "The kids at the new school thought they would give him a hard time, this new boy from Freeport. So they put a towel down where he was supposed to sit in gym class or something. And he threw it off and said to them, 'Don't you *ever* do that again!' I told my husband, he's not the one [of our boys] we need to worry about."

Wright III is the sort of person that Custer would have wanted with him at Little Big Horn: willing to fight to the last stand. Only it is not blind faith in a charismatic leader that gives Wright III his almost religious resolve. Nor is it greed, as H. Walker Royall surmises in the lawsuit he would eventually bring against Wright III and his father. Nor is it Lake Jackson uppitiness, as some in Freeport wager, the Gores having moved in the 1980s to that leafy subdivision ten minutes away from Freeport. Nor is it orneriness or just plain opposition to the marina project, as the city claims. No, it is none of those things. It is love.

In countless interviews with local media, Wright III does not speak about saving his father's business, though Wright Jr. has been the head of the business for twenty years now. Nor does he talk about saving "the family business" or even "Western Seafood." He talks about saving "my grandfather's business."

Normally tense and a brooder by nature, Wright III becomes instantly relaxed in Pappy's presence, grinning broadly and encouraging him to talk, cueing his memories with old stories. As a child, Wright III spent his happiest hours with his grandfather. Like many children, he found that the ordinary rules of bedtime and good manners didn't apply around Grandpa. His father, Wright Jr., is driven and organized and serious. ("My dad decided he wanted to go to military school when he was 12," said Wright III. "He put himself on the train!") Pappy Gore, on the other hand, was a natural-born prankster who taught Wright III how to curse like a sailor at the age of three. Together they invented a game that turned Pappy's car into a heart-thumping "roller-coaster ride," as Pappy liked to call it. Pappy would rev up the engine and activate the electronic garage-door opener. Then, timing the insanity for maximum risk, he put pedal to the metal just as the door began to rise, making the ninety-degree turn from the street into the driveway, speeding into the garage and "don't stop 'til you see the afterlife."

Fun-loving and unpredictable, Pappy Gore had the kind of wild streak it takes for a man to look at a place as godforsaken as Freeport was in the 1940s, sell everything he has, dig in his heels and say, "I'm going to make my fortune here, come hell or high water." And then work like the devil to make it happen. Wright III knew every detail of that story. It was the stuff of family legend. And the man who had lived it was flesh-and-blood proof of the American Dream and of that most important of Texan values: loyalty. Pappy Gore had been loyal to everyone and everything he'd loved in his life—Isabel, Wright Jr., Raymond, Gary, Western Seafood, his dozens of employees—and he deserved nothing less from his firstborn grandson. He would have that loyalty in spades. Wright III would save his grandfather's business, or he would die trying.

And so Wright III came to look upon Walker with a seething contempt that he could barely articulate. Yet to an objective observer, Walker hardly seemed worth the amount of attention that Wright III devoted to him. The city council proudly takes credit for the marina idea. At his deposition in the federal lawsuit, the city manager Ron Bottoms testified that the City of Freeport, through its economic development corporation, took the initiative in the deal. Lee Cameron, the director of the EDC, happened to know Ken Clayton, who was representing the estate of Robert Lee Blaffer II. "We actually approached him. He, in turn, approached the family, the heirs," said Ron Bottoms. "They were receptive to the idea." Then one of the heirs contacted Lee Cameron. "It was not Walker," recalled Ron. "It was one of the other heirs . . . they expressed an interest. I guess they got together and decided that Walker would be the—kind of the lead person as far as representing the—the—heirs, and that's how the relationship came to be."[3]

Judging by Walker's subsequent public interactions with Freeport, it seems hard to believe that he was very interested in the city or the deal to begin with. One gets the impression that it was simply a case of noblesse oblige. The city called upon Walker; he answered the call. And what a fuss and bother afterward! Now a website painted him as being at the center of a scandal in Freeport.

Wright III knew that having a website is one thing; driving traffic to it is another. In early April 2004, just around the time the website went up, the Gores, through a corporate entity, rented a forty-foot billboard on the main drag leading into town. It was big and bold, announcing the name of the website in black and red letters on a bright yellow background.

It didn't take long for word to travel up to Dallas, where Walker Royall lives. He wasn't happy. On April 8, 2006, Walter Herring of the Dallas office of Fulbright & Jaworski LLP, a major Texas law firm, sent a cease-and-desist letter by certified mail to Wright Jr. and Dennis Henderson, who was listed on the website as a sponsor. It warned that the firm had "reviewed the website located at scandalinfreeport.com" and found it to contain "numerous false, misleading, inaccurate, and defamatory statements about Mr. Royall." The letter pointed out that Walker is a "private citizen." Under libel laws, different standards of care apply to private citizens as against public figures. The letter said the site was "little more than a direct, defamatory personal attack on Mr. Royall and his reputation." As an example it cited the website's reference to the marina project as a "scheme invented by Mr. H. Walker Royall." To the contrary, Mr. Herring wrote, the "City of Freeport approached Freeport Waterfront Properties, L.P." to develop the waterfront. The letter took exception to the colorful phrases, "Walker takes your property, you get the bill, you get the boot." In fact, wrote Mr. Herring, "no homes will be taken by the planned development between the City and [Freeport Waterfront Properties]."

And then he got down to brass tacks. Mr. Herring took issue with the website's statement: "We've established that Dallas resident H. Walker Royall is richer than anyone who lives in Freeport." Mr. Herring noted: "In fact, we are unaware that you have undertaken any reasonable review to determine Mr. Royall's financial status." And finally, Mr. Herring took issue with this alleged libel: "Walker started his extensive collection of Porsche sports cars as a teenager." The counsel advised, "In fact, Mr. Royall does not own a Porsche." (Interestingly, Mr. Herring did not say that Walker never owned Porsches as a teenager. He only said that Walker didn't own one at present.)

In general, the letter maintained, "[t]he list of false statements and defamatory innuendo (e.g. 'greedy developer like Walker') on the site is too extensive to innumerate in this brief letter ... many [of your statements] are contradicted by the very documents you reference" on the website. Legal action was threatened "not only for your vicious and defamatory attack on Mr. Royall, but also damage from your tortious interference with Mr. Royall's business relationships" if the website was not taken down immediately.[4]

There are some in the big leagues of real estate development who revel in the public spotlight. They view real estate development as a financial and psychological dogfight, a take-no-prisoners type of capitalist pugilism. Ugly words are mere pellets aimed at their gargantuan, steel-plated egos. But the plainspoken culture of East Texas was not meshing well with the finer sensibilities of Turtle Creek, Dallas. First there was that meeting in Houston. Then the conference call that ended in the "disconnect." And now the website.

Wright III examined the letter, making a mental note of the part about the Porsches. That set him to thinking about what kind of cars Walker might currently own. Internet research revealed that he owned a Mercedes, so Wright edited the website accordingly. Other than that, he did not cease, nor did he desist.

Instead he ramped up the website so there was continually something new. He was convinced that without Walker's personal participation in the crucial decision—how much land the Gores would be able to keep—the matter could never be resolved. They'd keep spinning their wheels in fruitless mediation sessions, or pouring hundreds of thousands of dollars into lawyers' fees. Wright wanted Walker to come down to Freeport, to sit across the table from his father and explain why the 3,000-foot marina required *all* of the 330 linear feet of Western Seafood's land at its westernmost end. So he began taunting him daily on the website. He set up a tickler, the type one sometimes sees on tall buildings that shows the accrual of the national debt or some other perceived abomination to the public interest. The legend over the tickler said, "This is how long Walker has gone without speaking to us," and there was a big red stop sign over it for good measure. To make sure the message got across to everyone in Freeport, he put an ad in the *Facts* with a picture of a clock: "Why won't Walker talk to us?"

■ ■ ■

The taking of homes in eminent domain might just prove to be Freeport's very own Maginot Line. As the French learned in World War II, the Germans found a way around the line of fortifications that everyone thought was impenetrable. Now that Wright III had launched his website, posting the complete Maritime Trust study with its original blight data gathered by the city itself in 2001, there was cause for concern among the citizenry. *What does a promise never to condemn our homes mean if there's all this talk of blight?*

The city had been insisting that it would never condemn homes. But the master plan contained a smoking gun: it described 97 percent of the homes in the study area as blighted, and declared *every* home in the East End section to be "severely blighted." "Blighted" is a polite way of saying ugly, rundown, unfit for human habitation. In the old days, people used the word "slum." It doesn't take a master's degree in urban planning to know that a designation of "blight" is the first note of a death knell for a neighborhood under an urban renewal plan. Even under the new Texas law against economic development takings (which the city would argue didn't apply to pending projects like the one in Freeport), there are exceptions for blight, as there are in many similar state statutes. The master plan also identified a deeper malaise in Freeport: the town had "no sense of place." There was no central location where people gathered, milled about, chewed the fat. There was no place to go for essential services, such as a doctor or a barber. This was a town with an identity crisis. It used to have a downtown, a gathering place, a sense of life. Now it had nothing but boarded-up windows and memories.

Yet the Maritime Trust consultants saw potential. A very large employer, Dow, was plunked down permanently nearby. With 5,000 acres and just as many employees, Dow wasn't going anywhere. Freeport was only fifty minutes away from a major urban center, Houston. And most importantly, it was near water. Where there is water, there are things that people with leisure time and money can do: swimming, boating, fishing. The master plan also suggested biking and hiking along the levee path.

When the master plan talks about deficiencies, it is primarily talking about vacant land and empty buildings; but it is also talking about poor people. Visit the downtown study area and they are everywhere, chatting in driveways with neighbors, working on their cars, running after their kids, going about their business in the little houses. Now, planning consultants are far too polite and well trained to come right out and say that what a city needs is fewer poor people and more people with a lot of money to spend. The master plan lets you read between the lines. It mentions blight over and over, providing a detailed analysis of the blight, complete with appraised values per square foot of homes in the East End and a great big pie chart, lest anyone fail to grasp the subtleties.[5] Then it speaks in the language of modern urban planning: the downtown needs an arts district, it needs waterfront development. Toward the end, the master plan includes suggestions for community incentives to help homeowners in the East End repair their homes and generate more homeowner (instead of rental) presence there. These suggestions seem to have fallen on deaf ears in Freeport.

Wright III hatched an idea to distribute information about the master plan and its blight findings in the study area. Why not let people know that their homes were marked as blighted and what that means in the parlance of urban renewal and eminent domain? The majority of people who lived in those East End homes were Mexican American. They generally did not attend city council meetings. Most them had no idea that their neighborhood had been scrutinized and their homes judged to detract from the center of the "destination" that Freeport was soon to become. The master plan left the impression that they were partly at fault for Freeport's having "no sense of place." Wright III also thought the residents deserved to know that they would be paying for the marina with their own tax dollars.

So he created some informational door hangers to place at each home in the areas that were designated as "blighted." These door hangers told residents where to go on the Web to find the entire master plan and the draft of the development agreement, to see what their city government was doing with their tax dollars and learn what it means for a house to be described as "blighted" when talk of eminent domain is in the air. The door hangers also indicated that an interactive telephone system had been set up so people could get more information, in Spanish or in English.

Western Seafood employees distributed the door hangers to the "blighted" homes in the East End. Many residents became aware for the first time that some highfalutin consultants viewed their neighborhood as ripe ground for future projects. *They are taking away Trico and Western Seafood against the will of the owners. This thing called eminent domain means that someday they can take away our houses too.* Since the master plan relied on a blight study done by the City of Freeport itself, this lent the appearance that the city was thinking about condemning houses. Neither the master plan nor the development agreement explicitly called for the condemnation of residential areas, but both left room for possible future development. The master plan specifically suggested building a Port Freeport administration building as well as commercial development within the study area. All this was enough to get people talking about the marina development and wondering whether it was a good idea.

The folks at City Hall got red in the face. This was far too much information for Freeport residents to handle on their own. Apparently, city officials didn't put much faith in their constituency to think independently. "It's inciteful. My concern is those folks who are going to take it at face value," Ron Bottoms told the *Facts*.[6] Wright III countered by saying that the door hangers were supposed to be educative; they indicated where to go for further information. Bottoms said people had called City Hall and seemed upset, thinking they were losing their homes. "We've got nothing to hide," he said, and offered a number to call (presumably so people could speak with him). "This is an effort to undermine trust in the city and to try to derail the marina project." But while Bottoms spoke of openness in city government, neither the master plan nor the development agreement was available on the Freeport website. It is likely that most residents of Freeport would not have known about the existence of those documents or where to look for them if not for the door hangers. Most people would need help in understanding them, which Wright's website provided. As it was, anyone going to City Hall asking to see a copy of the signed development agreement had to submit a written request pursuant to the Texas Open Records Law.

The city that had nothing to hide immediately swung into action and launched a counterattack. On April 8, 2004, the official City of Freeport website said:

ATTENTION FREEPORT RESIDENTS!

En enspanol

Don't be misled by Door Hangers and Website!

Door hangers were distributed Wednesday, April 7, 2004 throughout the city that are not factual, and are misleading, and are attempting to use scare tactics to undermine your trust in your city government. The flyers attempt to mislead you that your home has been deemed severely blighted whereas the city has never made any such blanket determination. This is strictly an attempt to cause mistrust and to scare our citizens. The City of Freeport governmental authorities have nothing to hide and will be more than willing to answer any questions that you might have. Please call....

Again the information you were provided is inaccurate, and is meant to scare, and was distributed according to their website by **Western Seafood** and **Trico Seafood** headed by **Wright Gore** and **Dennis Henderson** respectively, both of which have challenged the City and have opposed the Marina Project.

The City of Freeport has never taken a home by eminent domain, nor do we have any plans to do so!

There is no scandal in Freeport.

The marina is a sought after project....

With regard to the allegations made by **Western Seafood** and **Trico Seafood** representatives that the City of Freeport diverted City funds to H. Walker Royall or any other individual is false. No member of its governing body, its administration, or any other individual has agreed to provide any money to H. Walker Royall or any other company, corporation or individual. The City has, along with the EDC, committed to a secured loan to Freeport Waterfront Properties for the development of the marina project.

The EDC has successfully negotiated with all property owners, with the exception of two commercial interests, **Trico Seafood** and **Western Seafood.** Both of which are in opposition to the marina with Western Seafood going so far as to file a civil suit against the City of Freeport.[7]

The editors of *Pravda* would have been impressed. This is a fine example of official backpedaling and dissembling if ever there was one. Rather than simply describe what the official purpose may have been when they undertook a blight study back in 2001, which may have been innocuous, the city decided to take the Clintonian tack of "deny, deny, deny." The fancy footwork trying to distinguish "money" from "loan" would be funny were it not so sad. For this partisan message was posted on an official government website, yet it singled out two corporate citizens (identifying their principals by name), as if they were not taxpaying citizens of Freeport. Indeed, over five decades in business, Western Seafood had paid hundreds of thousands of dollars in taxes to Brazoria County and the City of Freeport.

The website said that Western Seafood had gone "so far as to file a civil suit" against the city—neglecting to mention that the city fully intended to commence an eminent domain action against the Gore property, but had simply been beaten to the courthouse steps. The lawsuit commenced by Western Seafood in the federal court in Galveston was filed because of the city's attempt to get a permit from the Army Corps of Engineers—creating, in effect, an "inverse condemnation." The Gores had sued to stop a regulatory taking that no one had given them notice of, aside from the mystery fax. They had gone into court on an emergency basis to obtain an injunction to stop the Army Corps from granting the city a permit that would have resulted in cutting off Western Seafood's access to the Old Brazos River, putting them out of business entirely. Once they were all in federal court, they had been ordered by the judge to try working things out. When a federal judge orders you to do something, you do it. So like obedient schoolchildren, the EDC and the Gores had been meeting all winter, to no avail. The city wanted to shift the litigations out of federal court into what it believed would be a friendlier and quicker venue, in Texas state court, and they would soon be suing the Gores there.

Of course, the Freeport website didn't explain any of that. The main point was that the city didn't want the Gores to scare anybody. The city's April 8 posting set a pattern of identifying the Gores and Western Seafood by name in public, official city communications, criticizing them, using damaging innuendos or telling outright lies about them, while painting a rosy picture of the marina project with simplistic half-truths.

Meanwhile, the city had also launched a ground offensive. The *Facts* reported that "City officials, including firefighters, then began passing out fliers of their own, countering the first flier's claims."[8] Residents recalled seeing a city vehicle going up and down the streets with city employees hopping in and out, rolling up the fliers and sticking them into doorjambs. For good measure, the city also did a mass mailing that went out in the water bill to every household in Freeport—not just the few hundred in the East End that the Western Seafood employees had reached with their door hangers. A fancier mass mailing would go out in early October.

Also on April 8, the federal case was officially reopened and placed on the active calendar. This meant that Judge Kent thought there was no hope of settlement and it was time to stop pussyfooting around.

The "cruellest month … of memories and desire" was not shaping up very well.

CHAPTER 4

ON THE RIVER

Once a case is on a court's active calendar, the lawyers start fighting it out on paper. Usually this means the judge will decide who wins, which is commonly called summary judgment. That is where the Gores' federal case was headed, along with their mounting legal fees. The vast majority of lawsuits in the United States never go to trial. They are decided when lawyers file papers in court, arguing that there are no factual issues for trial, only issues of law to be decided by the judge. Using up enough paper to denude a small forest, they submit affidavits, attach cumbersome exhibits and submit legal briefs of fifty pages or so, breathlessly arguing that this case is so straightforward and its outcome so obvious that there really is nothing to argue about. These motions typically weigh about ten pounds. In a complex case, bringing or defending such a motion can cost a litigant tens of thousands of dollars or more. A judge often takes many months to ponder these motions. During that period of suspended animation, no amount of antacid poured down a litigant's gullet will suffice to quell the nagging realization that one's entire fortune rests in the acquired wisdom of a single person.

With the Western Seafood case back on the active calendar, Randy Kocurek wanted to see whether he could raise enough factual issues to have a trial. It was clear that under the Texas eminent domain law, the Gores' situation fell within the state's rather broad interpretation of the term "public use." Courts were supposed to give deference to the legislature when it had declared a "certain thing to be for a public use."[1] Like many states, Texas had a long tradition of taking private property and turning it over to private developers in the context of urban renewal projects or even for industrial uses.[2] Yet the case law in Texas also recognized that ultimately the courts had the last word on what a "public use" was. And under the existing federal case law at the time, there was some hope that Randy might be able to prove this was an unconstitutional private-to-private transfer. He amended the complaint to seek a declaratory judgment—in other words, asking the court to announce formally as a legal matter—that the City of Freeport could not condemn the Gores' property. The amended complaint also asked the court for an injunction that would stop the city from condemning or pursuing the Gores' property in the state courts of Texas.

On the law, they had to rely principally on language in *Hawaii Housing Authority v. Midkiff,* the leading U.S. Supreme Court decision on takings in the pre-*Kelo* world of 2004. *Midkiff* involved the big land oligopolies in Hawaii. As late as 1967, about half the land in Hawaii was held by seventy-nine private owners and the other half was owned by the government. It was difficult for the average person to buy property. The legislature passed a land reform act breaking up the oligopolies. A challenge to the law wended its way through the legal system, reaching the U.S. Supreme Court in 1984. Justice O'Connor, writing for the majority in *Midkiff,* stated that the land reform act did not violate the Fifth Amendment's public use clause because it accomplished an important public purpose—getting rid of pernicious land oligopolies. However, Justice O'Connor also stated that the transfer of property from one private party to another "for no reason other than to confer a private benefit on a *particular private party*" would be unconstitutional. (Emphasis added.)

In mid-April 2004, the lawyers in the Freeport litigation were back in federal court to discuss the injunction that currently barred the city from going ahead with its state court condemnation actions against Western Seafood. Anchors aweigh! The lawyers and the judge discussed the kind of mind-numbing mechanisms that turn the wheels of the judicial system and ultimately determine people's destinies. Should the state eminent domain proceedings, with all their arcane trappings, be brought under the jurisdiction of the federal court? That would be a highly unusual maneuver, to say the least. The lawyers were unsure of exactly how it would work, and to whose advantage. Should the state court cases be put on ice while the federal case with its constitutional issues was resolved? Randy was certainly in favor of that. John J. Hightower, the city's attorney, told Judge Samuel Kent that he was worried that with so much time passing, "the project is in danger of dying." He pointed out that the city risked losing the interest of the developer—the Blaffer family's Freeport Waterfront Properties.

> *Mr. Hightower:* The real reason this particular developer is important to us is that he owns most—a substantial part of the [marina] property. If he's not part of the deal, we'll be out trying to condemn his property to make the deal go. So that's why the concern is there.
> *Judge Kent:* I'm sure Mr. Gore's response would be, "What's good for the goose is good for the gander. Condemn them all."
> *Mr. Hightower:* I'm sure that's correct, Your Honor. The—and then, I guess, maybe the . . .[3]

So there it was, out in the open, and Judge Kent had called them on it. Condemning the Blaffer land was unthinkable. It would be like the town of Hyannisport in Massachusetts condemning the Kennedy compound in order to build a seaside resort—a sign of bad manners and ingratitude. After all, the Blaffers had given the town its City Hall building. Wasn't that swell of them? And the city had gone to the Blaffers asking them to do this deal. To then go and condemn their land would be so *rude.* The city elders wanted to avoid such a faux pas at all costs.

There may have been something else as well: the powerful lure of getting something for free. A marina and economic revitalization, with all that Blaffer land thrown in, and the city won't have to pay for it! No, the residents can pay with an itty-bitty half-cent sales tax and never feel the difference. What's a $6 million low-interest loan in the long run? Sure, the annual budget is only $13 million . . . and the marina won't pay taxes to the city for years, and we'll lose the Gores. (Aw, who's gonna miss the Gores, anyway? Hell, they moved out to *Lake Jackson.*)

Judge Kent asked for briefs on the subject of jurisdiction and the injunction. He was not inclined to enjoin (that is, to stop) the state courts from doing what came naturally on the condemnation.

■ ■ ■

The negotiations having petered out, the ball was thrown back in the litigators' court. Randy amended the federal suit. He upped the ante, throwing constitutional and civil rights claims at the city and the economic development corporation. The city had lawyers too, of course, and a seemingly unlimited legal budget. They not only defended the federal suit vigorously, but also brought separate actions in state court against Western Seafood and Western Shellfish (a distinct corporation that owned 100 linear feet downriver from the Western Seafood land; the city was condemning that parcel too). The Gores sought an injunction to stop the state court action from going forward until the constitutional claims—whether the city had the right to bring the eminent domain action—could be resolved in federal court.

Randy wanted to see if he could prove that an unconstitutional, private-to-private transfer was taking place in Freeport, of the sort that Justice O'Connor described in *Midkiff*. To do so, he would need to "take discovery." That's lawyerspeak for obtaining documents and asking witnesses questions under oath at depositions. Judge Kent was not enthralled with the idea of a lot of discovery in a case about eminent domain. Such cases are not traditionally seen as fact-specific, the way personal injury or patent or fraud cases are. He would give Randy one shot at a deposition: the city manager of Freeport. After all, wouldn't Ron Bottoms be in a position to know everything? At a hearing on the discovery issue, Judge Kent made clear his great faith in city managers.

As it turned out, Ron Bottoms, suave and agreeable as always, actually had little to contribute when he was deposed. He had secondhand knowledge of how the EDC had entered into the deal with the Blaffer family to develop their land, and only the most basic familiarity with the terms of the agreement. What the deposition did reveal was pretty much what everyone in Freeport already knew: that the marina deal came about as a purely private and congenial arrangement between the Blaffer heirs and the EDC, and that no other developer was ever considered. The entire project always hinged, from the get-go, on the involvement of the Blaffer land and Freeport Waterfront Properties.

Judge Kent allowed no further depositions. After an exchange of documents, he was willing to grant the request by the city (together with the EDC) to consider a motion for summary judgment; there would be no trial. The documents, according to Randy, contained "gems here and there" but no smoking guns. Without further depositions of government officials, the deal appeared to fall within the bounds of what the law described: a transfer of private property for the "public purpose" of the economic development of a depressed downtown. Randy was essentially cut off at the knees in his attempt to establish a record that this was a transfer of land primarily intended to benefit one private individual.

The lawyers rolled up their sleeves, the computers hummed, the printers spit out their mountains of paper, and the lawyers spun their endless supply of words into arguments. Then the Vietnamese trawlers began returning to the warm waters of the Gulf near East Texas for a new shrimping season. Western Seafood was paying out more and more each month in legal fees at precisely the time of year when it saw its greatest ordinary expenditures. This was 2004; the Gores didn't know that they had two more years of litigation ahead of them.

"Mama!" the shrimp trawlers greeted Isabel Gore. There she was in her seventies, still upright and strong with her no-nonsense expression, still settling accounts. It was time for the trawlers to buy supplies and start running up new accounts. Time to see how much was owed from last season at Marine and Industrial Specialties. "We owe *that* much, Mama?" Marine Industrial was filled with laughter and excitement, everyone hoping for a good season. While the trawlers went shrimping and the packers iced the shrimp, Randy was litigating.

On the motion for summary judgment, the city (and the EDC) argued that the taking fell within the meaning of the public use clause of the Texas Constitution because it was for economic development, a recognized purpose under Texas law. The city also maintained that, contrary to what the Gores alleged in their amended complaint, the condemnation of the Western Seafood land was proper under the Texas Development Corporation Act. This latter point appeared at first to be a rather tiny tail on a very big dog—a hypertechnical argument that no one cared very much about. It might eventually be the tail that wagged the dog.

The Texas Development Corporation Act was enacted in 1979 to encourage the economic development of Texas towns and cities. Originally, it only allowed municipalities to create not-for-profit economic development corporations, which could receive outside funding and work in cooperation with a city. But that changed in the late 1980s when a series of amendments to the law allowed state and local funds to be used for economic development, specifically local sales and use taxes. That is how, for example, the half-cent EDC sales tax came to be imposed in Freeport for the marina project. The Gores' complaint alleged that Freeport had not properly incorporated, or formed, its economic development corporation, and therefore it was not authorized to build the marina under Texas law; and further, that even if the Freeport EDC had been properly formed, a private marina was not a project of the sort to which cities are supposed to apply development funds under the meaning of the Texas Development Corporation Act.

Judge Kent was not impressed with these arguments. He held that the Freeport EDC had been properly formed and had the power to build a private marina anywhere it chose in Freeport. Moreover, Judge Kent wrote, the public use requirement was met under the Texas Constitution and its case law. "Texas courts have adopted a liberal interpretation of the public use requirement [and] Texas law recognizes redevelopment as a public purpose; therefore Plaintiff cannot show a violation of the public use requirement of the Texas Constitution."[4] The judge turned last to the federal constitutional arguments. In the pre-*Kelo* world, the main case that controlled, in addition to *Hawaii Housing Authority v. Midkiff,* was a landmark case called *Berman v. Parker.*

Berman (1954) involved the taking of a department store in a slum area of downtown Washington that was slated for urban renewal. The owner of the store objected to his viable business being torn down as part of a plan to bulldoze surrounding slum areas. The U.S. Supreme Court refused to cherry-pick and deferred to the judgment of Congress in enacting the law that gave rise to the plan to raze the neighborhood. The Gores argued that *Berman* should not control in their case because this was not a slum removal situation—nor was the city fighting the evil of land oligopoly, as in *Midkiff.*

Judge Kent made clear just how far *Berman* and *Midkiff* had entered the consciousness of the American judiciary, and indeed the American legal understanding of property. He began by acknowledging exactly the extent of the peril to private property rights: "This case involves a municipality's efforts to take, through eminent domain, one private party's property and transfer it to another private party to promote the public interest in a healthy local economy. These circumstances present stark and startling evidence of the potential for governmental interference with individual property rights. The grave implications of a broadly construed public use requirement have not escaped notice of this Court or of commentators." Judge Kent cited an article by an academic named Thomas Merrill, pulling out a statement that described the public use clause as a "dead letter," and also quoted an article by none other than Ralph Nader—not exactly known for having milquetoast opinions—in which the public use requirement of the Constitution is described as having been rendered "meaningless, essentially giving governments carte blanche to take property for any reason whatsoever, including crass political purposes or speculative, transient economic purposes."[5] Strictly speaking, these references are what lawyers call "dicta." That is, they don't "count" as law, but are there for the court to express itself or lay the foundation for a future opinion. There are a whole lot of dicta in Judge Kent's opinion. One gets the distinct impression that he would have preferred to rule the other way, but felt his hands were tied by *Berman* and *Midkiff.*

"The public 'use' identified by the City," wrote Judge Kent, "is more realistically characterized as a public benefit that will, according to the City's predictions, flow from the new private owner's development of the property." In other words, once the town council rustles up a wing and a prayer, it can lawfully tell you to fork over your property. Pre-*Kelo*, this federal court was giving the existing case the most expansive interpretation possible under federal law, but Judge Kent was not prepared to go out on a limb and carve out an exception in an economic development case. Instead, he treated the Freeport case as an urban renewal case—even though it did not involve an urban renewal plan or slum removal. Judge Kent admitted that his holding might strike "a rational and neutral observer as an unduly broad reading of 'public use' resting on a rather speculative plan of urban renewal," but added that "it is consistent with the prevailing interpretation of the Public Use Clause."

That is an odd statement indeed for a judge. Did Judge Kent believe it was not incumbent upon *him* to be rational and neutral? As for the urban renewal plan, it was less than speculative; it was nonexistent. In fact, the city elders had twisted themselves up like circus contortionists to convince the poor of Freeport that there were no designs to renew any of them, that nary a home would be touched—ever. No urban renewal plan was formally adopted by the city or voted on by the citizens. To the contrary, the city through its EDC simply entered into a contract for a private marina and then sought to take, through eminent domain, the land it had promised as a condition of that deal, all because the deal held out the promise of better times. Judge Kent was willing to make the leap from these facts to a lofty enough public purpose, even though the deal obviously benefited one private landowner over another.

Now, for a judge to rule as he feels constrained to under the law is one thing. Schmeering on the schmaltz is another. If only Judge Kent could have stopped himself where the actual legal verbiage ended. Unfortunately he couldn't resist laying on nearly a full page of what was surely meant as an apology to the Gores for putting them out of business with a swipe of his judicial pen. But what emerged was a stunningly condescending ode to the sometimes sad but inevitable march of "economic progress."

Reminding the Gores that "America increasingly wants her waterways devoted to trendier pursuits than regional transportation and commercial fishing," Judge Kent waxed poetic about the good old days when Galveston was filled to the gills with the maritime industry. Alas, such throwbacks as "ship's chandlers, drydocks, marine surveyors, I.L.A. halls, seamen's unions … mosquito fleets, net repair shops, and even tattoo parlors and rough-and-tumble drinking establishments have all given way to vast yachting operations, imitation, generic restaurants, souvenir shops, and museums."[6] He then proceeded to draw an analogy:

> Salem, Massachusetts was the international capital of the worldwide whaling industry in the early nineteenth century, but outside the confines of the National Whaling Museum, a present-day visitor will not find a single whaling ship or any vestige whatever of the South China trade.... But for all its love of hoary tales of barnacled ships and grizzly sailors, the Court cannot freeze time.... This Court rules as it must today with a heavy heart. But as with the Village Smithy at the dawn of the age of automobiles, the future is often merciless in its mandate for change, and even the best among us must stand aside as successors emerge.[7]

Actually, the whaling industry went out of business partly because of advances in technology and fashion that made whales less prized for their blubber and bones. Then whatever interest in whale hunting remained in the United States and many other nations was regulated virtually out of existence through international treaties after overhunting had put many of the species close to extinction. The analogy didn't make sense; shrimping is not an outmoded technology nor is it part of a cruel practice left over from a Herman Melville novel.

Wiping out Western Seafood, the judge's dicta suggested, is no big woof because, gee whiz, it was slated for the mothballs soon anyway and everyone knows that freshwater shrimping has gone out of style. The judge made reference to the "rapidly emerging shrimp farming industry"—which in truth accounts for only a small percentage of shrimp from American shrimpers. It seems that to Judge Kent, and indeed to some in Freeport, the crime that Western Seafood committed was staying too long at the fair. It kept on making a profit long after all the other fish houses on the Old Brazos River had gone out of business. That's because Pappy Gore was *right*; he knew there was a future in the American shrimping industry. And because doing it the Gore way—working harder than everyone else, being fair to everyone, going into related businesses that help see you through the down markets—was a winning formula. They were being pushed off the river not because they couldn't compete with American shrimp farmers, as Judge Kent implied (and isn't it a bit daft for a federal judge to digress into such a discussion?), but rather because they had *successfully* competed for years against foreign, farm-raised shrimp, often awash in chemicals, being dumped on the U.S. market without any steps by Congress to check the influx until recently. And they had survived. Our judicial system should reward such success, not punish it.

But in the world of economic development takings, none of this mattered. The Gores were in the way, and they were unfashionable. The fate of Western Seafood would be determined not by the free market, but by five men voting on the city council, and by a federal judge who believed that a viable business, still earning a profit, should be shelved in a museum to make way for a plan that even the court called "speculative." This is public use. This is now the American way.

■ ■ ■

Throughout the summer of 2004, the tickler on Wright III's website kept counting the days since Walker Royall had communicated with the Gores. The situation was becoming more urgent. August 5 was the day Judge Kent ruled on the motion for summary judgment. After months of entreaties, suddenly the cloud lifted and Walker decided to come. He called Wright Jr. and they spoke. The two gentlemen were always polite with each other; it was how they both were raised. Walker sent a cordial letter to Wright Jr. on September 16, 2004, telling him, "I look forward to meeting with you on Tuesday morning. I hope that our face to face meeting will be productive and that we are able to come up with a solution that can help resolve this issue. I know that we are both interested in an amicable resolution." The letter confirmed that they would meet the following Tuesday at 11:00 A.M. at a restaurant in Freeport called On the River. Walker mentioned, "As agreed, you and I will be the only attendees of this meeting." Wright Jr. faxed back to him, "OK, Walker, I look forward to seeing you."

The EDC planned a meeting at On the Water for the same morning. Ron Bottoms would be there. The restaurant owner reserved the back room so the group could have a quiet place to meet. They ordered iced tea. The agenda was carefully, indeed rigidly planned: a half-hour to discuss the Gores, another half-hour to discuss Trico's property. Since sale of shrimp from Trico accounted for about 20 percent of Western Seafood's profits, their fates were closely tied together. And navigation issues had not yet been resolved.

The Gores were growing anxious waiting for Walker. They were concerned that they would entirely miss the half-hour slot that Ron Bottoms had allotted to them. Wright III and his father stood watching in the parking lot outside On the River. As they waited, a black Suburban kept circling the block.

Then Walker arrived, along with some of his colleagues from Sun Resorts, and they all started to go inside. Wright III and his father and Walker and Johnny Powers from Sun Resorts went into the restaurant and took a quiet table in the back. Just before they went in, Wright III noticed that the Suburban had pulled into the parking lot.

Walker talked about what a great project the marina was. He also told Wright Jr. that he was upset about the website and the billboard, and asked him to take them down. Wright Jr. said he couldn't do that as long as the eminent domain matter was ongoing. During the meeting, a couple of city officials approached several times, but Wright III objected and asked them to move on so the Gores and the developer could have a private meeting. Ron Bottoms took offense and told Wright III not to tell him what to do. Wright III recalled that while his father wanted to discuss the marina and the logistical problems of the 330 feet, Walker wanted to talk about the website. They seemed to be talking at cross-purposes.

The noon hour was approaching and the EDC meeting was breaking up. Wright III told Ron that he and his father still had ten minutes of time left for their meeting with the EDC. Maybe they could still salvage things; after all, everyone was there—even the people from Sun Resorts. But by now people were leaving the restaurant. At this point, the whole enchilada had unraveled so spectacularly that everyone left On the River without paying for the iced tea.

When Wright Jr. and Wright III walked out of the restaurant, there was a man sitting on the bench near the front door. He approached them and handed them a stack of paper.

"You've been served," he said.

Wright Jr. looked down at the papers he held in his hands. They were legal papers. Walker was suing him. The man walked away and got into the black Suburban and drove off.

There was a suit against Wright Jr., his son and his company for libel, defamation and civil conspiracy relating to the website. Walker wanted punitive damages as well as an injunction to shut down the website. The suit also named Dennis Henderson, who owned Trico. But there was another suit too. It demanded $36,000 for breach of contract over a lease agreement for warehouse space in the old Intermedics plant. This was strange, Wright Jr. thought. He recalled terminating the lease amicably with Walker over the phone more than a year ago, and the Intermedics buildings had been torn down. The plaintiff in the lease suit was Freeport Waterfront Properties, the same entity that was slated to be the marina developer.

The original plan for the afternoon was for Wright Jr. to drive his car with Walker and Johnny Powers down to the Western Seafood property, just a few minutes away, the better to come up with a hands-on resolution to the dispute. So off they went. Wright Jr. now found himself pointing out various landmarks to Johnny Powers and the young man who had just sued him. "The tour of the waterfront was primarily to explain to those two why it would be good for us all to distance our packing house from their marina," Wright Jr. wrote in an email. "Walker came up with a couple of 'solutions' including literally and physically moving that packing house upstream a couple of blocks. The most impractical idea I have ever heard."

Wright III raced back to the Western Seafood office, where he frantically called the company's insurer to tell them about the lawsuits. After much back and forth in the ensuing weeks, the insurance company agreed to defend the lease suit and the defamation suit for the business and for Wright Jr. But it was another story entirely to convince Wright III's umbrella policy to cover the defamation suit as against him. The defamation complaint alleged that the city had made a "fair offer" to purchase the Gore land and Wright Jr. had then "responded with an offer to sell his property for more than three times the appraised value." After the city and Wright Jr. "reached an impasse" and the city began eminent domain proceedings, the Gores began a "malicious smear campaign" against Walker Royall.[8]

As much as the defamation suit shocked the Gores, it was the suit over the warehouse lease that left Wright Jr. pulling at what little hair he had left on his balding pate. It was a property no one had been interested in, he recalled in testimony under oath. Walker's lawyer had served him with a notice for a deposition in the $36,000 case, so he drove up to Houston, where for two hours he answered a lawyer's questions about the lease.

The irony of it was that Wright Jr. had never much wanted the lease in the first place. The lawyer for the Blaffer estate had approached him about renting the warehouse, and offered a low price. The lawyer had urged Wright Jr. to hurry and make up his mind, because ownership of the property was in transition. He said the lease would have an unusual provision: it had to be terminable on short notice, because there might be a marina built there at any time. But Wright Jr. had been hearing talk of a marina since he was a boy. And the terms were good. If the warehouse had to be vacated, well, the lease could provide for termination. So be it.

When he first rented the property, Wright Jr. testified under oath, it was strewn with garbage and he had to clean it up. Then, what do you know? The marina project actually got under way. He and Walker talked on the phone. It was all perfectly friendly, Wright Jr. testified. The warehouse needed to be torn down; Wright Jr. understood that. They came to an agreement and he sent a final check. He thought it was resolved. Now Walker's lawyer, Paul L. Mitchell, was asking him about that phone conversation under oath, in a dialog worthy of a Beckett play:

Mr. Mitchell: When did this telephone conversation take place?
Wright Jr.: I don't know.
Mr. Mitchell: Were you a participant in the phone conversation?
Wright Jr.: Yes.
Mr. Mitchell: Was Mr. Royall a participant in the phone conversation?
Wright Jr.: Yes.
Mr. Mitchell: Was anyone else a participant in the phone conversation?
Wright Jr.: Not that I'm aware of.
Mr. Mitchell: Did you make notes of the conversation?
Wright Jr.: No.
Mr. Mitchell: Is there any documentation relating or referring in any way to this conversation?
Wright Jr.: No.

Mr. Mitchell: Did you confirm the conversation in a letter?
Wright Jr.: No.
Mr. Mitchell: Did Mr. Royall confirm the conversation in a letter?
Wright Jr.: He confirmed it in an invoice.
Mr. Mitchell: Other than the invoice . . . and I suspect there's going to be substantial doubt as to whether that confirms anything . . . did Mr. Royall confirm the terms of the conversation by letter?
Wright Jr.: No, sir.
Mr. Mitchell: Okay. Was the conversation tape-recorded?
Wright Jr.: I don't know.
Mr. Mitchell: Did you tape-record it?
Wright Jr.: No.
Mr. Mitchell: Did you tell anyone else to tape-record it?
Wright Jr.: No.
Mr. Mitchell: Did you tell anybody about this conversation? Other than your lawyers?
Wright Jr.: Not that I recall.
Mr. Mitchell: Is there anything about the conversation that you can recall that you haven't told me?
Wright Jr.: Well, I haven't described the subject of the conversation to you.
Mr. Mitchell: Well why don't you tell me to the best of your recollection . . .
Wright Jr.: Walker Royall called me in—with regrets, so to speak, that they were going to need, to need to terminate the lease early, because they were—the marina project, the commencement was imminent. I told him that, not to be concerned about that, that we had already heard about that, that demolition was due and we had removed our property from the warehouse a good while back. So Walker suggested we go back in time to June 30th of '03 and call that the end of the lease and the termination date and we'd pay them $12,000 and that's the end of it. I had no problem with that at all. It worked well.
Mr. Mitchell: Okay. I'm sorry. I didn't mean to interrupt. Go on.
Wright Jr.: And it was an amiable conversation and one that appeared to be good for both parties.[9]

Did he *record* it? Wright Jr. was used to doing business the way Pappy did; his word was his bond. What sort of universe had he stepped into?

■ ■ ■

The Gores' peaceful life had turned into something out of a Lewis Carroll tale, where everything that had once been normal was now distorted and ugly. A knock at the door in the evening and everyone freezes. Is it a process server? Check through the window first. No, this time it's just a salesman.

There are fights with insurance companies. Dinner conversations about motions and briefs. Lawyer's bills. Subpoenas. The federal judge on whom we have pinned our hopes hands down a decision that compares the shrimping industry to the village smithy—as if Western Seafood didn't still employ dozens of people and make a profit in one of the most competitive businesses around. One minute Isabel is named Woman of the Year by the Chamber of Commerce, and the next minute we are being vilified around town as Lake Jackson snobs who are preventing Freeport from moving on and up. And how much of this should Pappy know? How much can he stand to know?

The decision from the federal court could not have been worse for the Gores. Walker was serious about the defamation claim. The city would not relent on the Western Seafood land and was ready to ramp up the condemnation cases in state court.

The fall of 2004 truly began to take on a *Through the Looking Glass* quality. All of a sudden, the city council was interested in its signage and advertising ordinance, a part of the city code that had been on the books since 1968 and had never been much cause for worry. But things had changed since the marina issue hit the fan. For one thing, the Gores had been speaking their minds, a lot, mostly in a little local paper. There had been political ads. The publisher of the local paper had been speaking her mind too. And there was that enormous canary-yellow billboard telling the whole world that there was a "scandal" in Freeport. The city elders started reexamining sections of the city code that had lain unmolested for years. Mayor Jim Barnett said that two "huge, ugly billboards" on Highway 288 "had caught the attention of city officials."[10] Could one of them have been the billboard that the Gores had rented to promote their website?

There is a local paper in Freeport called the *Sentinel*. It's published by Wendi Ross, who loves the newspaper business and wants a place to write the things she feels strongly about. The *Sentinel* is a weekly broadsheet, usually about ten pages, with articles about doings in town. It is given away free and supported by ad sales. Ross works hard to keep the paper going. During the marina controversy, she started becoming more and more critical of the city government. Then in September 2004 she heard about a pending amendment to the city code. She had a telephone conversation about it with the city attorney, Wallace Shaw, and came away thinking that the amendment would mean she could no longer distribute her newspaper to homeowners in Freeport.

This exchange led to an ugly scene at a city council meeting. Wendi Ross, a soft-spoken, middle-aged woman, was publicly excoriated in a hall packed with spectators and a local reporter. Wallace Shaw hotly denied ever having told Ross that it was "illegal" for her to distribute her newspaper in Freeport. "I would never say something like that," he said to Ross. "Maybe you should contact me and talk to me about things before you start making public accusations."[11] Shaw is a spindly older gentleman, but he can rise to the occasion when a sharp rebuttal is called for. He said the conversation was about fliers, not newspapers.[12] But everyone in Freeport knows that Ross publishes a newspaper, the *Sentinel.*

Ross claimed that she was reduced to tears in her telephone conversation with Shaw about her newspaper. She said the city had "tried to squelch her paper as she has become more critical of its actions. She accused city officials of taking copies of her newspaper in bulk from public locations."[13] Wright III took the podium and asked the city council for an assurance that Ross would be allowed to continue to distribute her paper; Mayor Jim Barnett said he guaranteed it.

At that same meeting, the council was also looking to amend provisions of the code that related to handbills and circulars. They didn't want another surprise like the one they had received with Wright III's door hangers. Section 113.03 had always required people to get a written permit from the city manager before handing out a flier in Freeport. But the code didn't say that the city manager had to approve every word of it. That would change. "[W]e felt as though our 'freedom of speech' was being censored by the city manager," wrote Steve Alford, a Freeport resident affiliated with the grassroots group Citizens for Freeport, in an email.

After all that melodrama, the amendment regarding handbills and circulars was tabled for the evening, along with an amendment concerning signs. According to the press report, the "proposed amendment drafted by Shaw would have basically banned off-premises signs, a designation that includes billboards."[14] Councilman Jim Phillips pointed out that the planning commission had recommended a more limited amendment. The council decided to take up the whole issue of regulating signage in a special session—a private meeting of the council, conveniently out of earshot of the public. A lot less melodrama that way. Signage regulations were issued a few weeks later. They did not affect existing billboards; but Lee Vela, a spokesman for Clear Channel Communications of Houston, a billboard communications company, said the city's new regulations imposing height limitations for on-site signs would put new businesses at a competitive disadvantage in Freeport.[15] Just what Freeport needed—to make things *less* hospitable for new businesses.

For the moment, the signage regulations did not directly affect the Gores. Wendi Ross emerged from her scuffle with the city council determined to keep on publishing the *Sentinel.* The Gores' ad was still up on the billboard. Eventually, the billboard company would decline to renew their contract after receiving a letter from Walker's attorney, advising it about the libel suit. In the meantime, the 2004 shrimping season drew to a close, and despite the bruising legal fees, Western Seafood managed to squeak by.

Then one day the Gores opened their mailbox and there it sat. It looked like a magazine, big and glossy. *City of Opportunity Newsletter 2004,* it said in huge letters across the top. It had a picture of a seagull that looked about to fly right off the page, and a beautiful palm tree in the background. At the bottom was the City of Freeport logo and on the back was a photo of the Gulf of Mexico at sunrise, the waves gently lapping at the shore. Far off in the distance was a shrimping boat, its rigging silhouetted against the warm, beckoning horizon. The newsletter cost the city $11,000, not exactly pocket change in the Freeport budget.

The purpose of the newsletter was to update citizens on various city projects, such as annexation of new land for Bryan Beach, a citywide cleanup plan and demolition of dilapidated buildings. The newsletter devoted a single paragraph to the aging sewer system, saying it would be replaced over ten years and announcing that the city had received two Community Development Block

Grants "to assist with meeting the timelines set out in the plan." These grants are given under the Housing and Community Development Act of 1974. Essentially, they are development grants for very poor neighborhoods to build infrastructure, with the ultimate goal of eliminating slum conditions. Communities that receive them are known under the law as "entitlement communities." What's more, Freeport's projected budget for 2004–2005 showed a $959,000 grant from the U.S. Department of Housing and Urban Development. Considered against the total annual budget of $13 million, the size of that HUD grant underscores just how poor the city is. One has to ask: Does a city that needs to go begging for *two* Community Development Block Grants in order to afford a *ten-year* sewer replacement plan have any business lending out $6 million on a non-recourse loan to a developer for a private marina? On top of that, the city was condemning viable, taxpaying businesses in order to do it, and turning the property over to its landowner of choice, along with an open-ended tax abatement.

The centerfold of the newsletter, however, was the real attraction. In huge, fancy type it announced "The Freeport Marina Project." There were watercolor artist's renderings of the marina and a waterfront plaza, as well as an aerial photograph of the Old Brazos River showing where the marina would be. Pretty snazzy. "To ensure its development," the text said, "the City has agreed to lend the developer $6 million which is secured by the marina project land, plus $1 million in cash."

The phrase "$1 million in cash" has a powerful ring to it anywhere, but especially in a city where the median income is $30,000. Those words ought not to be written unless they are absolutely accurate. In this case, what the city wrote was wrong. Having signed the development agreement, the city knew full well that Walker Royall's limited partnership was not obligated to pony up $1 million in cash. Perhaps the "$1 million in cash" that the newsletter mentioned was the equity that Walker was supposed to put into the deal. But the agreement made clear that the equity contribution would kick in only if building expenses went over $6 million. Even then, he would get a credit for the $750,000 that he and the city agreed the Blaffer land was worth. And the city would have to furnish the first $800,000 ($400,000 on its own behalf and $400,000 as a loan to Walker for his half).

In simple terms, what the development agreement really said—and the *City of Opportunity Newsletter 2004* did not explain—is that Walker would never have to put in *more than* $1 million of combined cash and land equity. The way the agreement was structured, it was quite possible that the marina could be built without his having to spend a dime. Legally, there's nothing wrong with that. There is something wrong, however, with misleading 13,500 Freeport residents in a mass mailing, while in the next breath defaming the Gores. For as thousands of Freeport residents opened their mail that day, there it was:

> A lot of rumors and mis-information have surrounded the advent of the marina project. Initially, Western Seafood representatives were in favor of the project and for over a year indicated that they wanted to be a partner in its development. They later filed a lawsuit to stop the project altogether. Because these property owners retain ownership of a small, but key, area of the development, and because the city felt the project was so vital to the community prosperity, another way had to be found to acquire the property.
>
> The city has assured the affected property owners [i.e. the Gores] that they will be fairly compensated for their land. The city needs only a small portion of property to complete the project, property that is currently used primarily as boat dockage. The main portion of the company's business will remain unaffected by the project.
>
> Recently a federal judge ruled in Freeport's favor, agreeing that the City was legally justified in using its power of eminent domain. . . .[16]

The Gores had never seen themselves as partners in the marina project. If anything, Wright Jr. thought the city had made *itself* a partner with Freeport Waterfront Properties by entering into a complex development agreement that deeply enmeshed it in the creation of the marina. He wasn't a party to that agreement. No one asked him to be and he didn't care to be. Apparently people started talking around town after he and Wright III went to the meeting up in Houston. But his concern when he attended that meeting was to make sure people wouldn't be killing each other on the river. It seemed to him that people weren't taking into account the navigation issues on the Old Brazos. They wanted to build the marina docks too long, jutting out in the deepest waters of that narrow channel. Where would the shrimp boats sail? How would the yachts maneuver?

The newsletter hauled out some of the same canards that the city had used on its website, for instance, "They later filed a lawsuit to stop the project altogether." In fact, the Gores filed a lawsuit to stop the city from filing a permit application with the Army Corps of Engineers and cutting off their navigation rights on the Old Brazos River, rendering their waterfront property worthless. Western Seafood owns "a small, but key, area of the development.... The city needs only a small portion of the property." If only a small portion were what the city wanted, the fighting would have been over long ago.

Western Seafood paid annual taxes of approximately $18,500 to the City of Freeport in 2004. That made them a major taxpaying contributor to the *City of Opportunity Newsletter 2004.*

■ ■ ■

Things looked grim. Then in November, word shot around eminent domain circles that a case called *Kelo v. New London* had been granted certiorari by the U.S. Supreme Court. Randy Kocurek immediately brought a motion in federal court before Judge Kent for a stay of all proceedings in the Western Seafood case and a stay of the state court condemnation cases, pending the outcome of *Kelo*. No one could deny the importance of the *Kelo* case. It held the potential to turn the world of economic development takings upside down. Some fifty years had passed since the High Court had agreed to hear a case challenging the scope of the meaning of the "public use" language in the takings clause of the Fifth Amendment. Judge Kent agreed to put the Western Seafood case on ice. Around the country, similar orders were issued in takings cases. Home and business owners had the long winter to await the outcome, to see if the Supreme Court would stop the economic development takings locomotive in its tracks.

As the winter months passed, the Gores, like so many others, had time to wonder: How did it ever come to this in America? How can my neighbors covet what is mine ... and then take it? They would not be the first to wonder such a thing. James Madison had given considerable thought to the very same question.

PART II

THE LUST FOR LAND

CHAPTER 5

MADISON'S BEEF, WEBSTER'S SHOWDOWN

The summer of 1789 was, in James Madison's words, a most "nauseating" time. But when it was over, he and his fellow Federalists had accomplished what they set out to do: they kept the deal they had made with the anti-Federalists at the Constitutional Convention in 1787, salvaging the Constitution from the latter's growling jaws. The Federalists had favored the elegant and sparely written Constitution that had emerged from the convention, which provided for a strong national government, radically changing the structure of the United States from the days when it was governed by the Articles of Confederation. But the Constitution had been vehemently opposed by the anti-Federalists, who feared a powerful central government with weak state governments. So a deal had been struck: the anti-Federalists were promised that if the Constitution was ratified, a Bill of Rights would be added during the First Congress. It fell to James Madison to draft the bill. Suggestions poured in from the state conventions, detailing what the states wanted to see in the Bill of Rights. No one mentioned a takings clause, but Madison wrote one anyway.

Eminent domain troubled Madison enough to use precious political capital on it.[1] Just what was his beef? After all, Americans tend to wax poetic about the sanctity in which the founding generation held property rights. Surely the passion of the patriots for such rights was unsullied as against one and all.

Well, pish! A man like Madison could not afford to harbor such romantic delusions in the thick of revolutionary-era politics. He was a member of the landed upper class, and he wanted to hold on to his land. The problem was, he had witnessed the war-induced frenzy of the last decade, when normally civil people had nearly gone stark raving mad, grabbing the land of their former neighbors with a fierceness that no one could have predicted. Having access to information about the development of law and civil society from up and down the seaboard and the territories westward, Madison was well positioned to see the various faces that Americans could show when it came to private property. He had seen in action the "majority" he so often theorized about in his political writings, and what he saw wasn't pretty.

The revolutionary and postwar periods were replete with greed, cunning, factionalism, violence, ruin, rush to judgment and revenge. Of course, there were the feel-good stories too: tales of fortunes made, freedom won, a new country rising from the smoke of war. And there were the great Northwest Territories, which sat like gleaming jewels on the northwest banks of the Ohio, waiting to be scooped up by settlers who felt hemmed in by the estates of the old colonial gentry. Those who were savvy enough to get there early could make smart deals with the land companies that had bought up gargantuan chunks of America and were selling it at wholesale prices. Come one, come all, and grab a piece, for this is America and anyone is welcome; your cash is good here. You just better hope your property deed isn't later "undone" by another land speculator, some fast-talking, politically connected con artist.

By 1789 it was evident that Americans could be fair and methodical as bureaucrats or judges, planning carefully and compensating judiciously in eminent domain matters, as had been done for more than a century of colonial rule. But we could also be vengeful local majorities, casting all caution to the wind after a bitter, hard-fought war, confiscating properties from Tory Loyalists with breathless speed and rapacity. Or we could be wily land speculators throwing our weight around in legislatures through lobbyists to further our investment interests, foreshadowing the buccaneer capitalists of the next century.

The land seizures were not taking place on the sly; the Continental Congress set it all in motion on June 24, 1776, with a declaration that all property of adherents to the Crown would be subject to confiscation.[2] The individual states took it from there—with a vengeance. State legislatures passed acts confiscating Loyalist estates.[3] Indeed, during the Revolution and in its aftermath, many of the state legislatures went positively slaphappy seizing Loyalist farms and houses, as well as stripping them of official positions they held in the community and the salaries that came with those positions. These state laws were hardly models of due process. For example, Pennsylvania's Confiscation Act, passed in 1779, enabled the courts to indict any man as a Tory "on the oath of one credible person." If he failed to appear "after four weeks' advertisement" (and many had fled during the war), his property was confiscated. "Many a loyal though cautious patriot could thus be robbed of his all by malicious or prejudiced neighbors," wrote Allan Nevins. "The partial motive of greed behind this legislation was obvious, for two-thirds of the property of New York, including the Crown land, was owned by British or Tory interests."[4]

At the same time, Loyalists were being forced to settle their debts on very unfavorable terms. While part of the motivation for the seizure laws was revenge, a larger part was fiscal. During the early years of the Republic, people were "consumed with the topic of the public debt and federal securities issued during the Revolutionary War."[5] Debates raged over how—indeed, whether—to pay the war debts, both in the national government and at the local level. In this climate, seizing Loyalist property became a sort of national sport. It not only provided a visceral sense of satisfaction for a war-weary people, but also helped fill the public coffers and put a dent in the elephantine war debt.

All this revenge and land-lust and old-fashioned political chicanery was not lost on Madison. In preparation for drafting the Bill of Rights in 1789, he "hunted up all grievances and complaints of newspapers, all the articles of conventions, and the small talk of their debates."[6] When he had a chance to vote against such land grabs, he did. As early as 1784, he supported the Bill Prohibiting Further Confiscation of British Property.[7] As a member of Virginia's landed gentry, educated in ancient languages and philosophy at Princeton (then called the College of New Jersey), Madison was deeply suspicious of the "vices" of legislatures as well as the "sudden impulses" of the majority, to which legislatures could fall prey. In addition, he took a dim view of quick-fix solutions that compromised property rights. Madison opposed the paper money bill pending before Congress, arguing that it was unconstitutional and worked the same sort of injustice as would occur if one cheated a person in a land deal.[8] The frenzy to confiscate Loyalist property, and the ease with which it was accomplished, bore out Madison's theory of the danger of factions and disgruntled majorities. This was a theory he had discussed in *The Federalist No. 10* and would present in great detail at the First Congress.

Madison was a realist about human nature. This quality showed early in his life, in his concern about the power of majorities, and it was confirmed later on when he came to know the British industrialist and early socialist writer Robert Owen (whose descendant Kenneth Dale Owen would marry Jane Blaffer, the great-aunt of H. Walker Royall). Owen visited Madison at Montpelier, where they discussed issues relating to human progress, especially the plight of the poor in the growing class of industrial laborers. Owen argued that the poor are entirely victims of external "circumstance," which forms a man's character, and that character is entirely outside a man's control. However, men could be transformed by external circumstances (including education) that impose equality and eliminate competition and privilege.[9] Madison was not buying into it. He didn't believe that human nature could be changed from the outside in, or that education by itself could make men better human beings. He didn't agree that the burgeoning industrial revolution in Europe and the human misery it was beginning to spawn could be cured by trying to change human nature. "[F]or Madison the problem with [Owen's socialist theories] lay much deeper, because the British reformer failed to understand that the system he decried, and many of the specific difficulties he proposed to cure, were rooted not in deficient and corrupting institutions, but rather in the natural proclivities of man."[10]

Even after the chaos of the war years ebbed away, Madison saw other changes taking place in the country that involved the use of eminent domain. These changes, while signaling great economic growth and optimism about the future, gave pause to a realist like Madison. States were choosing new cities in which to establish their capitals, condemning land and building new state houses and avenues to accommodate them. In Madison's home state of Virginia, the capital was moved to Richmond and the state legislature appropriated gobs of money to build a new seat of government there on land taken through eminent domain. Canals were the latest thing in transportation, and states were condemning land in order to build them. They were also chartering private corporations to build canals and endowing them with powers of eminent domain.[11]

By the time Madison offered his final draft of the Bill of Rights in 1789, he also had the example of the wrangling over the Northwest Ordinance. The settlement of the Ohio Territory had begun many years earlier, and the Continental Congress had finally produced a bill establishing a territorial government after considerable political haggling. All the fuss was over a very real fear: land companies buying up property in the Ohio Territory were afraid that later legislatures would rescind the land grants made to them when Johnnie-come-lately speculators showed up with fresh dough. Things like that had been known to happen. Lobbyists were working overtime to get a contracts clause with real teeth in it and prevent this sort of disaster. In the end, the Northwest Ordinance got a turbocharged contracts clause, intended to ward off crooks and con artists, and a takings clause that provided for "full compensation" in the event that public emergencies made it necessary to take any person's property "for the common preservation."

In many ways, the Northwest Ordinance foreshadowed the constitutional and social wave of the future with respect to American private property. The Northwest Territories were enormous, stretching from the Ohio River to the eastern banks of the Mississippi and north to the Great Lakes and the Canadian border. After much politicking and soul searching, the states had agreed to cede their individual claims to the lands west of the Alleghenies and allow them to become nationalized. The war was over and suddenly, in effect, the federal government had its own stupendous colony. The Northwest Ordinance would be the test of how the newly independent United States would govern a colony of its own.

Given the example of the Northwest Ordinance, which Madison and Jefferson had approved of, surely Madison could not countenance a federal Bill of Rights that failed to send as clear a message on the importance of private property rights. What's more, only two of the states, Massachusetts and Vermont, had takings clauses that allowed for compensation in their early constitutions. But the fight over the takings clause in the Massachusetts Constitution was a cautionary tale. It was a compromise that grew out of bitter tension between farmers and merchants over seizures of Tory land. In the end, property owners responded by ramping up property ownership requirements for voting—just at the time when restrictions on voting were loosening, not tightening, in about half the colonies.[12] Massachusetts was an example of how the protection of property rights had the potential of going hand in hand with factionalism and restrictions on the right to vote. Madison had his work cut out for him in crafting a takings clause and fitting it into the Bill of Rights in such a way as to promote the liberty interests of private property without getting people's ears smoking over property-related issues like voting and land seizures.

Madison understood the practical limitations of a federal takings clause. The takings clause of the Bill of Rights would apply only to the federal government, which was only tangentially involved in takings. In 1789, almost all eminent domain proceedings were brought by the states. Indeed, a large part of the Bill of Rights served only an educative function in his view, since at that time the rights enumerated there did not apply to the states. (The Bill of Rights would not apply to the states until after the Civil War and the passage of the Fourteenth Amendment, which brought about the "incorporation doctrine.")*

Madison was deeply concerned about the power of majorities, or the mob, to wield power in a republic, and he believed it important to weave into the Constitution as many impediments as possible to the exercise of majority power. Yet in 1829, after he had left public life, Madison wondered whether he had been too inflexible on the issue of suffrage as a young man. Later in his life, after he had spent more time off the plantation, he came to think about things a bit differently. When he wrote the takings clause, the majority of Americans did not own property. Madison feared that giving everyone the right to vote ultimately endangered those who actually *did* have property. He wrote in 1829 that if you extend

---

*That is, courts interpreted the amendment to mean that all of the rights enumerated in the Bill of Rights—including the Fifth Amendment and the takings clause—applied to actions taken by the states.

the right to vote "equally to all," then "the rights of property or claims of injustice may be overruled by a majority"—a majority that has nothing to lose. He pointed to laws impairing the rights of contract that were emerging with great popularity in the states. (Examples would be laws that wiped out debts, cancelled long-term contracts for toll bridges and ferries, and otherwise hurt corporate and landed interests.) Yet Madison also began rethinking his old position and came to recognize "that there are various ways in which the rich may oppress the poor; in which property may oppress liberty; and that the world is filled with examples; it is necessary that the poor should have a defence against the danger."[13]

Having watched the explosive growth of the country in the first quarter of the nineteenth century, Madison had the foresight to see that the balance of land ownership in America would not always be so lopsided, because of the unique nature of the American continent, its society and government: "The United States have [*sic*] a precious advantage also in the actual distribution of property, particularly the landed property, and so in the universal hope of acquiring property. This latter peculiarity is among the happiest contrasts in their situation to that of the Old World, where no anticipated change in this respect can generally inspire a like sympathy with the rights of property."[14] Madison correctly predicted not only that a greater percentage of Americans would come to own property, but also that the hope of change, and change itself, would cause Americans to sympathize politically with each other's rights as property owners.

Madison realized, however, that a more pernicious and inevitable development lay around the bend. Namely, that the enormous economic engine of America would eventually swing the balance of power. Land ownership alone would not always be the ultimate road to autonomy and power in the United States. Perhaps it was his dialogs with Owen that helped him realize that "we will become a nation of capitalists and laborers," as he wrote with extraordinary prescience in 1829.[15] (By 1827, Madison was receiving the *Harmony Gazette,* a newspaper published by Owen's little utopian settlement in Indiana.)[16] He feared that this phenomenon would vest "complete power over property in hands without a share in it." Madison, who had once argued in favor of the rights of suffrage for freeholders only, warned of the day when the "propertied will have *too much* power." Here, the "propertied" meant those who have real property and capital.

There is something eerie about Madison's prediction when it is read in the context of economic development takings. Here we see what Madison feared: the encroaching power of capitalists over properties *in which they do not share ownership.* They can exert power over those properties (with the aid of municipal governments) through their superior economic might. They can buy from unwilling sellers, assume the costs of litigation on behalf of the town when necessary, and, most importantly, promise higher tax revenues for the municipality, making their development ideas an irresistible enticement. And they can do it because land ownership has become so diffuse and many property owners are relatively powerless in our society; in fact, many are downright impoverished. Today, rich property owners are rarely the targets of economic development takings. Over the last two centuries, the balance of power has flipped: our elected officials (and their appointed municipal bureaucrats who engage in the planning) do not tremble at the thought of their freeholder/voters. To the contrary, they look at communities as they would a Monopoly board, shuffling around the toy homes of the voters, deciding who will stay and who will go, substituting one business for another, a Sears for a small auto-repair business, a retailer for a spate of homes—all for the good of the community. Madison's prediction came true.

Madison witnessed the way American patriotic drive could flip like a switch to rapacious destructiveness. It would be up to future generations of lawmakers and community leaders to hold such darker, majoritarian instincts in check. Madison could not have imagined the strange and varied circumstances in which future generations would come to rely on the takings clause. Those tests would begin in the federal courts in a case during the first half of the nineteenth century, brought to the U.S. Supreme Court by a man Madison knew.

▪ ▪ ▪

Daniel Webster, the great nineteenth-century politician, attorney and orator extraordinaire, had to know the case was a stinker the first time it crossed his desk. It was 1847 and by then Webster had been practicing law for some forty-two years. He had argued at the Supreme Court more than 150 times and before state courts and commissions more times than he cared to remember. Surely he knew a loser when he saw one—and this eminent domain case, *West River Bridge Company v. Dix,* was a long shot at best. One can only imagine the groan he must have emitted when he reviewed the record on appeal from the Vermont Supreme Court, with the case poised for appeal to the U.S. Supreme Court.

There was also his age to consider. He was getting on in years and was tired of arguing constitutional cases before a Supreme Court he considered inhospitable to the legal and political views he had spent a lifetime championing. To Webster, the worlds of law and politics were often deeply entangled. As a congressman, secretary of state and senator he had fought bare-knuckled political fights that had frequently spilled over to influence the positions he took in his legal practice. Webster was a vehement defender of a strong national government, and he believed passionately in the protection of property interests and commerce unencumbered by ambitious state legislatures.

Then again, Webster was never one to turn away a paying client, sometimes playing fast and loose with ethics in a way that would shock the conscience of modern lawyers. And there was a flip side to the age factor: who knew whether he would get another chance to go to the Supreme Court on a case so perfectly aligned to push the buttons of his old political enemy, now the chief justice, Roger B. Taney? Ah, yes, Taney, appointed by that old populist dog, President Andrew Jackson. Taney was the Supreme Court justice whom Webster loved to hate. From the perspective of tormenting Taney, *West River Bridge Co. v. Dix* wasn't half bad. It encapsulated the essence of the previous two decades in American politics: the struggle between Jacksonian populists, who favored the will of the people, and the Whigs—formerly called Federalists—who favored a strong federal Constitution and a contract clause that had some teeth to it. Fortifying the contract clause had been a top priority back in the days when Webster's hero, John Marshall, had presided over the Supreme Court. But that was another day, indeed, another era. In 1847, Webster wrote to his son Fletcher, "At present, I am quite engaged in these old causes. . . . I am tired of the Constitutional questions. There is no Court for them."[17]

Webster was old and cranky. He had rheumatism. He probably had the beginnings of cirrhosis of the liver. After too many decades of high living and imbibing of fine wine, his body was rebelling like a despicable ingrate with the disease that would eventually do him in. Yet he had his principles to think of. Lately the Whigs had been clinging with growing ferocity to their vision of a strong, unified national government as they faced down the voices of disunion rising up across the nation, growing more strident every day. First it was the disputes over tariffs and now the issue of slavery that threatened to tear the Union apart. Webster was a Whig to the core of his being. Here was a chance to stand up in the High Court on a classic conservative Whig position—the preservation of private property rights in a corporate franchise.

The merits of the case were compelling, Webster thought. Those West River Bridge folks had been terribly cheated in what could only be described as an eminent domain scam. Indeed, it was theft by legislative fiat. Imagine it: a group of townspeople having the cheek to lobby the legislature to pass a law that allowed a public road to be laid right over a private bridge! The law wiped out the rights of the private bridge, which would never again collect a toll. The private bridge was miraculously transformed into a public bridge with one stroke of the legislative pen. And due to highly suspicious hemming and hawing by the township, the phantom "road" on either end of the bridge never seemed to get built.

Would the case be worth the bother? After all, everything seemed to be going to hell in a handcart, Webster feared. The Federalist dream of his forefathers was crumbling before his eyes as the Taney Court increasingly deferred to state legislatures, dismantling much of the work of the Marshall Court, which Webster had helped to forge as a young attorney. How had the country drifted so far from its Federalist origins, from the early ideals of the sanctity of property rights? Weren't we still a country grounded in the principles of natural law, organized in a government of our own choosing for the preservation of liberty and property? The West River Bridge clients shall not be denied, Webster decided. He would take their case and argue the despotic dangers of eminent domain.

There was another, equally pressing factor to consider: Webster, as usual, was broke.

Daniel Webster's extraordinary mind was one of the greatest of his generation, grasping the monumental issues of the day and propelling them toward his agenda of national unity. Time and again he would wrestle his intellectual opponents to the ground on issues like the tariff, abolitionism and state nullification of federal laws, giving stirring orations that were reprinted in newspapers and read by thousands. His legal counsel was sought out by banks, corporations and wealthy individuals. And yet the debts continued to mount. Besides, the *West River* case was an excellent match for Webster's political sympathies. Eminent domain was something he eyed with suspicion, as it involved stripping property owners of their vested rights.*

Webster still remembered the sting of losing the *Charles River Bridge* case. To him that case represented the dismantling of the Marshall Court and the rise of Chief Justice Taney and the Jacksonian populists—and he didn't like it one bit. Webster had represented the Charles River Bridge Company, which ran a toll bridge over the Charles River between Charlestown and Boston, a franchise granted to it by the state legislature. The company was for all intents and purposes put out of business in 1828 when the Massachusetts legislature responded to the kvetching of local residents about the toll by enacting a law that created the Warren Bridge Company.

The Warren Bridge was designed to span the Charles River a mere 260 feet away from the Charles River Bridge; the plan was that it would collect tolls for six years, after which it would be a free bridge. Needless to say, at that point no one would have much use for the Charles River Bridge anymore, although there were about thirty years left on the company's exclusive franchise. Webster argued that the state had, in effect, taken his client's property

*A vested right is simply a right that is presently held; it has "kicked in," so to speak. (Today, for example, people talk of vested rights in pension plans or stock options.) Early American judges took a keen interest in vested rights for a simple reason: they didn't trust legislatures. They feared that legislators could get too big for their britches and could overrun property rights too easily. Chief Justice Marshall was concerned about this danger and his fears about the loss of vested rights propelled him to raise the importance of the contract clause of the Constitution as a pivotal building block in his vision of empowering the federal Constitution and, by extension, the federal judiciary.

by eminent domain in violation of Massachusetts law without just compensation, even though the land had not literally been appropriated. In fact, the proprietors of the Charles River Bridge had not been paid a penny in damages. Though Webster did not use the words, his argument described what would now be called a "regulatory taking." He lost in state court.

The case then headed to the U.S. Supreme Court, where Webster held out some modest hope of prevailing under the contract clause of the U.S. Constitution. He would argue that the law creating the new bridge interfered with his client's contract with the state, which contained an implied right to be the exclusive bridge in that area. Chief Justice John Marshall and Justice Joseph Story, great champions of the contract clause, still sat on the Court. Webster had raised his eminent domain argument before the Massachusetts Supreme Court, where he took quite a beating, and there he left it. In 1831, technically speaking, he had no federal eminent domain claim before the U.S. Supreme Court. But he did not count on getting blindsided by opposing counsel.

The first go-round before the U.S. Supreme Court in 1831 was a close call. The justices deadlocked (since one of them was absent). Then the case languished, put over term after term as justices died or retired. In 1835, Chief Justice Marshall died and President Jackson made his move, packing the Court with Jacksonian loyalists, including a new chief justice.

Roger B. Taney had been Jackson's attorney general and close advisor. In 1833, President Jackson slipped Taney into place as secretary of the treasury with a recess appointment, after Taney had loyally helped him bob and weave in political maneuvering with respect to the second Bank of the United States. In 1834, all hell broke loose on the Hill. The Senate majority, Webster among them, voted to censure Jackson for removing deposits from the Bank of the United States. To top it off, they also voted to reject Taney's recess appointment. Jackson had tried once before to get him onto the Supreme Court when Justice Duvall retired, only to have the Senate shoot down the nomination. But with Marshall gone, Jackson finally succeeded in getting Taney and another loyalist, Philip Barbour, on the High Court in 1836. The nominations were confirmed during a mysterious executive session of the Senate, of which no records were kept.[18]

Later that year, with Taney firmly ensconced, the lawyers on the *Charles River Bridge* case were called back to the U.S. Supreme Court to reargue the case. Imagine Webster's chagrin at facing Taney, who now held the upper hand. Taney was a "consummate Jacksonian." He even eschewed the knee britches of the sort that Marshall used to wear and instead wore long trousers as a symbol of his democratic affiliations.[19] Webster didn't need a crystal ball to figure out which way this case was heading.

This time around, the defendants brought in the big guns. Senator John Davis of Massachusetts, a well-known lawyer and rising political star, argued for Warren Bridge in a tour de force that foreshadowed an age of laissez-faire capitalism. He told the Court, in essence, that although the Charles River Bridge investors had gotten a tough break, that was part of the cost of doing business and a risk that everyone assumes in a bustling economy. The right of the government, Davis argued, "to impose embargoes ... to change public policy, to regulate intercourse with foreign countries, and to do and perform many other things—all of which may subject the people to great hazards and losses—has never and can never be questioned, whatever may be their influence upon trade or individual property."[20] This was all grandiloquence, considering that the new bridge was just a way to wriggle out of an obligation to pay tolls made in a fair-and-square deal back in 1785.

The defense team had yet to throw its curve ball. Knowing full well that eminent domain was off the table at the federal Supreme Court, Davis's co-counsel, Harvard law professor Simon Greenleaf, went ahead and raised the subject anyway, catching Webster off-guard. Step by step he dismantled the lingering attachment of American courts to natural law, both in the form of vested rights—so close to the heart of the Marshall legacy and so key to the protection of private property—and as "implied rights," which was the linchpin of Webster's case. (That is, even though the statute that granted the franchise to the Charles River Bridge Company didn't say the company would be the only bridge in that location, the logic of justice under a system of natural law dictated that result under the tradition of "implied rights.")

Greenleaf told the court that the Charles River Bridge Company could not possibly have an exclusive, implied right to operate a bridge at that location for a specific number of years, unmolested by anyone. For the government of Massachusetts to give up the right to hold sway over that location would require it to surrender a portion of its sovereignty; and that would mean the government was bargaining away its power of eminent domain—which it could not do! The power to take private property for public use, said Greenleaf, is essential "to the constitution and well-being of civil society."[21] What he failed to mention was that all the lawyers had hashed out the eminent domain arguments in state court, where they had been thoroughly rejected. Indeed, the state court had said that there would be no compensation because there had been no act of eminent domain in the first place. But now the eminent domain cat was out of the bag in federal court—the very place it was not supposed to roam. What an exquisite corner Greenleaf had backed Webster into.

Now Webster was well and truly angry. Greenleaf reported to a friend that Webster was downright abusive to him when court reconvened several days later. Sulking through his oral argument, Webster tried to bring the justices back to a more central theme, the broken contract, comparing his client's bridge franchise to the land grant ultimately upheld by the U.S. Supreme Court in other famous cases involving contracts honored under the contract clause of the Constitution. He pointed out key cases such as *Dartmouth College v. Woodward,* in which a group of board members was stopped from making Dartmouth College a public institution; and *Fletcher v. Peck,* involving the notorious Yazoo Land Grant fraud, in which the Georgia legislature was told by the Supreme Court that it would have to honor the contract made by an earlier, crooked legislature that had taken bribes in exchange for selling millions of prime acres to conniving land speculators. "[T]hey cannot be treated or considered as mere laws ... they are contracts," Webster argued, "for this [money] was paid...." When the contract clause runs smack up against a "taking," a citizen's vested rights take priority.

When the arguments were all done, Webster was not optimistic. He wrote to Jeremiah Mason, an old colleague, handicapping the outcome: "The Bridge case will be decided today, & decided wrong.... The Court is revolutionized. Politics have gotten possession of the Bench, at last, & it is in vain to deny, or attempt to disguise it." He predicted that the older judges, Joseph

Story included, would adhere to the Marshall vision of protecting individual vested rights. They "will be for reversing the judgment of the State Court; the four new judges [the Jackson appointees] for affirming. . . ."[22] In the end, only Justice Story sided with Webster on the merits of the case. Chief Justice Taney wrote the majority opinion. He said it is not enough to claim the bridge had such an extraordinary right by "implication." A right to operate to the exclusion of all competitors must be spelled out in the contract.

Taney was taking a far broader view of the law as the protector of the community at large, and in particular a nation that was growing by leaps and bounds and offering opportunity to the average man in a way that an earlier generation could not have imagined. "The object and end of all government is to promote the happiness and prosperity of the community by which it is established," Taney wrote. "And in a country like ours, free, active and enterprising, continually advancing in numbers and wealth, new channels of communication are daily found necessary, both for travel and trade, and are essential to the comfort, convenience and prosperity of the people."[23]

Taney danced around a good many of the facts in the case, which clearly suggested that the legislature had intended all along for the bridge to take over for the ferry service that Harvard University used to operate in that location, and to have an exclusive right to operate there for a specified number of years. But Taney nonetheless made a clear departure from the doctrine of "implied rights," held dear by an earlier generation of judges steeped in the traditions of natural law and the whispery shadows of Enlightenment philosophy.

Reaction to the case divided largely along party lines. Conservative businessmen and corporate interests saw *Charles River* as a sign that Whig influence on the Court and the federal government was waning. Though Justice Story had done his best, lashing out in a stern dissent and giving one last hurrah for the contract clause and vested rights in private property, the days of the Marshall Court were truly over. Webster asked Jeremiah Mason to keep his ears open for a good private position for Joseph Story in Boston: "Justice Story has decided on leaving the Bench, & I think he is right. He can add nothing to his reputation by staying on it, & will only subject himself to continual mortification . . . on all great questions [he will be] voted down."[24] To the Jacksonians, it was an obvious victory for the power of legislatures and the states' rights movement.

Taney, Webster and Story agreed about one thing: at the heart of cases like *Charles River* was a battle over economic policy. How would the hand of the law guide this rapidly growing nation? Conservatives like Webster and Story believed that confidence in the inviolability of private property and contract—a deal made is a deal kept—was essential to getting people to invest and the best way to build the economy in the long term. But populists like Taney had a different vision: vested rights must be sacrificed where necessary for the sake of unbridled competition and the rise of the little man. The principle of natural law and the Lockean idea that the central role of government is the preservation of private property were giving way to something new: the notion that the good of the many, the well-being of the "community," stands over and above the need to protect the property rights of the individual. This change started out quietly but would become ever more obvious in the eminent domain decisions of the twentieth century and finally in *Kelo,* when courts would pay great deference to the will of legislatures and take into consideration such factors as the need for jobs and economic growth in the community.

Webster saw the *Charles River* decision as virtually decimating the contract clause of the Constitution and he was deeply disturbed by it on a personal level.[25] This sort of loss was hard to take for a man who had argued some of the most important constitutional cases of his time, the sort that continue to be part of the standard fare of first-year law students nearly two hundred years later: in particular, *Gibbons v. Ogden* (the regulation of interstate commerce) and *McCulloch v. Maryland* (the distribution of power between the state and federal governments).

Not only was the Court taking a different direction, led by Taney in his man-of-the-people trousers, but the entire nation had been set on a course of grassroots democracy. Webster was growing nostalgic for the days when his interpretation of the Constitution had gotten a better reception at the High Court. During a major commercial case in 1847, he wrote to a client: "I hope for success & should have no doubt, if the Court was composed as formerly. But when I look up the Bench, I see, that Marshall &

Thompson & *Story* are not there."[26] To Webster, the rising level of activism in state legislatures and the willingness of the courts to defer to legislatures were a worrisome trend. Webster, after all, was not just a practicing lawyer but a lifetime politician. He knew that the decisions made in the lofty chambers of the U.S. Supreme Court and the appellate courts of the states would trickle down to local politics, where the powerful could trample the weak and where corruption and influence peddling could easily infuse the political process.

Webster marveled at how emboldened the state legislatures had become. For instance, the Massachusetts legislature had passed a law taxing passengers of steamships—and not allowing them to disembark unless they paid the tax. Other northeastern states had similar laws, the goal being to control the entry of paupers and other immigrants. States such as New York and Massachusetts saw no reason for the federal government to stick its nose into such matters. Webster was involved in these "Passenger Cases," arguing that only the federal government had the power to regulate interstate commerce in this regard. While he waited for the Court's decision, he wrote to his son Fletcher: "It is strange to me how any Legislature of Massachusetts could pass such a law. In the days of Marshall and Story, it would not have stood one moment. The present Judges, I fear, are quite much inclined to find apologies for irregular and dangerous acts of State Legislat[ures."[27] The passenger tax was defeated by a hair—the vote was 5–4. Taney and the other Jacksonians were in the minority, but Webster and his generation were running out of steam.

For Webster, *West River Bridge v. Dix* would mean another long-shot argument before the Taney Court. At first blush, the case must have seemed like *Charles River Bridge* all over again. Here was a toll bridge owner from Vermont, weeping over a calamitous investment. His company had been incorporated by the state in 1795 with an express grant to collect tolls for one hundred years, and had poured a lot of money into building a stone bridge over West River in the town of Brattleboro. Suddenly his future profits were wrested from him by a group of disgruntled townspeople who were tired of paying tolls after forty years. This particular group, unlike the folks in Massachusetts, didn't come up with a plan to build a second bridge at taxpayers' expense. Thrifty New

Englanders, they had a better idea. They lobbied the state legislature to pass a "highway act" that allowed county courts to take any real estate or corporate property in order to facilitate the building of a highway. Lo and behold, a few years later, a petition was filed in the local court near Brattleboro, asking for a resurvey of the existing road and requesting that all of the rights that the West River Bridge Company had in its toll bridge "be taken for the purpose of making a free road and bridge" across the river, and complaining that the existing bridge was a "sore grievance" which should no longer "be endured."[28] The town wanted to terminate the West River Bridge Company's ownership of the bridge, its right of way over the river at that location, and more importantly, its right to collect tolls (i.e., the franchise) for the remainder of the hundred-year contract.

The rising tide of Jacksonian democracy had caught up with Webster at last, as state legislatures were flexing their muscles. Here was a law that undercut the vested interests of a businessman who had built a bridge and who had a contractual right, a solid deal with the state. Now the state, exercising eminent domain through its legislature, was doing exactly the sort of mischief that Madison had warned about: coming along a generation—or an election—later and pulling the rug out from under a solid deal.

Webster argued that the plan for the public road was nothing but a sham, contrived to bring the condemnation case against the bridge owner in order to end the toll and destroy "the force and obligation of a contract" that existed between the West River Bridge Company and the town. To add insult to injury, the amount of compensation awarded to the bridge owner at the trial had been woefully inadequate. First, Webster argued that the bridge owners held a franchise, which is a very special type of right; it is not ordinary property like land or shares in a corporation, but rather a type of sovereignty, temporarily extended from the state to the holder of the franchise. Having temporarily given away a bit of its sovereignty, the state cannot now use eminent domain against it. Webster, no stranger to political shenanigans, noted the potential for political mischief. "What prevents the State from granting the same charter to some political favorite tomorrow?" he asked. Once the legislature has the power to impair a contract and take a state contract from one citizen under eminent domain, he argued, what will stop the legislature from turning around and selling it to others at a better price?[29]

The case was covered by the press, including the local Brattleboro paper, the *Weekly Eagle*, which sent a reporter to Washington for the occasion. The reporter came away with the clear impression that Webster and the opposing counsel were arguing from entirely different approaches, almost as if they were arguing different cases—a very unusual phenomenon before the High Court. The "ground taken" by Webster, the *Weekly Eagle* reported, was that the law revoking the franchise "conflicts directly with . . . the constitution of the United States which forbids the several States to pass any law 'impairing the obligation of contracts.'" But the town's counsel, Mr. Phillips, "on the other hand, bases his arguments on the principle of 'Eminent Domain'—that the State has the right to take private property, and even vacate franchises granted by itself, for the public good. The question is one of great importance, as affecting chartered rights, and its decision is looked for with much interest."[30]

The Court ruled against Webster's client, the bridge owner. It stated in no uncertain terms that eminent domain "is, as its name imports, paramount to all private rights vested under the government." Simply put, there was nothing out there that the government could not put under the thumb of eminent domain. *West River* swept away a major impediment to the exercise of eminent domain, helping to clear the path for the twentieth-century cases that used the police power to define the scope of what a legislature could take in eminent domain. In those cases, eminent domain would be used toward social and cultural goals, often mixed with political agendas—especially through urban renewal and later with economic development takings.

West River may have been about a single bridge, but a bad precedent at the High Court can set a mighty legal machine in motion, as the *Weekly Eagle* noted. Webster couldn't have agreed more. He saw the beginnings of a pernicious trend and warned that the Court's failure to keep eminent domain "within some safe and well-defined limits [will make] our State governments . . . but unlimited despotisms." The states' rights movement and popular democracy were in the ascendant, and state legislatures were feeling their oats as never before. "They will soon resolve themselves into the will of the existing majority as to what shall be taken, and what shall be left to any obnoxious natural or artificial person," Webster wrote. It didn't take much of a stretch, he believed, to go from the circumstances of the *West River* case to a time when "the legislature or their agents, are to be the sole judges of what is to be taken, and to what public use it is to be appropriated, [and] the most levelling ultraisms of Anti-rentism or agrarianism or Abolitionism may be successfully advanced."[31]

CHAPTER 6

BLIGHT, BEAUTY, BOUNTY

Daniel Webster turned out to be more correct than he could have imagined. In the twentieth century, eminent domain would come to be used as a tool for all sorts of "ultraisms": the massive relocation of more than a million people and the leveling of large chunks of cities in the name of urban renewal and modernist urban planning; historic land redistribution in Hawaii (precisely the "anti-rentism" of Webster's *West River* premonition); and finally "economic development takings," the fodder of municipal politicians, bureaucrats, real estate developers and influence peddlers, all jockeying for position in the management and payola of America's towns and cities. Each of these "ultraisms" would chip away at the autonomy of the American property owner. The major theme that allowed eminent domain to bust out of the dreary box of public projects like utilities and road building and into the sexy light of the cultural zeitgeist can be stated in one word: blight.

The thing that enabled Webster to make his prediction back in 1848 was history. When he argued *West River,* he had been in politics nearly four decades and was as well versed in the law as any man of his time. He surely knew that municipal governments since early colonial times had been taking land in eminent domain not just for public uses such as roads, but also, on occasion, in the furtherance of *private* interests. The takings clause of the Fifth Amendment has always been a malleable thing, and the more leeway allowed in its interpretation, the more potential for political mischief. Even in the early nineteenth century, while some private takings were similar to the ones we have today for public utilities, not all cases fit so neatly into the "public use" box. They sometimes had a more dubious connection to the community at large. With the rise in the power of state legislatures, it's understandable that Webster's imagination made the mental leap to a time when eminent domain could be used to advance political agendas.

Early American takings started out innocently enough. The government recognized that private interests on occasion would have to give way where the greater good was concerned. This idea first emerged in connection with the mill-dam acts, which were passed to allow gristmills to flood their upstream neighbors so long as compensation was paid. The mills were privately owned, but the government closely regulated their fees. People considered the practice fair in much the same way we regard takings for public utilities to be fair today.[1] The government's regulatory role, plus the widespread and immediate benefit to the public, softened the blow for property owners. The United States was a rural economy and the farmers had to get their corn ground up somewhere.

Bit by bit, mission creep snuck in. Soon corporations were using the mill-dam acts as precedent for statutes that harnessed water power for mills that were private in nature (for iron, lumber, textiles). Since eminent domain is a matter of state law, the courts differed on how narrowly "public use" should be read. In some states, a mere showing of a public "benefit" was enough.[2] For example, New Jersey in 1832 was the site of a cantankerous fight over land on the Delaware River, where a mill owner wanted to toss out the owners of the land and set up seventy mills. The property owners argued that such a taking would render the "public use" clause meaningless. Relying on the mill-dam acts as precedents, the court wrote—174 years before the *Kelo* case—that "the ever varying condition of society is constantly presenting new objects of public importance and utility; and what shall be considered a public use or benefit must depend somewhat on the situation and wants of the community for the time being."[3] By 1870, eminent domain was being used for private water power development on rivers in Maine, Connecticut, New Hampshire, Wisconsin, Indiana and Tennessee. Not all states, however, hopped on the bandwagon; New York, Georgia and Alabama rejected the practice.[4]

During the late nineteenth and early twentieth century, canals, railroads, bridges and roads were built across America. To get the job done, corporations were routinely granted powers of eminent domain as the states and territories were molding this enormous expanse of earth to their will. And yet municipalities did not run amok. Eminent domain was still perceived as an action closely tied to necessity, for the marshalling of natural resources or the taming of the land. A number of factors could have contributed to the self-restraint that still abided in the land.

In the early part of the nineteenth century, important conservative figures such as Daniel Webster and his colleague Justice Joseph Story—who not only served on the U.S. Supreme Court but helped shape American law and legal education at Harvard—opposed the expansion of eminent domain powers. There were also others who viewed eminent domain with suspicion. Just as the Taney Court had looked askance at anything that smelled of a monopoly in the *West River* case, populists in the mid-nineteenth century were dubious of anything that smelled of oppression of the "little man."[5] Beginning in the 1850s, states such as Ohio, Iowa and Kansas began to implement reforms in eminent domain compensation. Many features in those reforms are still used today in takings. They include, for example, the practice of the city paying the compensation into court before taking title to the condemned land, and the expanded use of juries to determine compensation.

And there was another big fly in the ointment that kept towns and cities from going slaphappy with eminent domain: municipal financing began to dry up around midcentury. The early nineteenth century saw a period of explosive growth in America, when towns and cities were digging canals and building roads as fast as they could clear the trees or move the dirt. Much of this was done through "[l]and grants and subsidies, financed by high interest bonds."[6] Legislatures and the courts started to put the brakes on this trend after nine states defaulted on bond obligations.[7] What developed in the case law and in state constitutions was a far more skeptical approach to state debt. State legislatures made clear that this wasn't funny money to play around with anymore and amended their constitutions to put limits on state debt. Courts struggled with questions of whether debt taken on by quasi-public corporations—of the type that were often endowed with powers of eminent domain—should be considered public debt, subject to state constitutional limitations.

In the twentieth century, states and municipalities began to figure out ways to work around this roadblock. One way was to establish public corporations that enabled projects to be done that were not bonded with money guaranteed directly by the state. As a result, the initiative for projects shifted to the county and city level, where money could be borrowed and bonded.[8] This trend put money, and hence power, into the hands of local officials who headed up public corporations, such as economic development corporations, which have powers of eminent domain. Public financing of large-scale eminent domain projects occurs routinely today, both in economic development takings such as the Freeport marina (for which the city planned to float a $3 million bond to help generate the $6 million it was loaning the developer) and in classic public projects such as ballparks or roads, which often come with a mixed bundle of state public authority and city bonds. It isn't hard to imagine how the nineteenth-century suspicion of municipal financing served to slow the pace of eminent domain activity through the latter half of that century.

Finally, before the New Deal it hadn't occurred to many local legislatures that they held the magic wand to revitalize their sagging waterfronts or depressed downtowns. Tinkering with the economy, strictly speaking, was not government work. But such notions are taken for granted today. During the oral argument at the Supreme Court in the *Kelo* case, no one blinked an eye when Justice Ruth Bader Ginsburg, speaking of the town of New London, Connecticut, pointed out that "the community had gone down and down and the town wanted to build it up." Therefore, she asked the attorney for the homeowners, wasn't the town justified in condemning working-class homes and building a row of expensive waterfront condominiums to increase tax revenues? When the government came to a point where it was predisposed to meddling in the economic, aesthetic and cultural life of American cities, it certainly helped set the stage for economic development takings.

States had figured out how to raise money again; everyone had an idea to peddle for saving their local community in the New

Deal age; and America was on the cusp of modernism in urban design. All that was needed was something to jump-start the process.

▪ ▪ ▪

One day in the spring of 1942, a congressman named George Arthur Paddock from Illinois decided to take a walk in Southwest Washington, D.C. Mr. Paddock was shocked—shocked!—to find blacks living in slum conditions there. He saw "housing without central heating; without indoor toilet facilities; without running water; indeed, without any of the amenities that would presumably have been considered absolutely necessary in his native Evanston, Ill., a wealthy Chicago suburb."[9]

Slums in Washington, D.C., were nothing new, but these neighborhoods had lately seen overcrowding because of World War II, and Representative Paddock was alarmed at the thought that an epidemic might start in the neighborhood and spread to Capitol Hill and "hamper the war effort." He gave a speech before the House of Representatives to alert official Washington to the potential crisis and called for the immediate enactment of a housing code for the District of Columbia.[10] The first few measures seemed sensible enough: a law already on the books was amended to speed up the condemnation of dilapidated structures, and a large chunk of money was set aside under the Lanham Act to house defense workers near the District of Columbia (ostensibly to avoid overcrowding inside the District).

But once the politicians got their hands on the potential for all that epidemic-containing, soul-redeeming redevelopment of prime real estate, they couldn't let go. After all, the Senate District of Columbia Committee had begun an investigation of the slums and it had to yield something fruitful. Two camps began to form: those in favor of knocking everything down and bringing in hotshot real estate tycoons to build private, low-cost housing, and those in favor of knocking everything down and doing private development, with a smattering of public housing.[11] This being Washington, a compromise was reached the old-fashioned way: a law was passed that would breathe fresh life into a Washington bureaucracy. Hence the District of Columbia Redevelopment Act of 1945, which directed the National Capital Planning Commission to create a plan for Southwest Washington, D.C. The plan envisioned the redevelopment of a 76-acre parcel near the Capitol and the Mall, in the heart of the District of Columbia. By 1950, the National Capital Planning Commission was ready to begin bulldozing a section of Southwest called Development Area B. Close to ten thousand people lived there; nearly all of them were black. Area B had the most serious slum conditions of all the tracts in the Southwest redevelopment areas. It also had a thriving commercial area called Fourth Street. Some of the stores on Fourth Street were slated for the wrecking ball.[12]

An important thing had happened while the Planning Commission was drawing up blueprints for Southwest: another statute was passed by Congress. The Federal Housing Act of 1949 would change the face of American cities. Title I of the act was plain in its mandate, saying that "every American deserves a decent home and suitable living environment." Title I would open the spigot from which billions of federal dollars would flow into the states. The strategy was unambiguous: knock everything down and start over again. According to a presidential advisory committee, "Millions of dwellings must be demolished and large areas must be cleared.... *A PIECEMEAL ATTACK ON SLUMS WILL NOT WORK!* We must clear our slums and we must add good new housing to the supply.... [W]e must get at the causes as well as the symptoms of the trouble."[13]

Mandates don't get much clearer than that. Within the blink of an eye, municipal bureaucrats started lapping up federal dollars, razing slums and dislocating poor people as if they were expecting an invasion of friendly aliens for whom they had to make plenty of room. Martin Anderson, in his seminal book *The Federal Bulldozer,* wrote that between 1949 and 1963 as many as 609,000 people were displaced by urban renewal projects.[14] Only one-quarter of them, he estimated, were assisted in finding new living quarters by government officials; most muddled through on their own. Yet even with the unmistakable mandate from the federal government, there remained a nagging constitutional question: was all this bulldozing and shuffling of human beings in the name of blight removal actually constitutional? Even as cities all around the country were going at it with gusto, no one was sure.[15] But the U.S. Supreme Court settled the question in *Berman v. Parker* (1954).

The Berman firm was the executor of the estate of Max Morris, who had owned a department store on Fourth Street, in Development Area B, Tract 60.* It was slated to be bulldozed so a private developer could put up office buildings, parking garages, residences and, of course, other stores. The family wanted to keep the store in business. Berman argued that it was one thing to knock down old houses that lacked indoor toilets and electricity so as to build new ones, but quite another to take away this perfectly good business only to turn the land over to another private businessman—which was the plan for Fourth Street. "It was actually a densely populated, predominately back neighborhood," wrote Charlotte Allen, who lives in that neighborhood today, on the very street where Morris had his store. It was "dilapidated on some blocks, tidy and middle class on others." Fourth Street "was then the commercial heart of Southwest, with block after block of thriving small businesses."[16] The majority of Southwest was slated for private development, which seemed unfair to the Morris heirs. The federal district court agreed with Berman in principle as to his particular property, but ruled that the statute was constitutional because it also condemned properties that were "injurious to the public health, safety, morals and welfare."[17]

The U.S. Supreme Court thought there was no need to pussyfoot around this way. To define the limits of the police power that may be exercised by the legislature, wrote William O. Douglas, would be "fruitless." Why stop at public safety or public health? "Miserable and disreputable housing conditions may do more than spread disease and crime and immorality. They may also suffocate the spirit by reducing the people there to the status of cattle.... They may also be an ugly sore, a blight on the community which robs it of charm, which makes it a place from which men turn." Douglas, writing for a unanimous Court, was troubled by the thought of individual property owners coming forward on future redevelopment plans and picking them apart, property by property. He urged "judicial restraint" and deference to the legislature and its redevelopment plan as an unquestioned, integral whole. Douglas made clear that it was up to the legislature to determine

*Tract numbers refer to the United States Census tracts.

the scope of the plan, and that it would be difficult indeed to imagine a purpose that would not fit within the confines of the police powers of the Constitution and be enforceable by the Court: "Public safety, public health, morality, peace and quiet, law and order—these are some of the more conspicuous examples of the traditional application of the police power ... they merely illustrate [it]."

Any federal or local bureaucrat who had doubts about Title I of the Federal Housing Act of 1949 could now breathe easy. *Berman* became the galvanizing case that sent a message to a restless nation: boundless opportunities existed to use eminent domain in order to take that which did not belong to them in the higher cause of the new urbanism and modernist design. No longer would the poor have to live in outdated, substandard housing, in communities that had risen up helter-skelter during our 150 years as a disorganized, unplanned nation. The past would be razed and the future would be laid down in Mies van der Rohe simplicity. And the poor who had to be displaced from their communities would just have to get jiggy with it.

From urban renewal to economic development takings there runs a continuous thread called blight. For blight, as a generation of urban planners and legislators would come to learn, is rather like beauty: it is in the eye of the beholder. To say there is blight is not quite the same thing as saying one beholds a slum. The word "slum" conjures all sorts of dire images: vermin, overcrowding, dangerous stairwells, poor ventilation, lack of heat or hot water, and the like. But blight encompasses more subtle and often highly subjective conditions, including how streets and lots are laid out. People today might be shocked to see the rather ordinary structures and neighborhoods to which the "blight" label has been applied.

Reading the Federal Housing Act of 1949, it's easy to figure that the goal is improved housing for the poor. Simply replace bad housing with good housing. The statute provides funding for slum clearance and urban redevelopment. However, there are loopholes big enough to drive a bulldozer through. Essentially, the area to be cleared by the federally funded bulldozer has to be "primarily residential"—either *before* the federal government pays two-thirds of the cost to clear it or *after* it is cleared. This means a city could tear down a residential slum and then build a commercial development. It could also tear down a slum area that was not primarily residential and then build *expensive* residences. Under Title I, the federal government is only paying to clear out the slums.[18]

After all, the name of the statute is not the "Federal Low-Income Housing Act." Somehow, the drafters of the law simply assumed that all those poor people displaced by the bulldozers would miraculously find their way back into their communities. For the most part, they didn't. Suddenly towns and cities were flush with federal money to bulldoze slums, and with nothing but their consciences to compel them to replace the low-income housing that had previously existed there. Federal money was flowing in to build low-income housing under other parts of the 1949 law, but the question of who would get that housing was often tinged with racial politics, especially in the 1950s. Early on, it was evident that the urban renewal program was impacting minorities heavily. The program was ruefully referred to in the black community as "Negro clearance" or "Negro removal"; and the Los Angeles Community Redevelopment Agency was dubbed the "Chicano Relocation Agency."[19]

Welcome to the age of urban renewal.

Berman v. Parker is a prime example of promises made and broken—in this case, right under the noses of the congressmen who had passed the District Redevelopment Act in the first place. The statute was the *cri de coeur* to uplift the downtrodden who lived in the worst sections of Southwest, a mere stone's throw from the Capitol steps.[20] According to census records, before the renewal (in 1950), some 9,559 people lived in Tract 60, of whom 9,071 were black, and there were 2,373 housing units. (Max Morris's store was in Tract 60.) After the renewal (in 1960), 7,000 of the black residents were gone and the neighborhood was full of office buildings. One-third of the 622 housing units were occupied by blacks. The median income had more than doubled. The figures for the neighboring Tract 56 were more jarring. In 1950 there were 9,071 black residents, whom urban renewal was supposed to save from ghetto life; in 1960 there were 1,056 black residents, clustered into low-income housing at the southern end of the tract.[21] In all, "only 310 of the 5900 new residences constructed after the condemnations were classified as affordable to the displaced residents of the area, and within a few years the neighborhood became majority white."[22] Poor black neighborhoods became upscale white business and residential neighborhoods, while black residents were left to fend for themselves in fringe neighborhoods, pushed farther away from the center of the city. It was a pattern that came to be repeated time and again across America.

Of course, the Supreme Court couldn't have known all this when it ruled on *Berman* in 1954. But would it have made a difference? Justice Douglas clearly relied on what the government had laid forth as a grand plan: the National Capital Planning Commission said that one-third of the housing would be "low-rent housing with a maximum rental of $17 per room per month." If the development had been built as planned, there would have been more than a thousand such units. In the end, though, as a legal proposition it didn't matter exactly what got built. And that is the enduring lesson of *Berman.* Douglas made it clear that Congress had the power to remake Southwest in any fashion it chose, and the Court would not look over its shoulder as a super-legislature: "If those who govern the District of Columbia decide that the nation's Capital should be beautiful as well as sanitary, there is nothing in the Fifth Amendment that stands in the way."[23]

The story of eminent domain in the twentieth century is largely a story of idealism gone haywire. It's worth noting that *Berman* was decided six months after *Brown v. Board of Education,* the famous school desegregation case. (Actually, if one discounts the summer months when the Court is not in session, *Berman* practically followed on the heels of *Brown.*) This was a Court flexing its liberal muscles at the dawn of the civil rights era, ready to use its police powers to reshape America from the ground up.

■ ■ ■

Eminent domain would become the great forklift with which idealistic urban planners would pick up millions of pounds of American earth and mold our cities to their modernist vision. Open an urban planning textbook to the index and you will see dozens of entries under eminent domain. Over the decades, real estate developers, urban planners, municipal bureaucrats and others involved in shaping urban environments started teaching to the test: an important way we change things around in a city is by using eminent domain. Just seven years after *Berman,* Jane Jacobs, in *The*

Death and Life of Great American Cities, cautioned against the overuse of eminent domain and questioned its fairness. The ensuing four decades have borne out her concerns. As Jacobs noted in her brief to the Supreme Court in the *Kelo* case, eminent domain was used liberally after *Berman* to reshape American cities, with a disproportionate impact on black Americans.[24]

The *Berman* case was a turning point in the history of American property rights, but not just because of the sweeping, expansive nature of Justice Douglas's language, which left virtually no limits to the relationship between the police power of the state and the takings clause of the Fifth Amendment. The case was a turning point because it christened the great mother ship of urban renewal, allowing eminent domain to set sail over the American landscape and pick up passengers who were like devotees of a new municipal religion. Legal cases don't become important when they sit on the shelf unnoticed; it is when they live and breathe in the public consciousness, influencing the choices people make, that cases are important. *Berman* was important because people felt empowered by it to fight blight and refashion neighborhoods.

If you can fight blight, why not create beauty? If beauty, why not bounty?

The police power of the state molded itself to all sorts of social goals. Daniel Webster's prediction in the *West River* case was coming true: eminent domain was now a tool of political opportunism, wielded in the service of social and political philosophies. This trend in the common law was pulled along by Congress, which created the Community Development Block Grant Program in 1974. This program was intended to give communities more flexibility and control over local projects and reduce delays and red tape. The program was expanded in 1977 to include the Urban Development Action Grant.[25] UDAG projects sound a lot like modern economic development takings. UDAG funds were combined with slum clearance projects and "could be used for virtually any private development that produced new jobs and increased local tax revenues." The funds were often used for infrastructure improvements that would lure "tax rich businesses and jobs."[26] Many people questioned whether this really helped the poor at all, or simply made it easier for large businesses to operate on prime downtown real estate. For example, UDAG funds were used to construct high-end projects like Boston's Copley Place Hotel and a Neiman Marcus department store. In fact, "half of all downtown malls constructed between 1978 and 1985 received UDAG financing."[27] Clearly, the idea of the poor making way for economic development (supposedly for their own eventual good)—with some form of federal funding thrown into the mix—was becoming well established in the popular imagination.

Urban Development Action Grants accounted for a very small portion of the federal budget. Indeed, by the late 1970s, the age of big bucks for urban renewal was waning.[28] But developers and cities had learned important lessons from a quarter-century of dancing to the tune of Title I and its progeny: that commercial development could rise from the rubble of poor neighborhoods, and that when private developers work with government, they get the bonus of eminent domain, a convenient tool for assembling land.

An early experiment in seeking bounty from the fountain of eminent domain took place in the gritty Detroit neighborhood of Poletown. It was one of the first large-scale economic development takings.

Poletown, Michigan, was a place that by all rights should never have made it onto any historian's map. It was just a working-class neighborhood of Detroit, composed of single-family homes, churches, schools and businesses. The residents were about one-half Polish Catholic and one-half black. They had jobs in nearby factories and quietly went about the business of pursuing the American Dream. Yet Poletown has acquired a kind of infamy in legal and social-science circles, forever equated with the idea of government folly and waste. It was not destroyed on grounds of blight, like so many neighborhoods taken in the post-*Berman* years, for it was not blighted. Poletown was a living, breathing neighborhood that more than three thousand people called home. It was reduced to rubble because those in positions of power were of a single mind, and they believed its sacrifice was necessary to the survival of the city as a whole.

In 1980, Detroit was in dire straits. With an 18.3 percent unemployment rate, the city was willing to grasp at just about any straw that General Motors threw its way. GM had a plant in the vicinity that was getting old and needed to be retooled. But retooling was very expensive, so GM said it was willing to build a new plant in Detroit that would provide six thousand jobs. All Detroit had to do was provide the land. But not just any land: it had to have five hundred contiguous acres and be accessible by highway and rail, free from toxic waste, cleared of any structures and suitably cheap. The deal had to be ready to close mighty quick, and tax abatements were demanded, too. Otherwise, GM would take its business and its six thousand jobs elsewhere.

Like an ugly duckling asked to the prom by the captain of the football team, the city fell over itself in its effort to accommodate GM. After surveying the possibilities, in the fall of 1980, the authorities fixed upon the Poletown neighborhood because of its configuration and its proximity to transportation. The city did not regard the thousands of people who lived, went to school, owned businesses and worshipped in churches there as an insurmountable impediment.[29] They would be cleared out—and fast. In addition, the Detroit City Council granted GM a twelve-year, 50 percent tax abatement for the new plant.

Naturally, GM required clear title to the entire contiguous parcel, with no recalcitrant sellers or hangers-on. Detroit's contract with GM required the city to deliver title by May 1, 1981, according to Alan Ackerman, an attorney who represented business owners in certain aspects of the Poletown litigations. That was an extraordinarily short period of time in which to assemble such a large parcel of land free and clear of title encumbrances. There was only one way to acquire so much land from so many people so quickly: through the coercive power of eminent domain. The city filed suit against the home and business owners on November 24, 1980, to acquire title by court order. In the end, 1,500 homes were condemned, along with 144 businesses, sixteen churches, two schools, a hospital and an abandoned concrete factory (which cost a fortune to demolish). In all, some 3,400 people were uprooted.

One might have expected that factions would emerge among the powerful in Detroit, but the opposite occurred. "There was a sense of inevitability about the whole thing," recalled Ackerman. "You had massive pillars of the community" such as the archdiocese, Mayor Coleman Young, Governor Bill Milliken, the UAW and GM "all supporting something."

It is also possible that an element of racial politics was involved—one that is seldom addressed in the retelling of the Poletown story, which has taken on the white liberal mythology of being purely the saga of a mighty corporation steamrolling over a distressed city. The truth may be rather different, especially when one considers the integral role that race has played in the history of eminent domain in America.

Coleman Young was Detroit's first black mayor. He was not a man to be trifled with. He had come up the hard way and had stood up time and again to some of the biggest bullies America had to offer. Consider his confrontation early in his public life with the House Committee on Un-American Activities, which investigated him in connection with his role as a labor organizer in the automobile industry. Young mocked the committee members, refused to answer their questions, and famously corrected the way Frank Tavenner, the committee's counsel, pronounced the word "Negro." ("It's Negro, not *nigra*.")[30] In essence, Young told the committee to bugger off. They took no further action against him.

When Young took office in 1973, Detroit was a city in transition. There was a nearly fifty-fifty balance of white and black citizens, with blacks gaining in population and white flight diminishing the tax base. Mayor Young was faced with a rising crime rate, double-digit unemployment, and the general economic decline of the rust belt. Yet he showed himself to be a savvy player, ahead of his time in his ability to partner with the private sector in development projects, finding ways to attract businesses and keep them in Detroit. Indeed, according to Wilbur C. Rich's hagiography, it was Young who approached GM with the idea of building a new plant within city limits.[31]

Young also knew his way around Washington; the contacts he established in the Carter administration would prove invaluable during the Poletown crisis in 1980. When push came to shove, he was able to rustle up an extraordinary (for 1980) $138 million in HUD loans and grants to help cover Detroit's costs for the project. It's reasonable to posit that in Young's view, GM was not the barbarian at the gate, but rather the savior of jobs—indeed, the savior of the city itself, a city with an increasing black constituency.

Before committing to the deal, the Detroit Community Economic Development Department conducted a cost/benefit analysis to determine whether the project was worthwhile. No matter how favorably they projected the benefits, their analysis showed that Detroit would still lose money in the long run.[32] And even in 1980, GM was making noises about future automation of some jobs. Yet to refuse the deal was politically untenable, as GM had made clear it would take its business elsewhere.

This left Mayor Young, a shrewd politician, with what may not have seemed to him a terribly difficult choice. Obviously, many whites in Poletown, and blacks too, would have to lose their homes. But since the 1950s large numbers of people, most of them minorities, had been dislocated in massive urban renewal projects all over the United States. And the dirty little secret of urban renewal, no doubt well known to many black Americans at that time, was that the black populations who were removed from blighted areas seldom, if ever, returned to those neighborhoods after they were "renewed." But this time, the relocations would not be in vain: six thousand jobs would be created. Or so GM led Mayor Young and the City of Detroit to believe.

Between October 8, 1980, when GM made its formal offer to acquire the site, and March 13, 1981, when the Michigan Supreme Court handed down its decision holding that the taking was lawful, Poletown was in a state of chaos. Many homes had already succumbed to the wrecking ball. Fires were rampant night after night, and scavengers combed through empty houses at will. With piles of debris lying right next to occupied houses, parents feared for their children's safety. It would not be long before chain-link fences would be erected around the churches and activists would take part in civil resistance, occupying a church until the last moment before bulldozers destroyed it.

Unlike the subjects of many large-scale blight takings that had occurred in the past, many of the white residents of Poletown were not going quietly into the night. A small grassroots contingency of residents emerged, led by local Catholic priests, who organized a "necessity challenge" to the condemnation of Poletown—that is, they brought a legal challenge to the right of the city to take the land. The necessity challenge—which became the famous lawsuit known as *Poletown Neighborhood Association v. City of Detroit*—soon expanded into an all-out, citywide rumble. The priests found themselves going toe to toe against their own diocese.

Many residents reported feeling betrayed not only by their local government, but by the Church, which sided with the government, the UAW and GM. Midway through the ruckus, Ralph Nader blew into town to fan the flames. Coleman Young once described him as "foam[ing] at the mouth" every time GM was mentioned.[33]

The parties were put on an accelerated briefing schedule in the necessity challenge. The Michigan Supreme Court wrote the landmark decision so hastily, in fact, that Justice Ryan submitted his now widely quoted dissenting opinion several days later, and admonished the majority for acting too quickly on so grave a matter. An examination of copies of the file-stamped original briefs shows that the court had the reply brief in hand less than a month before rendering its opinion. Given time for oral arguments, it is likely the court made and wrote its decision in about two weeks. Such complex matters of state constitutional law are typically disposed of over a judicial term. It is a measure of the desperation that the rust belt must have felt, and of GM's omnipresence, even at the highest court in Michigan, that the jurists rushed through a decision they normally would have pondered for at least six months.

The majority of the residents did not join in the necessity challenge. But many of the businesses in Poletown did challenge the amounts the city offered in compensation. These valuation challenges proved difficult and bitter. Detroit fought dozens of such mini-suits, going to trial over the compensation to be paid to the owners of everything from a shoe repair shop to a hospital.

These lawsuits arose in part because of a mistake made by the city, which in its haste to move forward had failed to make proper offers in the first instance for the value of the movable fixtures of the businesses. As a result, the city ended up going to trial and paying hundreds of millions more in compensation than it had planned on initially. Surprisingly, despite the working-class or even rundown image of Poletown purveyed in the media over the last two decades, there was substantial value in the 500-acre community, as an examination of even a few of the valuation proceedings will show. Alan Ackerman, for example, represented a barrel company and an oil distributor. "The city offered $350,000 for the oil distribution company," he recalled. At trial, the company got $5 million. Similarly, Ackerman recalled that the city had offered $12 million to Poletown's hospital at the time of the taking. At trial, the hospital was awarded "in the range of $35 to 40 million."

The original acquisition estimate for the *entire* project had been $62 million. Estimates differ on how much the Poletown taking finally ended up costing Detroit (or more accurately, federal taxpayers, the State of Michigan and the City of Detroit, in that order), but the consensus from a variety of sources is in the range of $300 million. GM snapped up the site for a mere $8 million.[34]

Clearly, the ugly duckling's date with the football captain turned out to be far more expensive for her than anyone could have imagined. But this scenario may be inevitable when governments—which don't have to answer to shareholders or boards, or otherwise account (at least in the short term) for horrendous fiscal stupidity—get involved in the real estate business. Cost overruns have also occurred in New London, Connecticut, the site of the *Kelo* case. The damage there has been protracted political bitterness as well as financial strain.

But what about all those GM jobs? A Cadillac assembly plant was built, but it seldom operated at the double-shift, 6,000-job capacity that had been projected. It sputtered along, providing about 3,000 jobs at its peak. The city had no recourse, having entered into a lopsided deal; GM had council-approved, long-term tax abatements and no obligations to employ anyone.

Nevertheless, the Detroit elders soon repeated the Poletown strategy, making a similar deal with Chrysler. In the decades that followed, the city became the equivalent of a real estate welfare queen, forgetting how markets work and demanding, again and again, that land development projects be ginned up through eminent domain. Unfortunately, Detroit's experience of getting hooked on eminent domain is not unique. A study conducted by Samuel R. Staley and John P. Blair of the Reason Foundation concluded that "in some cases eminent domain has become a tool of first resort (and sometimes the only tool)" of urban economic redevelopment.[35]

Since most eminent domain proceedings are brought in state courts, there are no official tallies of how many such projects there have been around the country, or how many properties have been involved. Perhaps because it is a round number—and a rather dramatic one—the figure of 10,000 has been cited many times in the press to describe the total number of homes seized in economic development takings. As far as we can know, this figure appears to be too high; yet it has taken on a life of its own. According to numbers published by Washington's Institute for Justice, the libertarian advocacy organization that represented the homeowners in the *Kelo* case, eminent domain was *threatened* in connection with 10,000 properties and actually used in connection with 3,717 properties between 1998 and 2002; we don't know how many of those were economic development takings. Since 2002 there have been more such cases, including large projects involving either pure economic development takings or "blight" loophole takings in Florida, Ohio and New Jersey. Using loose definitions of "blight" is another common way to take private property and engineer the development of cities.

In the summer of 2004, the Michigan Supreme Court, which had let loose the Poletown debacle in a spasm of rust-belt panic, had the chance to look back on what it had wrought. A suburban county called Wayne, having already gobbled up a thousand acres of private land, wanted still more to make way for a technology and business park adjacent to a newly expanded airport. Since Poletown, taking property for private businesses had become as endemic in Michigan as rooting for the Wolverines.

But a revolt was brewing. Some homeowners wanted to challenge the taking. And in a twist worthy of Hollywood, the suit was brought to the Michigan Supreme Court by none other than Alan Ackerman, one of the attorneys involved in the Poletown episode. Back then he had represented business owners in valuation trials, figuring there was no way to fight what he and many others saw as the overwhelming tidal wave of establishment power. After watching twenty years of economic development cases in Michigan, Ackerman felt enough was enough. Apparently, so did the Michigan Supreme Court. Awash in regret, the court reversed itself in *Hathcock v. County of Wayne,* deciding that the drafters of the Michigan Constitution had never meant for public use to have so broad a meaning. The court summoned up the ghosts of Poletown by closely following the blistering language and train of thought laid out in Justice Ryan's famous dissent. We made a mistake in 1981, the court said, and now we are putting it right.

The court concluded that in 1963, when the key constitutional language was written, the public could never have understood "public use" to mean the taking of private property for unfettered enjoyment by other private owners, with the sole public purpose of raising tax revenue or generating jobs. Much like the reasoning used in federal cases in the nineteenth century, the court found that property could be taken and given to other private entities only if there was absolute necessity (such as railroad tracks) or an operation that guaranteed continued public monitoring (such as a waterworks). A third exception was a circumstance in which the very act of condemning the land served a public purpose, such as eliminating a slum. But that circumstance was not present in *Hathcock*.

After the *Hathcock* decision came down in the summer of 2004, those who had been mainlining economic development takings in Michigan had no choice but to quit cold turkey, and that would take some getting used to. An op-ed by a Michigan academic named John Mogk that appeared in the *Detroit News*, for example, bore all the symptoms of acute economic-development-takings withdrawal: "Detroit has used condemnation power to facilitate construction of the General Motors Poletown and Chrysler east side auto assembly plants, Brush Park and Jefferson Village neighborhoods, Comerica Park and Ford Field, integral parts of the city's theater district and sections of the Detroit Medical Center. The city's future hinges on creating greater economic opportunity.... [In] overruling *Poletown* ... the court has rendered a decision that cripples Detroit in its efforts to economically rebuild the city."[36]

One might point out that if economic development takings have not worked to revive Detroit after twenty-three years, perhaps it's time to give something else a whirl. The Michigan economy, to be kind, has been in the doghouse for decades; and the long-term affects of putting the kibosh on economic development takings remain to be seen. The state has a year's head start on other states that have passed similar legislation since the *Kelo* decision came down, and it will provide an example of how things can go right or wrong after the plug is pulled on government subsidy of private development. One thing we do know, at least anecdotally: *Hathcock* had a chilling effect on eminent domain generally in

Michigan. Alan Ackerman, who has practiced in the state for decades and depends to a large extent on doing valuation trials in many kinds of eminent domain proceedings, said his practice fell off by 40 percent in the year after *Hathcock*. People are predicting a similar chilling effect in Ohio from the recent *Norwood v. Horney* decision. *Norwood* was the first eminent domain case to be brought to a state supreme court after *Kelo*, and it resulted in a narrower reading of eminent domain powers in Ohio.

The *Hathcock* decision, though it got scant attention in the general media, rocked the little clubhouse of eminent domain. For the first time in recent memory, a state's high court had *narrowed* the definition of public use. To eminent domain watchers, the event was cataclysmic for two reasons. First, it came out of Michigan, the mother ship of economic development takings. Second, it was issued in July 2004, while another challenge to economic development takings was winding its way up to the United States Supreme Court: *Kelo v. New London*.

In the spring of 2004, a small group of homeowners from a neighborhood in New London, Connecticut, asked the U.S. Supreme Court to hear their case, which challenged an economic development taking in their neighborhood. Though the homeowners' lawyers, the Institute for Justice, kept tabs on important cases pending around the country, there was no way of knowing how those other cases would turn out, or whether *Kelo* would even be granted certiorari by the High Court. (That is, whether the Supreme Court would agree to hear the case. Lawyers call this "granting cert.") Those decisions would not be announced until the fall of 2004, when the Court reconvened after its summer break. Therefore, when the *Hathcock* decision hit the presses in July 2004, it breathed fresh life into the *Kelo* homeowners' request to be heard by the Supreme Court. If Michigan could rethink what it had done in Poletown under the state constitution's public use clause, couldn't the Supreme Court take the time to reconsider the meaning of "public use" under the federal constitution? It had been a mighty long time since the Court had done so. The Supreme Court very rarely hears straightforward eminent domain cases. Over the past fifty years, regulatory takings cases have come before the Court more often, and even they are not common.

Sure enough, when autumn rolled around and the Supreme Court was back in session, cert was granted to the *Kelo* case. The Institute for Justice began to roll out its formidable public relations machine to raise the profile of the case. For the first time in history, eminent domain was starting to look just a little bit sexy.

CHAPTER 7

KELO

Fort Trumbull is like a lot of old industrial neighborhoods in America—a shadow of its former glory. It sits where the Thames River meets the Long Island Sound in the city of New London, Connecticut. In 1997, a small, private, nonprofit community development corporation had a vision: the town with its grimy waterfront and abandoned Navy lab could be transformed into a "hip little city" with offices, luxury housing, a marina, a museum and a hotel with a conference center.[1] This dream coincided with an aggressive push on the part of the state to get Pfizer to build its new global headquarters in Connecticut. The plans for the hip little city would entice Pfizer to come, and would complement the headquarters once it was built. Of course, the hundred or so working-class homes in Fort Trumbull would have to go. No one imagined this would pose much of a problem. Connecticut law allowed for economic development takings, like the Poletown model. Sweep the place clean in the service of a big corporate neighbor. The New London Development Corporation would not even have to prove blight in order to remove those houses. This would be an easy project.

Ten years later the land still sat vacant. More than one hundred families and businesses had been bought out under the threat of eminent domain, their homes and businesses bulldozed. The nonprofit development corporation had gone through $73 million of state money and was still locked in a Promethean battle with the city council—begging and haranguing, demanding $4 million of city money. The governor had sent in professional mediators. Along the way, a lady named Susette Kelo and eight of her

Fort Trumbull neighbors, who had refused to settle with the nonprofit and give up their homes, brought a landmark eminent domain case to the U.S. Supreme Court.

■ ■ ■

Susette Kelo's adventure began the way many economic development takings begin: with a notice from a local development corporation, telling her that she would have to move out of her house. That notice arrived in 2000. Like those sent to her neighbors, it informed her that her home, which she had not put up for sale, was about to be purchased by the New London Development Corporation (NLDC)—a private, not-for-profit 501(c)(3) corporation—on behalf of the City of New London. The sale was part of the Fort Trumbull Municipal Development Plan. Kelo is proud of her home, a Victorian that she renovated herself. The other homeowners who eventually joined in the suit to stop the project felt similarly attached to their property. One of them, Wilhelmina Dery, was born in her home in 1918, and she had lived with her husband in that house for some sixty years.

John Brooks, the NLDC's manager of the Fort Trumbull Development Project, would beg to differ about the quality of the neighborhood. He described it as "a slum." That is a startling assertion, since Wesley Horton, the attorney who argued for the city and the NLDC at the U.S. Supreme Court, took pains to make clear that this was not a blight case. "There is no blight that's been alleged in the condemnation papers," he told the court.[2] When asked about this, Brooks said that Horton was defending the municipal law (which allows economic development takings), but that the city could just as easily have condemned the properties under a more general blight standard or as a public works project. Interesting, since the folks at the Institute for Justice and the Supreme Court—indeed, all of America—were under the impression that this was an economic redevelopment project aimed at revitalizing New London.

Brooks also disputed the much ballyhooed "water views" enjoyed by Susette Kelo. Even the Supreme Court opinion mentions that Susette Kelo "prizes [her home] for its water view."[3] Brooks said that the homes of the nine individuals who challenged the taking were located in the middle of the Fort Trumbull peninsula. Susette Kelo "never had water views until we knocked down the houses all around her house," he said, with a note of impatience in his voice. "*Then* she had a water view." At first blush, the question of whether she had a water view seems petty, but it is not. It goes directly to the class issue that simmers just below the surface of many economic development takings cases.

One of the phenomena that drive many economic development takings is the changing nature of waterfront property. American waterfronts used to be the sweaty turf of longshoremen, heavy industry, cheap hotels and hard drinking. In shore towns, they were filled with little seaside bungalows. As many of these communities waned, the only people who stuck around were those who had little choice in the matter: the poor and the working class, whose jobs—if they were lucky enough to have them still—kept them rooted there, along with family ties. For many years, no one was terribly interested in these depressing stretches of land. Their decaying wharfs and factories and seaside attractions sat there like lapsed capitalists. Who would actually want to live, shop and stroll among the stigmata of that grimy past? But of course, to think in such a defeatist way underestimates American ingenuity. What was needed was to see the potential for charm. Yes, *charm*.

Or as the television anchor Anderson Cooper does at the beginning of his show: a 360° turnaround. Turn a situation around so thoroughly that you have obliterated what now exists and substituted something entirely new, so that the past will be forgotten and the replacement only faintly suggests what was there before. Doing this requires a lot of bulldozers to remove the ugliness, so it can be replaced with things that are delightful and charming: condominiums with water views, restaurants with water views, river walks with water views. Better yet, yacht marinas that place one in a boat directly *on* the water. Charm. Beauty. Elegance. In the blink of an eye, the town goes from cheap to chic. And this brings in substantial tax revenue to the municipality. Hard to argue with that.

Now the awkward question arises: who shall enjoy these water views? The poor and working-class people who had them to begin with? They are the ones who were stuck living in the waterfront community (or decided to stick it out there) when times got rough.

They stayed for decades, paying taxes, shoveling snow from their driveways, attending PTA meetings, raising money for the local Kiwanis Club and the Veterans Day parades. Don't they deserve a reward for all that commitment? Or should we do the smart thing and toss the views to the wealthier people who will come along and buy the waterfront condominiums, or the developers who will build the luxury hotels, or the Gen-Xers with their techie jobs, or the affluent retired Boomers who will move into the lofts in the converted Navy building and make our town hip at last?

Here is where the eminent domain sticker shock comes into play. Say a city condemns the home of Mary Condemnee in Waterfront Town. Mary has lived for decades in a modest house that she and her husband bought when they married, after World War II. Its current market value, given how rundown the neighborhood has become, is about $200,000. Her mortgage is paid off. She planned to live her whole life in that house and leave it to her children. The city buys her out and turns the neighborhood over to a private developer—lock, stock and barrel. The developer bulldozes Mary's house and those of her neighbors, and builds condominiums and a private marina. Prices start at $499,000 for a one-bedroom condo. As a publicity stunt, the developer offers Mary a unit in the building, with free maintenance and no taxes for a few years.

But if Mary lives past the point where she has to start paying the enormous real estate taxes and the maintenance on the luxury condo, she won't be able to afford it. And she is afraid the value of the condo will fall; she has seen a lot in her seventy-five years, and that is what has always happened in the beachfront communities of her state. She fears having to take out a mortgage. Who wants a mortgage at her age? The grim reality is that Mary will have to move far from the waterfront. Once the developer gets done revitalizing her neighborhood, it will be richer people who have the view and the ocean breezes that she once had. The tight-knit community she knew for sixty years will be dispersed forever.

This is precisely the scenario that has been playing out in Long Branch, New Jersey, where a group of octogenarians are fighting for their homes. This is one of the ways America's coastlines are being condo-ized for the upper classes.

Rose LaRosa owned a home in Long Branch, a seaside town in New Jersey. Long Branch is the site of a massive redevelopment project aimed at remaking the once quiet town into a clone of Miami Beach, with wall-to-wall condominium development, retail venues and high-end restaurants. LaRosa's father bought the house in 1942. Like many of the other homeowners who are being forced out of Long Branch, she is elderly; this is a common phenomenon in economic development takings. Many of the elderly residents have resisted buyout offers from the developer, claiming that the offers are not enough to enable them to buy seaside homes again. A real estate broker in the area noted that it is difficult to find comparable homes in Long Branch because "The town took them all."[4] The developer offered units in the luxury condominiums, which were retailing for more than the amount at which the town had appraised the homes, but none of the blue-collar, elderly homeowners (or younger homeowners with small children) were interested in swapping their private homes for what they considered to be essentially apartments. They were also concerned about the eventual maintenance and tax costs, which would kick in after an initial waiver period.

The Long Branch homeowners challenged the taking in court, arguing that the project was a pay-to-play scenario. They alleged that the city attorney had been on the board of the developer's parent corporation, that things were just a bit too close for comfort in a typical New Jersey sort of way. The judge dismissed the complaint. The case is now on appeal.

What fueled the rage of the Long Branch homeowners was not only that octogenarians were being ejected from their homes, but also that their heirs were denied the right to inherit what clearly had become extremely valuable property. Through a combination of luck and loyalty, these homeowners had hung on to oceanfront property that savvy real estate developers were now salivating over. Perseverance had played a large role in it, since Long Branch had gone through many bleak years, as had other little seaside towns in New Jersey. But now the residents of Long Branch were being kicked out so that richer people could take their place and enjoy the ocean breezes and the continuing appreciation in property values. The message is clear: if you are working class and fortunate enough to be sitting on waterfront property, your luck is about to run out.

For several years, the poor and working-class residents of Riviera Beach, an Atlantic coastal town in Florida, fought a mushrooming eminent domain battle against their own mayor, the very man who said he wanted to "rescue and save them." Riviera Beach is prime real estate, near Palm Beach and West Palm Beach. At the moment, it is something rare in Florida: a place where people of modest means live very close to the water. The city revved up its plans to relocate some five thousand residents and take title to about one thousand homes and businesses, many of these from people unwilling to sell. The land was to be turned over to a private developer to build a 400-acre waterfront condo and yachting facility. Riviera Beach would become a town for rich people. Its smooth-talking mayor at the time, Michael Brown, a black man who grew up poor in Riviera Beach, did not hesitate to invoke the name of his saintly departed mother in defense of his plans. He insisted this was the way to raise revenue and rescue the city's residents—even if thousands of them would have to be ejected in order to accomplish that goal. No doubt he figured out that the town's ritzy neighbors would prefer to have a rich cousin living next door, rather than the dubious moat of the poor and working class that separates their communities now. It's a regular little manifest destiny thing they had happening down there: *connect the Palm Beaches!* The demand for yacht marinas and condominium resorts along the Florida coast seems to be insatiable, and that means tax revenue. You just have to get all those poor and working-class people out of the way first.

Under Florida law, economic development takings were not allowed. There was, however, an exception for takings involving blight. In other words, a city could condemn private property and transfer it to a private developer if the purpose of the taking was to eliminate blighted conditions. Gotta get rid of slums, right? That's a loophole a politician and his council can work with. Indeed, the words Mayor Brown used in discussing the Riviera Beach project were indistinguishable from the way economic development takings are described. The mayor said in interviews that he was on a mission to "save" Riviera Beach by providing jobs and tax revenue for the city. He pointed to "blight" as justification. Jackie Lorial, a lifetime resident of Riviera Beach, took offense at the blight label. "When we read that this is a blighted community,

A map of downtown Freeport shows the planned marina area, running east along the vacant Blaffer land from Cherry Street (near the white, square Western Seafood packing house) to the Pine Street Bridge.

View of Old Brazos River looking east toward Gulf of Mexico, the guillotine gate and Pine Street Bridge in the middle distance. The white square structure is Western Seafood's packing house. *Courtesy of Western Seafood Co.*

(L to R) Wright III, Beth, Wright Jr. and Josh Gore pose on the docks of Western Seafood in the 1970s. *Courtesy of the Gore family.*

Isabel Gore in the Western Seafood office, 1955, with a photo of baby Wright Jr. on the shelf behind her. *Courtesy of the Gore family.*

Wright Winston (Pappy) Gore Sr. with Senator Jimmy Phillips, 1959, holding the Texas Shrimp Conservation Act, which Mr. Gore helped develop. *Courtesy of the Gore family.*

The Old Brazos River, 1950. "All up and down the river, nine fish houses . . ." Pappy recalled. "Now there's one." *Courtesy of the Gore family.*

Pappy Gore during a quiet moment in the office of the Western Seafood fish house, early 1950s. *Courtesy of the Gore family.*

A very young Pappy Gore, working for the Falgouts at a Gulf station on Galveston Island. *Courtesy of the Gore family.*

Pappy Gore outside Western Seafood, 1964. "I worked," he said, "from can 'til cain't." *Courtesy of the Gore family.*

that—that hurts. That hurts the self-esteem. That hurts our—even how we react to our own grandchildren, our children."

The residents of Riviera Beach, many of whom have lived there for decades, would be cut a few measly checks—the developer hinted at offering "at least the assessed values" of the homes—and then their neighborhoods would be chopped up and scattered to the four winds. Nicki Bie, a Riviera Beach resident, said in an interview on *Hannity & Colmes,* "What are we going to get for leaving? We are not going to get this quality of life. We're literally blocks away from the Intercoastal. We're about a mile away from the ocean. And what are they going to give us for that? It will never be comparable." Letters to the editor of local Florida papers indicated that residents of nearby towns worried about where all these people were supposed to end up. One thing was clear: wherever they landed, they wouldn't be enjoying waterfront views and ocean breezes. Those have increasingly become the luxuries of the rich. And there is something particularly cruel—indeed, un-American—about taking a property from someone who had the foresight or just the dumb luck to buy waterfront real estate such as in Long Branch or Riviera Beach and took care of it for decades and who wants to stay there and leave the house to their children. Especially since current measures of compensation do not allow the homeowner to share in the enormous increase in value the property will reap after renewal.

The Gore family in Texas is aware of how the land on the Old Brazos River has appreciated in value over the decades since Pappy and Isabel bought their parcel from Till Falgout. "And you'd think that you acquire property over so many years, even if something happened to the business, well, at least we'd have all this waterfront property," said Beth Gore. "Maybe some day we could sell. Maybe that would be a ... that could be everyone's retirement. At least we would always have that. And over the years Wright has acquired more and more property in Freeport. And now you just wonder if that was the right thing to do."

"I don't think it's a public use to give rich people better views than the people living there now," said Dana Berliner at a University of Chicago roundtable in the fall of 2004. Berliner, a senior counsel of the Institute for Justice, was discussing what she described as condemnations brought for "politically powerful parties" in order to "acquire desirable property. And that is something we're seeing a lot of, particularly on the waterfront."[5] So the question of whether Susette Kelo had a water view from her pink clapboard house in Fort Trumbull was actually a question loaded with class distinctions.

▪ ▪ ▪

Heaven knew Fort Trumbull was a city that needed a jolt. It had been languishing since the 1970s; and in 1990 a state agency officially declared the city a "distressed municipality."[6] The average income in the city of 26,000 was $31,800. After the Naval Undersea Warfare Center closed permanently in 1996, the city's unemployment rate was double that of Connecticut overall. The military yard had been the lifeblood of the community for many years, employing 1,500 people. It had occupied 32 acres—which the federal government gave to the city.

Then in the late 1990s, an idea was hatched in Governor John Rowland's administration: let's bring Pfizer to Connecticut. There was vacant land in New London right near Fort Trumbull. But good grief, look at the place! Pfizer would have to be enticed, in much the same way that GM had to be convinced to bestow its corporate beneficence upon Detroit in 1981. Fort Trumbull would have to be cleaned up. The state had to find a way to funnel money to the city and have the city do the necessary redevelopment.

Political players in the state with connections to Governor Rowland's office reached out to Claire Gaudiani, the president of Connecticut College and a former president of the New London Development Corporation. The NLDC had raised money privately in the past and had done various small-scale rejuvenation projects in the downtown business area. Gaudiani was asked to resurrect the NLDC, which had been inactive for some time. Within two years, tens of millions in state money would be flowing directly into the NLDC. This left the elected city leaders on New London's city council—who believed they were supposed to initiate major policies for their city—standing by like Cinderella at the ball.

Soon, a carefully choreographed dance began. A "Pfizer Concept Plan" was put down on paper, showing a clear vision of Fort Trumbull that the state was prepared to offer up to Pfizer, with new housing units, a hotel and a marina. Of course, Fort Trumbull was currently a blue-collar neighborhood. Four days later, the NLDC's planning firm formally recommended a plan for redeveloping the Fort Trumbull neighborhood with condominiums and townhouses, a marina and a hotel and conference center. A month later, Pfizer announced that its board had approved building the global headquarters in New London. This announcement was followed within days by the first infusion of $5.35 million to the NLDC from the state.[7] In 1999, Pfizer's president, George Milne Jr., sent a letter to the NLDC predicting that his company might use up to a hundred rooms a day in the new hotel.

This was a golden opportunity for the New London Development Corporation. It is not a creature birthed by the city government, but was formed in 1978 by "area businessmen to do community-based, smaller projects such as business loan programs," according to John Brooks, manager of the Fort Trumbull Development Project. Back then, he said, the projects were "fairly low key." The NLDC did attempt a large, mixed-use waterfront development in the late 1980s using donations and grant money, but it "never got off the ground."

The NLDC is a private charitable organization, whose corporate existence is independent of the City of New London. Its employees are not elected, nor are they municipal employees, answerable to elected officials. Nevertheless, the NLDC *does* have powers of eminent domain, delegated to it by the city under Connecticut law (which allows for municipalities to give agents such power when it is convenient or necessary). This doesn't make the NLDC a freak. To the contrary, all across America there are thousands of private nonprofits, quasi-public corporations and government agencies endowed with the power of eminent domain.

Unlike a municipal economic development corporation, the NLDC is not awash in city money. It can and often does solicit private donations. At the same time, as a community-based nonprofit it has received enormous sums of state money, which has created a rather brazen little creature. Indeed, the NLDC has often been at odds with the city it was set up to serve.

The NLDC is quite open about its "partnership" with Pfizer. The influence of Pfizer, and the extent to which Pfizer's wishes and concerns were incorporated into the Fort Trumbull project, should not be underestimated. The NLDC has made no attempt to hide it. On its website, the nonprofit explains that the project involved three partners: the State of Connecticut, Pfizer, and the City of New London—in that order. The NLDC talks about the involvement of its partners in matter-of-fact terms. In the space devoted to Pfizer, complete with the corporate logo, the NLDC website describes what it calls a "public-private" community partnership: "With a corporate culture that emphasizes participation and contribution in the community, Pfizer management participates on the NLDC Board of Directors and NLDC committees. Employees also take on active roles in the corporation's planning and community development activities."

Having a corporate gorilla like Pfizer as its wing man, the NLDC began bringing home some serious pork from Hartford. With $15 million to support its planning activities, the NLDC was operating with a staff of eight, on a scale it had never experienced before. Working on that staff was not a bad gig: David Goebel, the chief operating officer, worked "three days a week for a salary of $84,414, higher than the full time salary of the city's director of development and planning."[8] By 2000, the NLDC had secured a promise of $73 million from the State of Connecticut—$23 million in grants and a $50 million bond—to raze ninety acres of Fort Trumbull and make it construction-ready. But first, the NLDC had to put the development plans through their proper paces: initial approval from the city council, a series of neighborhood meetings, and submission of the plans to state agencies.

The city would have to put up *and* shut up. Back in 1997, the city manager, Richard Brown, had said, "We should be consulted now, not after a deal is arrived at."[9] Clearly, no one was listening. The city council approved the redevelopment plan. To do otherwise was politically untenable: they would be known as the council that turned away $73 million in state money and spurned the Pfizer global headquarters. The city delegated its powers of eminent domain to the NLDC. This wasn't the city's project and there were 115 homes and small businesses to be condemned; let the NLDC do the dirty work.

The project was an ambitious one: the ninety-acre parcel to be cleared included an old Amtrak railroad station and two wastewater treatment sites that would require environmental cleanup and expensive pipe removal. Simply grading the site would be an enormous undertaking. And there was the matter of all those houses. Parts of Fort Trumbull were still viable working-class neighborhoods, where hundreds of people lived. They would have to be compensated and relocated. In comparison with the heavy environmental tasks, this looked like the easy part.

But of course, it wasn't. The NLDC negotiated buyouts with most of the property owners. Under threat of eminent domain, deals were made with small-business owners and homeowners, and a small group of holdouts emerged: Susette Kelo, Charles and Wilhelmina Dery, Thelma Brelsky, the Christofaro family, William Von Winkle, Richard Beyer. In December 2000, the Institute for Justice became involved in the case. Two parcels were at issue in the *Kelo* case: parcel 3 and parcel 4A. Going into the Fort Trumbull project, no one quite knew what was to become of parcel 4A, where many of the homes were located, including Susette Kelo's. The plan designated parcel 4A as "park support," which is a clever euphemism for who the hell knows what we'll do with it, but we'd better grab it now while the grabbing is good.

Soon the NLDC found itself fighting a two-front war: against the holdouts who wanted to keep their homes and were mortified at having to surrender, and against a city council that was getting pretty tired of being bossed around by a nonprofit that had morphed into the Hulk and was hitting it up for millions of dollars. Meanwhile, two opposition groups had formed in New London: the Coalition to Save Fort Trumbull, a preservation group, and Lower Our Taxes, a group determined to keep city taxes down, which vehemently opposed any city money going to the project.

In the legal case and in the press, the Fort Trumbull project was all about economic development: retail, residential, restaurants, a marina. The word "condominiums" was tossed about liberally, but the hotel for the Pfizer business guests was the linchpin. To hear the NLDC tell it, however, "This was a street and infrastructure project." According to John Brooks of the NLDC, "One-third of the land is not developable. That includes the city's wastewater treatment plants, and the rail lines." The NLDC saw their mission as cleaning up the ninety-acre site, building new roads, grading the land for one office development, a Coast Guard museum, a hotel and some multifamily residences (one of the

Warfare Center buildings would be left standing and converted to residential use). The residences, Brooks said, will be "all rental. No condos will be built." It is difficult to understand how such a project would even begin to revitalize New London, especially given the shifts in the economy and the market. The hotel that Pfizer promised to fill with a hundred weary travelers every night will still be built, because the developer has already plowed $1 million into designs and permits; but Pfizer has made clear that it no longer needs the hotel and doubts it can send people there.

The State of Connecticut had asked the City of New London, "as a gesture of support" for Fort Trumbull, to contribute $4 million to the project in addition to the land it was condemning. The city did not exactly leap to its feet to comply. Two years after talk of the project began, the city cautiously agreed to fund the "last dollars into the project" up to $4 million. This left open the possibility that the city might not have to kick in any money at all. As it turned out, that $4 million would become a bone of contention that the city and the NLDC would gnaw, nip and wrestle over like pit bulls for the next five years.

As early as 2003, the NLDC had spent nearly all of its $73 million, and the city was refusing to cough up the $4 million in "finishing money," arguing that it was intended to "fund the final trimmings of a project that today is far from complete."[10] "Far from complete" was putting it mildly. The money had been spent on infrastructure, much of it roads. The Massachusetts developer brought in to construct the buildings, Corcoran Jennison, hadn't hammered a nail yet. The blame for this state of affairs could not be laid entirely at the feet of nine holdouts with their tiny parcels, though the NLDC sometimes tried to lay it there, citing the pending litigations as stalling the development. The developer said it could not obtain financing while the lawsuits were pending.[11] But even if the NLDC had been free to knock down the homes of the holdouts, it would not have been able to make the ninety acres construction-ready in 2003. (Pretty much the same situation prevailed in the winter of 2006–2007.) The NLDC wanted the $4 million from the city to install underground utilities and a riverwalk; but $4 million was only half what was needed to build the riverwalk and rebuild sections of streets in various areas and remove pollutants from the former industrial sites.

In the city council there was some confusion over the ultimate goal for the sprawling site. Major elements of the plan continued to shift: now you see the marina, now you don't. Now you see the Coast Guard museum over here, now you see it way over there. Years into the project, the council continued to demand more detailed explanations of what the plans were and what was being done with the money.

The NDLC was not shy about blaming the city council for stalling the project. Its president, Michael Joplin, said the council's refusal to supply the $4 million was "a fool's choice." At a meeting in April 2004, he lashed out at the council: "There can be no more waiting. How much time are we going to waste? Are you going to tell me we used eminent domain, we tore homes down, only to have the city renege?"[12] Joplin sounded like an armchair psychiatrist. According to *The Day* of New London, he said that "the city has a perverse attitude, a 'deep denial that we can't improve ourselves,' calling its leadership a 'disorganized group of people who just reach for what they can.'"[13]

The city council was in no mood to be psychoanalyzed by the NLDC. Councilor Lloyd Beachy was reluctant to fund a $4 million bond when funding from the state might be reduced in future years, leaving the city with a high tax burden on a ten-year note, which would soon require a half-million-dollar interest payment. He foresaw a long period of capital improvements to the Fort Trumbull area, during which sacrifices would have to be made in other parts of the city: "We will be unable to bond for other projects we need," Beachy said, "because we will be busy digging more holes back in Fort Trumbull."[14]

The fight over the $4 million grew increasingly ugly. Eventually it would get to the point where the city council and the NLDC leaders couldn't be in the same room without a paid mediator to keep everyone calm.

▪ ▪ ▪

Meanwhile, the Fort Trumbull homeowners were fighting in the state courts, where they managed to obtain an injunction that kept the bulldozers at bay. In the fall of 2004, the U.S. Supreme Court agreed to hear Susette Kelo's case. Argument was scheduled for February 22, 2005. A remarkable circle of odd bedfellows began to converge and submit friend-of-the-court briefs. There were the "usual suspects," those one would expect in a property rights case, such as the libertarian Cato Institute. But right alongside Cato was the NAACP, arguing that eminent domain has historically been used in a way that unfairly impacts minorities and therefore broadening the power is dangerous to minorities and the poor. The AARP argued that economic development takings have tended to single out communities of the elderly. The Becket Fund for Religious Liberty put in a brief, arguing that churches were at risk because, as nonprofits, they will always pay lower taxes than businesses. The American Farm Bureau Federation argued the unfair economic leverage of developers over farmers. The list of strange allies went on, from the Goldwater Institute to the Southern Christian Leadership Conference. On the other side, the City of New London had about a dozen amicus briefs, including one from the Municipal League of Cities and urban planning organizations, who favor the use of eminent domain for economic development.

The Supreme Court would look first and foremost to *Berman v. Parker* (1954) and *Hawaii Housing Authority v. Midkiff* (1984).[15] If *Berman* was a rubber band that stretched the public use clause, then *Midkiff* was judicial Silly Putty. *Midkiff* involved a statute that changed the nature of land ownership in Hawaii to end the private ownership of vast, feudal-like estates and redistribute the land to longtime tenants through the use of eminent domain. Justice O'Connor, writing for a unanimous court, said that the Hawaii statute was constitutional because the use of eminent domain was "rationally related" to a public purpose; the sales were done to break up land "oligopolies," which O'Connor described as an "economic evil."

Midkiff was an instance of the "anti-rentism" that Daniel Webster had predicted 136 years earlier. When Webster was litigating the *West River* case in 1848, he warned that expanding the use of the Constitution's takings clause would eventually lead to no good. Specifically, he predicted that the time would come when eminent domain would be used to further political agendas, such as "anti-rentism." He was referring to the Anti-Rent Wars of the 1840s, when tenant farmers on some of the few remaining great estates in New York rioted, demanding that the landowners stop collecting rents from farmers who had worked the land for generations. The rebellions were put down, but not before a good deal of mayhem and even murder had occurred. The Anti-Rent Wars were precisely the sort of upheaval that Webster abhorred.

Over the years, eminent domain has popped up in the service of various political and cultural theories, especially those concerning poverty and urban planning in the 1950s through the 1970s. With *Midkiff* in 1984, the Supreme Court faced what was essentially an eminent domain case in the service of an anti-rent political agenda. When it came time to argue *Kelo,* everyone would be stuck with this anti-rent case, along with *Berman.*

At the time the *Kelo* case was granted cert by the Supreme Court, some states allowed economic development takings while others did not. Connecticut fell into the former camp; its state supreme court had decided in March 2004 that the takings in New London were constitutional. Four months later, *Hathcock* rocked the takings world; the Michigan decision was completely at odds with Connecticut's. It is not the role of the U.S. Supreme Court to resolve conflicts in state law, and the *Kelo* case went up on a federal constitutional issue. But the division among the states helped put the federal takings clause on the national radar screen. Suddenly, the public use clause seemed to be up for grabs. If the Supreme Court nixed economic development takings on federal constitutional grounds, then many states would have to follow Michigan's path—no matter what their state constitutions said—because citizens could invoke their rights under the Fifth Amendment of the U.S. Constitution. But if *Kelo* went the other way, then states that hadn't made up their minds about such takings might decide to walk in Connecticut's footsteps and either continue to use economic development takings or start using them. A lot hung in the balance.

From the outset, the Institute for Justice (IJ) was faced with some tough choices in arguing for the *Kelo* petitioners. *Midkiff* and, even more, the sweeping language of *Berman* seemed to have sealed their fate. IJ was not going to suggest that *Berman* and *Midkiff* had gone too far and should be reversed, as some libertarian groups had argued in amicus briefs. Instead, IJ asked the Court to keep *Berman* and *Midkiff* in place but set a limit on eminent domain—to "establish a bright-line rule: no economic development takings whatsoever." There were strategic risks in bringing this argument, too. Judicial philosophies at the Supreme Court have their own ebb and flow, with different alliances favoring "rules" and others favoring "standards" (or balancing tests) at various points in the Court's history. The legal scholar Kathleen M. Sullivan explained in a famous article, "The Justices of Rules and Standards,"[16] that the conservative justices today, most especially those who have gravitated toward Justice Scalia's orbit, can usually be counted on to favor rules, while the liberal justices tend to favor more flexible, fact-sensitive weighing of interests. Indeed, she pointed out that Justice Stevens once chided Justice Scalia—who favored a bright-line rule in a regulatory takings case: "'[L]ike many bright-line rules, the categorical rule established in this case is only 'categorical' for a page or two in the [law books] before it gives way to an exception."[17]

This was a tricky balancing act, because when the Institute for Justice came before the Court in *Kelo,* its primary task was not to persuade the conservatives on the bench, who were predisposed in the homeowners' favor. By arguing a bright-line rule, IJ took the risk of preaching to the choir while alienating the liberals on the bench. It may be no coincidence that Justice Stevens, who had made clear his distaste for bright-line rules, ended up authoring the majority opinion in *Kelo*. On the other hand, to ask the Supreme Court to roll back takings jurisprudence to the state of the law before *Midkiff* and *Berman* may have seemed the riskier course. When cert was granted to the *Kelo* case in 2004, Justice O'Connor still sat on the Court. She was universally regarded as the swing vote. For most Supreme Court practitioners, the name of the game, in a case where deep divisions were expected on the Court, was to persuade Justice O'Connor. It may well have seemed like a suicide mission to go in and say, well Justice O'Connor, you were wrong in *Midkiff,* please reverse your own decision.

On February 22, 2005, the line of spectators who wanted to get in to see the oral argument in the *Kelo* case snaked all the way down the grand marble steps of the Supreme Court building and around the block. There had been intense publicity before the oral argument. The central hallway outside the courtroom was packed with attorneys scheduled to argue cases on that day's calendar. The courthouse deputies kept "shushing" everyone. The lawyers who were there to argue *Kelo* were surrounded by their entourages.

The attorneys from the Institute for Justice, Scott Bullock and Dana Berliner, looked solemn and pensive. They stood in a group surrounded by well-wishers, caucusing quietly. A little further down the hall, Wesley Horton, the attorney for the City of New London, was standing with his family. He appeared positively jovial, rocking back and forth on his feet a little and holding some papers casually in one arm. He looked as if he couldn't wait to get into the courtroom and start arguing.

The press gallery inside the huge, marble-pillared courtroom was packed to the gills. The major dailies and the wire services were there. A handout had been provided to the reporters ahead of time, giving a quick lesson in takings law to help everyone follow the argument.

As the attorney for the petitioner, Scott Bullock argued first. He had the tougher row to hoe because he was asking the Court to make new law, to carve a new rule. Alas, his "bright-line" argument was not going over well with the justices. They were struggling with how to square such a sharp cutoff in the meaning of "public purpose" with the sweeping language of *Berman,* which allows for the taking of private property for turnover to other private parties for purposes as amorphous as improving the human spirit. Logic led them, more than once, to ask why the homeowners' position would not require the Court to overturn *Berman* and *Midkiff.*

> *Justice Ginsburg:* The line you draw is between blight, which Berman says was in the public use ... but [not] depressed conditions ...
>
> *Mr. Bullock:* Yes, Your Honor. We think that is a line that this Court has drawn.... And the condemnations in Berman removed the problematic areas. It removed the blight.
>
> *Justice O'Connor:* Oh, but Berman spoke, in the opinion, said the determination of the legislature about these things is virtually conclusive, that there is only the narrowest, narrowest role for the judiciary. What kind of standard are you proposing we should get into here to second-guess the public use aspect?
>
> *Mr. Bullock:* Your Honor, it is clear that eminent domain power is broad, but there has to be limits, that's what we are really talking about here.
>
> . . . .

> *Justice Breyer:* . . . But there is no taking for private use that you could imagine in reality that wouldn't also have a public benefit of some kind, whether it's increasing jobs or increasing taxes, etc. That's a fact of the world. . . .
> *Mr. Bullock:* Your Honor, we think that that cuts way too broadly.
> *Justice Breyer:* Because?
> *Mr. Bullock:* Because then every property, every home, every business can then be taken for any private use.

Bullock went back and forth for quite a while with Justice Souter over whether increasing the tax base and creating jobs amounted to a "proper government purpose" and whether they constituted a "public use." Bullock insisted they did not. But in that case, Justice Souter asked, don't we then have to overrule *Berman*? Finally, Justice Scalia jumped in:

> *Justice Scalia:* Mr. Bullock, do you equate purpose with use? Are the two terms the same? Does the public use requirement mean nothing more than that it have a public purpose?
> *Mr. Bullock:* No, Your Honor.
> *Justice Scalia:* That's your answer to Justice Souter.

But Justice Souter wasn't very happy with that answer. Many of the justices wanted a balancing test of some sort. Bullock suggested that the economic development should have a "reasonably foreseeable" chance of success and that the city should meet "minimum standards" in showing that the project is on the up and up. At first relieved that they had a standard to chew over, the justices wasted no time in lamenting that the Court would have to "get into the business of saying" to a city, you have to do this or that with respect to a particular taking. Justice Souter asked why it isn't enough simply for a city to show "good faith" and let someone who objects to the taking prove bad faith.

Then it was Wesley Horton's turn to speak. Ironically, most of the drama occurred during his argument rather than Bullock's, even though Horton was not asking the Court to depart from settled law. He opened by saying, "The principal purpose of the takings clause is to provide for just compensation. Now, I want to very briefly . . ." An audible gasp swept through the room; normally one can hear a pin drop in the Supreme Court.

Justice O'Connor quickly cut Mr. Horton off. "Well, but it has to be for a valid *public use.*"

Horton paused. "Yes, it does, Your Honor," he replied. The audience collectively settled back into their seats.

The justices were disturbed by the idea of the government taking from A to give to B simply because B would pay more in taxes, and they questioned Horton about this again and again, sometimes playing devil's advocate and posing hypotheticals to Horton:

> *Justice Scalia:* . . . I just want to take property from people who are paying less taxes and give it to people who are paying more taxes. That would be a public use, wouldn't it?
> *Justice O'Connor:* For example, Motel 6 and the city thinks, well, if we had a Ritz-Carlton, we would have higher taxes. Now, is that okay?
> *Mr. Horton:* Yes, Your Honor. That would be okay. I—because otherwise you are in the position of drawing the line. I mean, there is, there is a limit.
> . . . .
> *Justice Scalia:* Let me qualify it. You can take from A to give to B if B pays more taxes?
> *Mr. Horton:* If it's a significant amount . . .

Horton then risked opening up his own Pandora's box. He unfolded a drawing of the contemplated development, showing the Fort Trumbull peninsula, and proceeded to point out specific parts to the justices, who peered over their enormous mahogany bench at this rare visual aid being shown in the august chambers of the Supreme Court. In the press gallery, everyone started scribbling furiously; no one had ever seen anything like it at the High Court. Horton proceeded to give the justices a grand tour, pointing out the state park, the site selected for the hotel, the nineteenth-century fort, and the place where the Pfizer headquarters now sits.

Finally O'Connor broke in: "Let's talk about the litigants before us today."

So Horton homed in on the disputed parcels, 3 and 4A. "Parcel 3 is going to be office space," he said, pointing to the drawing.

"Parcel 4A is for park support or marina support. Now, it isn't more definitive, but obviously, one possible use is for parking here because you've got a water treatment facility here."

Horton's remarks made clear that the city had no idea what it was going to do with parcel 4A. This naturally led to a discussion about a reasonableness standard, which had come up during Bullock's argument. Justice Breyer asked, "Could the courts, under this [takings] clause, at least review what you've just said for reasonableness?" Horton responded that a higher level of judicial review was not necessary, because the people displaced from their homes are being paid by the city government. Justice Scalia jumped on him: "Mr. Horton, you're paying for it, but you're also taking property from somebody who doesn't want to sell it. *Does that count for nothing?* Yes, you're paying for it, but you're giving the money to somebody who doesn't want the money, who wants to live in the house that she's lived in her whole life. That count's for *nothing?*"

Chastised, Horton responded, "No, of course not, Your Honor." He defended the position based on the difficulty of assembling land. Horton argued that abusive transfers from A to B purely for private gain would not be made because of high "transaction costs" for the city.

Finally, Justice Kennedy came back to the issue of compensation, which seemed to be troubling him. "[I]s there some way of assuring that the just compensation actually puts the person in the position he would be in if he didn't have to sell his house? Or is he inevitably worse off?" he asked.

Horton replied that in Connecticut, "we have relocation loans which are involved here." As soon as he uttered the word "loans," the entire audience simultaneously sucked in air.

> *Mr. Horton:* There was, it wasn't clear from our brief whether they were loans or not, and it is correct that they are loans. The other side pointed out that that was for all projects in the state. That's not true, I mean, there is $10 million involved in relocation funds.
>
> *Justice Souter:* But the loans don't make him whole. Isn't—
>
> *Mr. Horton:* That's true.
>
> *Justice Souter:* I mean, what bothered Justice Breyer I guess bothers a lot of us. And that is, is there a problem of making the homeowner or the property owner whole?

. . . .

Justice Breyer: What is the remedy? [A]n individual has a house and they want to be really not made a lot worse off just so some other people can get a lot more money—is there no constitutional protection? If this isn't the right case, what is?

Mr. Horton: Well . . . I would say in terms of just compensation, in deciding what the fair market value is today, you can certainly take into account the economic plan that's going into effect. You know—

Justice Kennedy: Really? I thought that that was a fundamental of condemnation law that you can not value the property being taken based on what it's going to be worth after the project. Just—

Mr. Horton: Well—

Justice Kennedy: Unless Connecticut law is much different from any other state.

Mr. Horton: I may have misspoken on that subject, Your Honor.

Justice Scalia (getting testy): What this lady wants is not more money. No amount of money is going to satisfy her. She is living in this house, you know, her whole life and she does not want to move. She said I'll move if it's being taken for a public use, but by God, you're just giving it to some other private individual because that individual is going to pay more taxes. I—it seems to me that's, that's an objection in principle, and an objection in the principle that the public use requirement of the Constitution seems to be addressed to.

Unlike oral arguments at the Supreme Court in the days of Daniel Webster, when they could drag on for days, this oral argument was over in half an hour. The case was so high-profile that the reporters practically tripped over each as they ran out of the courtroom like a herd of buffalo so they could file stories on deadline. There was actually another important takings case on the calendar right after *Kelo*—a regulatory takings case called *Lingle v. Chevron* that would affect rent control in California—but nobody was sticking around for it. Outside on the broad marble steps, a rather grim-looking Scott Bullock stood by his clients while they were interviewed by throngs of television and print journalists.

The case was all over the media that night and the next day. It's a measure of how new the subject of eminent domain was to the media on that gray day in February that when Lou Dobbs reported the story on CNN that night, he kept mispronouncing it, calling it "imminent domain." The case was much chewed over in the press during the weeks and months that followed. Law firms around the country briefed clients about the case and how it might impact real estate development and constitutional law. *Kelo* became one of the most impatiently awaited decisions of the term. Of all the closely watched cases on the Supreme Court's docket that year—which included cases on medical marijuana, Internet file sharing, race and juries—*Kelo* was easily the one with the greatest mass interest. No one can accuse the Supreme Court of lacking a sense of drama; it waited until the end of June to hand down the decision.

▪ ▪ ▪

It was a very close call: 5–4. The Court ruled in favor of the City of New London, finding that taking homes and property for the purpose of raising tax revenue and building up the economy falls within the meaning of the public use clause of the Fifth Amendment of the Constitution. The justices generally known as liberals—Stevens, Kennedy, Breyer, Ginsburg, Souter—were in the majority, with Justice Stevens writing the majority opinion.

Justice Stevens wrote in essence that the city would not be allowed to "take property under the mere pretext of a public purpose" if its real intent was to benefit a specific private party. But New London, said Justice Stevens, had a "carefully considered development plan." If only Justice Stevens could have been a fly on the wall at all the city council meetings where the New London Development Corporation and council members were at each other's throats over the ever-evolving plans, with the NLDC demanding money and the council repeatedly seeking further explanations of what the devil they intended to do with it.

In many ways it seemed that the world had been turned upside down in the *Kelo* decision, with the liberal majority on the Court invoking federalism and states' rights to justify its ruling. Stevens noted the need to defer with "great respect" to "state legislatures and state courts in discerning local public needs" under a "strong theme of federalism." But here, the majority was invoking federalism for the purpose of disempowering the individual property owner as against majorities in local legislatures and weakening his constitutional protections. The Court also decided against a more stringent level of review for economic development takings—for example, making sure there is some reasonable likelihood of the project's success—on the grounds that it would impose too great an "impediment" to the completion of such plans.

It was clear, however, that Justice Stevens's heart was not fully behind this opinion. He sent a very plain signal that states were free to do the opposite of what the Court had just decided: "We emphasize that nothing in our opinion precludes any State from placing further restrictions on its exercise of the takings power. Indeed, many States already impose 'public use' requirements that are stricter than the federal baseline.... [T]he necessity and wisdom of using eminent domain to promote economic development are certainly matters of legitimate public debate."[18] Stevens did everything but send an engraved invitation to state legislatures to convene hearings on the subject. In fact, he later said in a speech before a bar association, in August 2005, that he personally regretted the *Kelo* decision but had felt compelled by precedent to rule against the homeowners.

Justices O'Connor, Scalia, Rehnquist and Thomas joined in a dissent. (Thomas was so outraged he also wrote a separate dissent, arguing original intent of the drafter of the Constitution.) Despite her skepticism during the oral argument, Justice O'Connor wrote a blistering dissent in language that instantly zipped around the print media and the blogosphere: "The specter of condemnation now hangs over all property. Nothing is to prevent the State from replacing any Motel 6 with a Ritz-Carlton, any home with a shopping mall, any farm with a factory."[19] O'Connor wrote that the federal case law in takings boiled down to three types of cases. First, those where property is taken and transferred to public ownership, such as military bases or roads. Second, cases where property is transferred to private parties who make it available for the public to use; these are situations like utilities, stadiums, airports, railroads. Third, O'Connor described the line of cases such as *Midkiff* and *Berman*. Here's where the legal elastic band stretches to a certain point and then no farther. Although these cases involved transfers of private property directly to other private parties, the transfers achieved a broader public purpose because they ended a harmful condition that existed in society (blight in *Berman,* oligopoly in *Midkiff*). "Here, in contrast," wrote Justice O'Connor, "New London does not claim that Susette Kelo's and Wilhelmina Dery's well-maintained homes are the source of any social harm."

Justice O'Connor and the other dissenting justices were hip to the difficulty in ferreting out unfair deals entered into for the benefit of a particular powerful party: "For his part, Justice Kennedy suggests that courts may divine illicit purpose by a careful review of the record and the process by which a legislature arrived at the decision to take—without specifying what courts should look for." She explained that the "trouble with economic development takings" is that the private benefit and the "incidental" benefit to the public are merged." In this case . . . any boon for Pfizer or the plan's developer is difficult to disaggregate from the promised public gains in taxes and jobs."

Justice O'Connor was not buying the majority's "federalism" argument, saying that it was essentially a cop-out on the Court's duty to protect the rights of individuals against overpowering majorities. "The Court suggests that property owners should turn to the States, who may or may not choose to impose appropriate limits on economic development takings. . . . This is an abdication of our responsibility. States play many important functions . . . but compensating for our refusal to enforce properly the Federal Constitution . . . is not among them." O'Connor did not mince words on who would be most likely to suffer in a world in which "[a]ny property may now be taken for the benefit of another private property." The beneficiaries, she wrote, are likely to be those citizens with the greatest influence in the political process, including large corporations and development firms. "As for the victims, the government now has license to transfer property from those with fewer resources to those with more. The Founders could not have intended this perverse result."[20]

When the case was released by the clerk of the Court on June 23, 2005, few could imagine the instantaneous firestorm it was about to ignite.

CHAPTER 8

THE *KELO* BACKLASH

The *Kelo* decision instantly rocketed back to Freeport: "Court's Decision Empowers the City to Acquire the Site for a New Marina," read the headline in the *Houston Chronicle*. "This is the last little piece of the puzzle to put the project together," said Jim Phillips, the newly elected mayor of Freeport, in an interview with the *Chronicle* following the announcement. The city wasted no time in ramping up its case against Western Seafood. "With Thursday's Supreme Court decision," the article explained, "Freeport officials instructed attorneys to begin preparing legal documents to seize three pieces of waterfront property along the Old Brazos River from two seafood companies for construction of an $8 million private boat marina."[1] Within days, Randy Kocurek would be back in court fighting the city, which wanted to lift the injunction that had kept the federal case and the state cases on ice while *Kelo* was being decided. "My grandmother talked about how some people are happier than 'vultures following a gut wagon,'" wrote Jeff Murrah in a letter to the editor of a local newspaper. "I now understand what she meant. The city officials of Freeport have wasted little time in taking advantage of the Supreme Court's usurping of private property rights."[2]

The Gores were running at full speed on the litigation treadmill during that post-*Kelo* summer of 2005. They were trying to keep their lifesaving injunction from unraveling before their eyes in federal court, and to keep the noose of the defamation claim from choking them, and to keep the state court condemnation actions from making headway until the federal summary judgment decision could be appealed. Their existence had become like an insane juggling act in which the colored balls spinning through the air were their own lives, to be kept aloft at all costs, lest they fall to the ground and be scooped up by the eminent domain bulldozer. They were hoping for a favorable result at the federal court of appeals, and trying to stave off the state court eminent domain case once again. It never occurred to anyone that they might get a better outcome at the Texas state court.

The eminent domain proceedings in state court involved service of various legal papers, such as motions and subpoenas. The Gores refused to accept service through their attorneys; they saw no reason to help speed things up for the city that was treating them with such contempt. So process servers began coming around to their home in Lake Jackson and to the grounds of Western Seafood.

When a suspicious car pulls up in front of Marine Industrial, Wright Jr., who is extraordinarily light on his feet at fifty-eight, suddenly dashes away from the front counter into a back room. After his brother Gary determines that the occupant of the car is just a salesman, Wright is back as suddenly as he disappeared, his fair skin slightly flushed. "It was a false alarm," Gary explains. "Sorry for all the melodrama." Process servers also come around Isabel and Pappy Gore's home, trying to effect service of process on the Western Shellfish corporation, incorrectly believing that Pappy can accept service for that company. A nurse answers the door and the process server barges into the house, looking for Pappy. He spots him. Pappy knows what is up and tries to get away, leaning on his walker. The process server gives chase. Pappy, eighty-five years old but still game for a fight, tries to outrun him, walker and all, but can't. The guy serves him with the papers and walks out of the house. When a legal kafuffle ensues about the incident, the process server insists that the nurse had invited him in. Just another day for the Gores, fighting City Hall and trying to keep their property.

As Wright III kept track of all the lawsuits, spending hours on the phone with Randy, reading briefs into the wee hours, the shrimping season was on again in Freeport. The *Kelo* decision seemed timed by some mischievous greater power with a bad sense of humor. It was precisely when they needed capital to see Western Seafood through a season that would prove to be especially difficult because of unprecedented fuel prices, which affected both their suppliers (the shrimp trawlers) and their buyers (the wholesalers who take the shrimp to market). "Of course," said Wright Jr., "Asian shrimp competitors are hurt by high fuel costs too, because they have to travel very far to bring their shrimp to the U.S. market." But this year the Gores were being pushed to the wall by the burden of legal fees, which were approaching the $400,000 mark by the summer of 2005.

"I've been here thirty-five years, since we were married. We came down here," said Wright Jr. "All my life growing up I've been involved in that business. Driving the trucks, unloading the boats, going out on the boats, you name it, I did it all. There have been ups and downs, but these last three years have been downs like we've never seen before."

In addition to high fuel prices and the eminent domain wars, Western Seafood was challenged by the large-scale dumping of Asian shrimp on the U.S. market. When Europe banned farm-raised Asian shrimp because of concerns about the use of chemicals, the result was a dumping free-for-all in the United States. In 2004, the International Trade Commission stepped in and ruled that six countries had illegally dumped shrimp into the United States. The U.S. Department of Commerce similarly determined that six countries had dumped shrimp on the United States market. Since that time, tariffs have been imposed on shrimp imports from Brazil, China, Ecuador, India, Thailand and Vietnam.[3] It remains to be seen whether the tariffs will hold off the onslaught of foreign shrimp from countries where the shrimp industry is state-sponsored and labor is far cheaper.[4]

At the moment, as long as they have their land, the Gores are hanging on the old-fashioned way: through competition, and letting the market decide whether they survive or fold. Despite all the odds being stacked against them, they managed to break even in 2003 and 2004—"just barely," said Wright Jr. Even after Judge Kent declared the American shrimp industry ready for the wax museum in his summary judgment decision in 2004, the Gores broke even again in 2005 and 2006—and would have done much better had they not been shelling out serious cash for lawyers in state and federal court, not to mention the endless distraction and worry of the five pending lawsuits against them.

"And so, it's as though all the evil planets aligned," said Wright Jr., "and we're $400,000 into legal expenses and court costs at a time when we can least afford it. It's the worst possible timing for us to have to defend something like this."

Wright III carefully considered his options. Like thousands of people across the country, he had pinned so much hope on the *Kelo* case. Now, Justice Kennedy's hint was as clear as day: go to the legislature. It was the end of June and the Texas legislature was still in session, but soon would be packing up and heading out to Seattle for the meeting of the National Conference of State Legislatures. He needed to get up to Austin right away. This would be a three-front war: he would fight for Western Seafood in the courts, up in Austin, and on the streets of Freeport. The Citizens for Freeport were ready to start gathering signatures for ballot initiatives. In the meantime, Wright met up with his youngest brother, Alex, and his cousin Patrick Gore and moved to a motel in Austin.

▪ ▪ ▪

The Associated Press headline on the night of June 23 was short and sweet: "Cities Can Bulldoze Homes for Development." A tidal wave of popular outrage followed.

Within hours of its announcement, the *Kelo* decision caused a sensation. After decades in the dusty confines of law libraries, eminent domain had burst onto the evening news. Suddenly, everyone in America knew what it was and everyone was against it. Or so it seemed, since urban planners and city officials, who thought *Kelo* was fine and dandy, could barely get a word in edgewise in the media blitz that followed the decision.[5] An MSNBC website poll revealed that 98 percent of Americans disagreed with the Supreme Court's decision. When was the last time 98 percent of Americans felt the same way about anything? The very next day, Congress wagged its bipartisan finger at the Court, adopting a highly unusual resolution by a vote of 365 to 33. The representatives expressed "the grave disapproval of the House of Representatives regarding the majority opinion of the Supreme Court in the case of *Kelo et al. v. City of New London et al.* that nullifies the protections afforded private property owners in the Takings Clause of the Fifth Amendment."[6]

Newspaper editors around the country had a field day with a Supreme Court case that was easy for everyone to understand and had plenty of punch to its legal bottom line. Headlines read: "Eminent Mistake";[7] "Property Wrongs: A Supreme Blunder";[8] "Court: OK to Take from the Poor, Give to the Rich";[9] "Rush Is On to Calm Homeowners";[10] "High Court Rules on the Side of State Socialism";[11] "Court Expands Power to Seize Land";[12] "When 'Public Purpose' Means You Don't Count";[13] "Neighborhood Shudders at Eminent Domain's Reach; High Court Ruling Broadens Threat to Residents Confronting Developers";[14] "High Court Ruling Should Spur Christians to Action";[15] "Court Shows Homeowners Door: Development Trumps Property Rights";[16] "For Homeowners, Frustration and Anger at Ruling";[17] "Eminent Domain Ruling Has Dire Implications."[18]

Much of the news reflected sentiments like those of Terry Gannon, president of Citizens for Responsible Growth, who said in an interview with the *St. Petersburg Times,* "It used to be our home is our castle. Now our home is our castle until we see the bulldozers coming."[19] In a piece called "Stealing Home," the *Houston Chronicle* described the decision as a "bizarre anomaly." Perhaps "the government in China or Russia might take private property to hand over to wealthy developers to build shopping malls and office plazas, but it wouldn't happen in the United States. Yet, that is the practice the U.S. Supreme Court narrowly approved this week. Local governments, the court ruled, may seize private homes and businesses so that other private entities can develop the land into enterprises that generate higher taxes." The conservative commentator George Will, describing *Kelo* as the most important case of the term, cautioned that conservatives "should be careful what they wish for [in their] often-reflexive rhetoric" about judicial restraint and deference to the powers of elected branches of government. In *Kelo,* wrote Will, a liberal court had placed government power and its potential to cure all ills over and above the power of the little man. The decision had squashed "society's little platoons, such as homeowners and the neighborhoods they comprise."[20] According to Howard Troxler, a Florida columnist, "The U.S. Supreme Court has basically handed a big pile of crack cocaine to every state and local government in

America and said, 'Try not to get addicted.' The court will be forced to modify this ruling in time."[21]

Meanwhile, the blogosphere erupted in a burst of populist rage. Internet postings appeared on the very day *Kelo* was issued. It wasn't just the far right or the far left or the don't-tread-on-me libertarian crowd. Across the spectrum, from lawyers to laborers, bloggers were venting in disbelief, often in pretty salty language, over what the U.S. Supreme Court had done. "I totally disagree with the Supreme Court's decision that *GOVERNMENT CAN STEAL YOUR PROPERTY* for some kind of nebulous 'appreciable benefits to the community,'" wrote Rob, the self-described Bubba of Bombast, in a posting titled "Piss Poor Decision" on his Gut Rumbles website on June 23, 2005. "If these 'benefits' work elsewhere the way they do around Savannah, a select few will reap most of the money, and the 'community' can just kiss their asses."

A blogger who goes by the name Evil Conservative vented:

> We hear all the time how liberals and Democrats are all for the small guy, and how conservatives and Republicans are all about money and big business, but here it was the more liberal justices who voted to take away from the small guy, while the more conservative voted against it. So much for them being for the ordinary person. An LA Times writer claimed "Economic development emerged as the clear winner." A 5–4 decision is not a "clear" win. They are also wrong, it isn't a win for economic development, it's a win for cities to be able to squeeze ordinary people in order to get more tax revenue. It has turned the fifth amendment into a law to make more money for cities, while they continue to tax us more, and give us less services.

The blog Eric's Grumbles Before the Grave gathered enraged sentiments from around the country, including thoughts from the Cattalarchy blog:

> It's kinda like the Raich [medical marijuana] case, where the Supreme Court reamed the commerce clause pinhole into a gaping void which allows the feds to regulate anything. . . . Now they've interpreted the word public in Amendment V . . . to mean anything which benefits the public in general, including private businesses, rather than the more obvious interpretation of direct

> public use. Since you can argue that pretty much any private business benefits the public, now your local officials, who "know best," get to decide whether or not to bulldoze your fucking home.

And blogger Mover Mike sarcastically noted the silence from the Office of the Solicitor General, which did not submit an amicus brief on behalf of the White House, although every Tom, Dick and Harry in town had filed briefs in the *Kelo* case:

> This decision legitimizes the cronyism of the powerful developers with money and the politicians who need money. This decision is a terrible blow to private property rights. Where was President Bush? He was at one time considering filing an Amicus Brief on the side of New London, he who subscribes to an ownership society. Yes, we live in an ownership society, until a developer decides he wants to own our property.

Even the Founding Fathers reacted to *Kelo*—by turning over in their graves at an alarming speed. "Thomas Jefferson must be spinning in his grave!" wrote a resident of Tampa, Florida, in a letter to the editor. "As James Madison turns over in his grave, the least we can do is vote for congressmen who oppose loose interpretations of eminent domain," said the blogger Happy Mills, who tracks the heavy eminent domain activity in Fresno, California. "The upshot of Kelo is simple," penned the Milwaukee talk radio host Jeff Wagner on his website. "A man's home is still his castle—unless Starbucks wants to build a new coffee shop. That noise you hear is the Founding Fathers collectively turning over in their graves." And we had it on excellent authority from Townsend A. ("Van") Van Fleet that his great-great-great-great-great-grandfather George Mason, "who helped write the Fifth Amendment, is most likely rolling over in his grave as a result of this shameful decision by the liberal members of the Supreme Court," which Van Fleet called "Robin Hood in reverse."[22] With all this jostling of bones, it was inevitable that we would hear from Madison himself. He wrote a stern memorandum to Justice Stevens, taking him to task for the *Kelo* decision, as a result of which, he informed the justice, "I'm spinning in my grave."[23]

The outbursts on Scotus Blog, favored by the lawyer-and-policy-wonk crowd, were more circumspect but still bristling: "My worst fears have been confirmed." (Benjoblog) "This was entirely expected, but nonetheless infuriating." (Pegmanesque) "I thought this was the kind of thing that happened in France." (Disinterested Party) (France, eh? Now *that's* hitting below the belt.) "It's a sad, sad day for individual rights." (The Minards.com) "The Supreme Court just screwed the individual again." (The World According to Nick) "While I'm not quite ready to pull a Pournelle and declare the Republic dead, evidence suggests it is going downhill fast and/or on life support. First, this execrable ruling from the Supreme Court . . ." (The Laughing Wolf)

A more eloquent protest of *Kelo* came from Senator Gary Hart and his son, John Hart, who own land and practice law in Denver. "Perhaps the justices have to come from the West, like Justice Sandra Day O'Connor of Arizona, to fully understand what a monumental threat this is," the Harts surmised. They described the unsettling feeling that the decision left them with, the worry for every westerner about "his or her local government, which may decide that having Wal-Mart on your farm or ranch is better than having you on your farm or ranch," and they noted that this is a "blatant invitation for political corruption at the local level." Not everything, the Harts explained, is a matter of money:

> As Western landowners, we are particularly troubled by this cavalier approach to landowners' rights. How do you determine "just compensation" for land and property rights in cases where ownership of family ranches, parcels and mountain homes has spanned generations and long family and community histories? Family tradition, our ties with history and our past, must give way to shopping malls. Stories about the original Americans and prairies full of bison will be but past dreams of rolling foothills now covered by parking lots, littered with stray shopping carts.[24]

Just as odd bedfellows had joined ranks on the way up to the Supreme Court in two dozen friend-of-the-court briefs, they were bedding down together in post-*Kelo* outrage. Senator John Cornyn (R-Tex.), openly libertarian in his politics and one of the few Texas politicians to happily support the Gore family during their struggle, found himself on the same side of the issue as Representative

Maxine Waters (D-Calif.), a liberal, and Representative Bernard Sanders (I-Vt.), a self-described socialist. Waters said the *Kelo* decision is "the most un-American thing that can be done" and predicted it would weigh most heavily upon minorities and the poor. Tom Delay, usually not known for siding with Maxine Waters, chimed in and called the decision a "travesty."[25] Representative Richard Pombo, a conservative Republican from rural San Joaquin County, California, was more than ready to join forces with the other side of the aisle. Anger at the Supreme Court's decision "had united rural landowners with suburbanites and city dwellers fearful that cities will eye their homes for hotels, malls or any commercial use they think will generate more taxes," Pombo said in an interview with the *San Francisco Chronicle.*[26] In the seven days following *Kelo,* the U.S. House of Representatives spit out bill after bill with heroic titles like the Protection of Homes, Small Businesses and Private Property Act; the Eminent Domain Limitation Act; and the Private Property Rights Protection Act. Aside from situations of national emergency or war, Congress rarely moves so fast.

Once in a blue moon, a case comes along that, rather than quietly ending a dispute, ignites a national debate. This can happen only when the underlying controversy taps into a deep well of emotion; and it helps if one of the lightning rods of politics is involved, such as sex, race, religion, class or money. *Kelo* involved questions of money and class, and its outcome threatens to violate that most sacred of American domains: the home. What has emerged from the ashes of the 5–4 opinion in *Kelo* is a Supreme Court phoenix—a case that lives on in the political consciousness. Who would ever have thought that such a rare bird could rise from the arcane archives of the law of eminent domain? The surge of political activity resulting from the decision became known as the "*Kelo* backlash."

Debates about eminent domain found their way into local, state and national politics. In one month's time, legislatures in twenty-eight states had introduced more than seventy bills aimed at curbing local eminent domain powers, and legislators in five states proposed constitutional amendments to prohibit eminent domain for private development.[27] In South Dakota, legislators started working on a bill the day after *Kelo* came out.[28] South

Dakotans were serious about eminent domain; they passed a law that did *not* contain a loophole for blight. That would place them in a small minority in the coming year. Similar laws were passed in Florida, Nevada, North Dakota and South Carolina. By July 2006, twenty-nine states had passed some form of eminent domain reform, either placing restrictions on how eminent domain could be used, revising procedural requirements, or prohibiting the transfer of property to private parties. For example, Colorado changed the standard of proof for blight, requiring condemning authorities to show "clear and convincing evidence" of blight, while Utah created a requirement for written notice to homeowners of each public meeting that could affect their property. Missouri instituted a compensation reform for properties that have been in a family for fifty years—a "heritage" value that is tacked on top of the property's market value.

But in the majority of states that passed legislation or amended existing laws (Alabama and Maine are examples), the statutes still allow takings that look and smell an awful lot like economic development takings in neighborhoods that are "blighted." As a practical matter, that means it's déjà vu all over again. We began with *Berman* and we continue with *Berman* in those states: minority removal, poor-people removal. As Timothy Sandefur pointed out, government routinely causes blight by stifling growth through regulation and making it prohibitively expensive to build new housing. "There's something amiss," he wrote, "when developers find it easier to cannibalize existing owners than to build new homes or shops on [existing] vacant land."[29] And as the study conducted by the public advocate in New Jersey would soon show, blight is not a very hard thing to find when a willing city and a willing developer go looking for it.

There was such a hue and cry when *Kelo* was handed down, and it came from such varied and bipartisan quarters, that more than one governor issued a moratorium on all non-public eminent domain projects in their states. One of them was Governor M. Jodi Rell of Connecticut (a Republican). It might have been expected that *Kelo* would settle matters in New London, but instead the mudslinging grew more frenzied. The City of New London, like sore winners, slapped a bill for unpaid "rent" on the *Kelo* homeowners, reasoning that since the homeowners lost the case, they had effectively been living in city-owned property since 1999. The Institute for Justice vowed to "pull out all the stops" in Connecticut. It probably didn't help to quiet things down that Governor Rell likened *Kelo* to "the 21st century equivalent of the Boston Tea Party; the government taking away the rights and liberties of property owners without giving them a voice. But this time it is not a monarch wearing robes in England we are fighting—it is five robed justices at the Supreme Court in Washington."[30] Governor Rell called for a moratorium on takings until the state legislature could consider a pending bill on the subject. In the meantime, the city council's relationship with the New London Development Corporation continued to deteriorate with still more haggling over that blasted $4 million. Even before the *Kelo* decision, in March 2005, the council and the NLDC had entered into mediation workshops with a conflict resolution consultant, arranged for by Governor Rell; it seemed necessary since people had begun storming out of council meetings. The eminent domain moratorium would give everyone time to go to their respective corners and chill out. Negotiations over the homes of Susette Kelo and the other holdouts continued through 2006, although one of the elderly holdouts, Wilhelmina Dery, passed away in the midst of the turmoil.

While the United States Congress had moved with lightning speed to pass the House Resolution condemning the *Kelo* decision in grand language, passing actual legislation was another matter. A number of bills were introduced in the House in the immediate wake of *Kelo*. Some were rather neatly drafted, suggesting interesting reforms. Two bills simply exempted from taxes any compensation received in an eminent domain award or settlement (H.R. 3268 and H.R. 4603); neither of them got very far. Another bill proposed that treble damages be paid by any federal entity condemning a property, or by any state entity condemning a property if that state wants to continue receiving federal economic development funds (which are defined very broadly). These bills did not prevent the states from engaging in economic development takings, but set up clearly written disincentives to doing so.

Just as nature abhors a vacuum, Congress abhors laws that are clear and unequivocal. On November 3, 2005, the House passed H.R. 4128, known as the Private Property Rights Protection Act of

2005, which proposed a complicated scheme for withholding federal money from states that use eminent domain in private-to-private transfers of property. An alternative title to the act could have been "The Permanent Employment for Lawyers Act of 2005," because it revolved so closely around litigation. Any act of "eminent domain abuse" as defined under the statute has to be proven in a court—and the cutoff of federal money begins "two fiscal years following a final judgment on the merits." The state or city can keep the federal funds from getting cut off if it gives the property back or "replaces any property destroyed."

Since in most states it is difficult if not impossible to get a court to stop an eminent domain bulldozer while the parties haggle over legal issues, chances are there would be a lot of houses and businesses "destroyed" and therefore a lot of "replacements" occurring, and endless litigation over them and the related cutoff of federal funds. And exactly who was supposed to enforce this federal law? Apparently, ordinary Joes. Private citizens would have standing to bring actions under the act; it's not clear that anyone else was intended to do so. They also would bear the burden of proof and have to front all their legal fees—a mighty big risk in going up against a city or a state. Under H.R. 4128, the attorney general of a state wouldn't bring the suit for them, but would play the role of Big Brother, monitoring which towns and cities were doing economic development takings and reporting back to Congress. Most people don't have the money to hire a lawyer in an eminent domain case. In fact, many eminent domain lawyers work on contingency; it's often the only way people involved in eminent domain cases can secure legal representation. Citizens would have to fight their government to show a violation of a complex federal law, and to get their property returned or replaced. The result of a ruling in their favor would be the loss of billions of dollars in federal funding to a state—a point that might not be lost on judges who are elected.

After H.R. 4128 passed in the House, it went on to die a peaceful death in the Senate. Another bill, also called the Private Property Rights Protection Act (S. 1895), had been introduced in the Senate on October 19. Although it was dressed up with plenty of elegiac recitations about the Founders and property rights, at its core it had a deadly design. The bill clearly defined what constitutes a "public use" for purposes of eminent domain (such as government facilities, highways, schools, prisons, airports, public stadiums). Then it stated that any entity applying for federal funds of any kind would have to certify that it had not engaged in eminent domain other than for a public purpose, and anyone making a certification could be audited by the IRS. This bill, too, died in committee. Once the initial media storm over *Kelo* subsided, neither H.R. 4128 nor S. 1895 had the support to be put to a vote in the Senate. In the meantime, a narrower House Bill called the Protect Our Homes Act (H.R. 4088), which would have cut off Housing and Urban Development funds to states or local governments that participated in economic development takings, failed to come to a vote in the House. By November, the notoriously short attention span of the United States Congress had been distracted by the war in Iraq and other pressing matters. It was clear that the real legislative action would be in the states.

The debate entered local politics in many strange permutations. For example, in what can only be regarded as comic relief for those who live in New Jersey—a state that never met an eminent domain project it didn't like—two gubernatorial candidates, Douglas Forrester (a Republican) and Jon Corzine (a Democrat), tried mightily to outdo each other with demonstrations of outrage over *Kelo* during the summer of 2005. The mini melodrama in the Garden State illustrates how eminent domain abuses can become tangled up in local intrigue. Within weeks of the *Kelo* decision, Forrester called a news conference to announce solemnly the creation of a task force "to study the impact of the court's ruling."[31] He could not, however, pass up the opportunity to remind his audience of what he believed to be the eminent domain abuse involved in the proposal to build a golf course on Petty's Island, a project reportedly backed by a Democratic power broker who, he alleged, was close to Corzine. Forrester warned of the "sinister element of connections—political connections, pay-to-play connections—involved in eminent domain use."[32] Apparently it took the *Kelo* case to reveal this scandal to Forrester. Corzine soon fired back with his own seven-point plan—which he insisted he had formulated before *Kelo* was decided—for ridding New Jersey of the evil of eminent domain abuse, "except in rare and exceptional circumstances."[33] Whatever that means.

Not to be outdone by their neighbors across the Hudson, the challengers in the New York City primary race for public advocate, always a slugfest, were also slinging mud over eminent domain. In the post-*Kelo* world, it seems to be *de rigueur* for politicians at least to *appear* as if they despise eminent domain. The incumbent public advocate, Betsy Gotbaum, was attacked for publicly supporting the highly controversial Atlantic Yards redevelopment project on Brooklyn's waterfront—in which eminent domain had been threatened but not yet deployed—while at the same time insisting that she was opposed to such takings. Among Gotbaum's critics was a city councilwoman who introduced a bill to prevent the use of city funds to facilitate such takings. Gotbaum reasoned that the powerful and well-funded developer was still negotiating buyouts with the holdout residents, and besides, the developer had told her "he didn't want to use eminent domain."[34] That's a bit like saying that a robber who puts a gun to a man's head and takes his wallet did not obtain it by force, since he never actually pulled the trigger.

In Texas, where the Gores and Western Seafood were fighting for survival, two competing bills were in the legislature in the summer of 2005. In the immediate wake of *Kelo,* on July 22, 2005, the Texas House of Representatives unanimously (136–0) passed a bill to put a leash on economic development takings. The bill would have amended the Texas Constitution to narrow the meaning of "public use" to eliminate takings for private development. In response, Senator Kyle Janek introduced the more moderate SB 7, which created a statutory solution to the problem, with explicit exemptions for certain kinds of public use projects like ports—and for the new Dallas Cowboys stadium in Arlington as well as an urban renewal project planned for an empty high-rise in downtown Dallas.[35] The original version of SB 7 also contained a grandfather clause, which would have preserved the existing laws on the books for any condemnation cases pending in Texas at that time. Of course, that included the eminent domain cases the City of Freeport had already filed against the Gores.

Wright Gore III, along with his brother Alex and his cousin Patrick, had been in Austin lobbying legislators to take out the grandfather clause in SB 7. If it didn't come out, the bill would not help families like the Gores who were already caught up in an eminent domain nightmare. The Gores were hardly met with open arms in Austin. Controversy over the bill was intense. The debate spilled over into a special August session. Many legislators wanted to get out of town to attend the National Conference of State Legislatures in Seattle, and the last thing they wanted to do was deal with some desperate property owner flinging himself at their feet.

What's more, the Gores had opposition. During July, Mayor Phillips went up to Austin for the day. "There were about five of us," he said. There was Ron Bottoms, Mary Stotler, and Sandra Leavey, who sits on Freeport's redevelopment board and is active in downtown revitalization efforts. "We didn't go to lobby against the bill itself. We knew there was no hope" of that, the mayor explained, because "the reaction to *Kelo* was strong in Texas." He and his group were there to lobby for what Mayor Phillips called the "ex post facto" provision. Freeport, like many cities, wanted a grandfather clause. Property owners, such as the Gores, wanted it taken out.

Seventeen votes were needed to pass SB 7 in the senate. "We went around counting votes, begging senators to stick around for the vote," Wright III wrote in an email. The hallways of the Austin state house were packed with lobbyists, including those of the Texas Farm Bureau and the Waco Associated Realtors, who favored a strong property rights bill, and the Texas Municipal League of Cities, who wanted a bill that left the power of eminent domain as broad as possible. The scene that played out in Austin that summer was repeated in state houses across America, with one very individual exception: a man who called himself Sputnik.

Sputnik's appearance before the State Affairs Committee of the Texas Senate on July 2, 2005, certainly broke up the usual routine. It had already been an unusual legislative session, with the whole state capital turned upside down following the release of the *Kelo* decision. The committee had before it three bills that would limit the extent to which eminent domain could be used for private economic development in Texas. With its bills lined up neatly like ducks, the committee was prepared to hear testimony. But as so often is the case when testimony is presented before public bodies, the senate had pretty much made up its mind as to where this debate would go. Around the country there had been a great deal of grandstanding on the front steps of state houses; but inside those buildings, legislators were under pressure from lobbyists to keep a lid on anti-development legislation. The furthest the Texas Senate would go in the next several weeks—and that was all they had before the summer session ended—would be a statutory response. No one was going to go hog wild and start pressing for a constitutional amendment.

In the hallway outside the senate chamber, Wright III was awaiting his turn to speak, along with Sputnik, the chairman of the Texas Motorcycle Rights Association. Sputnik was easy to spot: he is a burly fellow and bald except for a Mohawk. He dresses in jeans and a leather vest, wears multiple earrings and has the word "freedom" tattooed on his forehead. He was there to lobby his legislature for an anti-*Kelo*, anti-eminent-domain bill.

A casual observer might think that Wright III, with his college education and good suit and ten-dollar words, would be the better lobbyist of the two. Wright III went first and gave a nice presentation. Senator Duncan even congratulated him for making such a moving speech. Before you place your bet, it's only fair to tell you that Sputnik successfully went up against the insurance lobby and convinced the Louisiana legislature to repeal their mandatory helmet law. (It's a safety hazard that impairs individual freedom, Sputnik maintains on his website.) Louisiana later repealed the repeal after too many brains got splattered on highways; but still, here was a master lobbyist at work. He had come to remind the men in Austin what life is like for those who live paycheck to paycheck, and to tell them how *Kelo* had shattered their already fragile sense of security.

> *Senator Duncan:* Uh, Sputnik? Uh, I've always wondered, what's your real name?
> *Sputnik:* What?
> *Senator Duncan:* What did your Mama call you?
> *Sputnik:* You don't want to know what my Mama called me. She don't care too much for my lifestyle.
> *Senator Duncan* (chuckling): OK. Well, I won't go there. Sputnik, go ahead …
> *Sputnik:* OK, Mr. Chairman, Committee Members, today you're probably bein' faced with one of the biggest issues you'll ever have to come against while you're in the legislature. This reaches to the very heart of bein' an American, and it must be addressed in two short weeks.

> Once you have started this, it has already gone to committee, you know very well if it is not settled this time, within the next two years, there'll be a lot of people losin' their homes because the cities are not gonna pass up the opportunity to do what they can *now.*
>
> Our right to own property is bad enough that if you figure my taxes on my property now, my monthly payments on my home now are more than I paid when I bought it 30 years ago. So we never really *own* it. At least we get to *live* there as long as we pay the fees. To tell us that someone else will pay more to the city, or the county, or the state, so we have to give up our home—
>
> You give us just compensation, but for the just compensation that I would be given for my home today, I would not even come close to replacing it, and I could not even live in a place that I chose to live.

Now Sputnik goes for the lobbying jugular:

> ... And I would not believe that simply a statutory law will solve this problem. I believe it will have to be a constitutional amendment. Because there's always ways for a good attorney, as a lot of you know, to get away, across, around the statutory law. But once it's in the constitution, it's gonna be a lot harder to battle.
>
> *Senator Duncan* (leaning forward, toward Sputnik): That didn't slow down the City of New London, because the Supreme Court has just held, constitutionally, that ... they just opened the door, constitutionally ...

Oh, foolish man, thinking you can outwit Sputnik:

> *Sputnik* (a little louder now): Yes, they have and that's why we need to close it *in Texas*. The Supreme Court doesn't say you *have* to do it; they said you *can*.

Senator Duncan leans back in his seat now. Sputnik has nailed him.

> *Sputnik:* But our state constitution *should* say you *cannot.* A statutory law simply will not meet the needs and I trust you all realize how very important this is as Americans in Texas and you will, with the bills and resolutions, come up with the right ideas, and the right solutions. Thank you.

The man with the Mohawk and multiple ear piercings left the chamber. Not only did he outwit the presiding senator while testifying, he also refused again, in the colloquy with Senator Duncan at the close of his testimony, to disclose his full name or the formal name of the organization he represented. Sputnik would say only that he represented the bikers who came under his "umbrella organization, the Texas Bikers," and that he also represented "his heirs." That is, the heirs to the property he and his wife own out in the country, which he would like to keep.

In the immediate aftermath of *Kelo,* Sputnik spoke for us all, because there is a little bit of Sputnik in all of us. Most of us don't live like him. We don't have the guts to ride a big bike—with or without a helmet. But buried deep in every American is the notion that we have the *right* to be like Sputnik if we want to be: the rebel *with* a cause. To be the man who rides the open road on a motorcycle, the outsider, the nonconformist. America is not America without men like Sputnik. He put a condescending politician in his place. He spoke eloquently for every little guy who has been or will be shoved around by an economic development taking. He hit the nail on the head when he said: "My son is fixin' to lose his home [to a road project]" and "my secretary is fixin' to lose her home [to a road project] and that's understandable," but to lose a home "that we have worked for all our lives and that we are guaranteed belongs to us" because a city or a county can make more money from someone else is a "total travesty."

It is a "total travesty" because it is degrading. Your city or town has said: you are not worth as much to us as someone else. A homeowner or a business owner who may have spent a lifetime in a town, whose family may have been there for generations, or who may be an immigrant who sacrificed to get there, is suddenly reduced to the sum total of the taxes he pays and nothing more. America traditionally has not been a country that measures people in such starkly economic terms. In a country that was relatively new and still engaged in exploration and settlement, citizens were prized for ingenuity and resourcefulness and generosity.

In truth, poor neighborhoods for decades have been evaluated by economic standards under blight statutes and subjected to urban renewal, but the principle was not articulated in the terms of "tax revenue." Instead, it was expressed as a form of benevolence:

we're knocking it all down for the sake of the poor souls who live there, because no one should have to live in such conditions. They'll find someplace else to live. They always do. Then we'll bring in private developers to build something decent: a commercial building, a mall, some residential units, a hotel. What's that you say? Low-income housing? Oh, sure, there'll be some of that too. All of this, of course, had the effect of vastly increasing tax revenues. But no one had the gall to say openly, in so many words, that the people who lived there were simply no damn use anymore. Today, under "blight eminent domain" statutes such as the one Ohio was considering after exhaustive post-*Kelo* task force hearings, what is really being done is economic development takings in poor neighborhoods. The only difference is that the city, before shooting the starting pistol, must make a finding that at least some percentage (sometimes as little as half) of the neighborhood is blighted. Under many blight standards, this is not difficult to do. After such a finding is made, the poor can be evicted and the city can build anything that will increase its tax base.

In essence, what has evolved over the twenty years since Poletown is a much franker way of talking about blight-related takings. What many in urban planning might not have wanted to admit years ago can now be shouted from the rooftops: it's about the tax revenues. At first, urban development involved a mix of political forces, including a genuine desire to improve cities. But it didn't take long for people to figure out that once land was cleared—especially if nothing got built on it for years on end, which was often the case with land bulldozed for urban renewal—cities could generate a lot of revenue by building upscale developments.

The sad part of the story about the *Kelo* backlash is that it took the condemnation of some houses in a white, working-class neighborhood to get the country up in arms over the scandal of it all. When the *Berman* decision came out fifty-two years ago, announcing that sixty-three acres of a black neighborhood in the District of Columbia could be bulldozed to the ground for the sake of beauty, charm and hygiene—and thousands of people were displaced, never to return—nobody marched in the streets. For decades, eminent domain was just one small part of the injustices being visited upon minorities in America. This was well known within the black community, but no one else took much notice of eminent domain as a social and political issue until it started creeping toward the middle-class majority.

As for the debates in the Texas legislature, Sputnik's plea for a constitutional amendment was not going to fly. The senate and the house of representatives jockeyed back and forth on a final bill, trying to reach a compromise. The normally gentlemanly atmosphere of the senate erupted in a filibuster because of a provision in the bill that prevents universities from using eminent domain to acquire land for dormitories and parking lots. Finally, the bill was signed in late August by Governor Rick Perry. But after a long hot summer of chasing down politicians in Austin, it was not clear whether Wright III, his brother and his cousin were going home to Freeport with the prize they had sought: a clarification on the grandfathering issue. The grandfather clause came out, but nothing new went in its place. The new Texas law was silent on the matter of pending condemnations; that was the compromise reached by the politicians. It remained to be seen whether the bill, with this maddening ambiguity, would help the Gores at all on the appeal.

■ ■ ■

Given the raucous nature of American politics, it didn't take long for the eminent domain news cycle to turn from tragedy to farce. Not long after *Kelo* was decided, Logan Darrow Clements, an impassioned libertarian and Ayn Rand disciple from California who seemed to have a lot of time on his hands, jumped into the fray. He started up a campaign to convince the folks of Weare, New Hampshire—the hometown of Justice Souter, who had voted with the *Kelo* majority—to teach the justice an objective lesson on liberty. Clements' idea was to get Justice Souter's property taken in eminent domain. The old family home, a farmhouse sitting on eight acres, would be condemned for the purpose of tearing it down and building a bed-and-breakfast called the Lost Liberty Inn, which would generate greater tax revenue for Weare. Clements' sojourn in New Hampshire made for great press and was followed nationally, delighting columnists and reporters from coast to coast. Justice Souter, who lives a rather reclusive life, found himself blinking at flashbulbs near his front door on more than one occasion. In the end, though, the townspeople rejected Clements' proposal in a vote on February 4, 2005. Many of them reasoned that economic development takings are simply wrong, and therefore it would be wrong to inflict such a taking on their neighbor Justice Souter. They voted instead for a measure calling upon the state legislature to enact stricter eminent domain laws. Justice Souter, thanks to his sensible neighbors, managed to dodge the bullet he had helped fire against his fellow Americans.

Pretty soon the bipartisan love-fest on Capitol Hill was over and the state legislative grandstanding had largely subsided. States that were truly serious about reforming eminent domain, such as South Dakota and Florida, had enacted their reforms without much fuss and muss. Those that were not serious did what governments do when the name of the game is appearances: they issued grave pronouncements and convened a task force to study the matter.

When it comes to pompous grandstanding in the face of adversity, no state surpasses New Jersey. Staring down one of the worst eminent domain records and one of the highest-profile cases in the country, that of Long Branch, Governor Jon Corzine appointed Ronald Chen to a newly created position as public advocate, making clear that one of his top mandates was to study eminent domain in New Jersey and make recommendations. Chen was perfect for the job from a public relations point of view because he had recently represented the owner of a small pub who fought back when Jersey City tried to condemn his pub and adjacent land so a very influential parochial prep school could expand its athletic field by ten yards. (This was rationalized as a "public use" because the school said it would occasionally lend out the field to public schools.) Chen hadn't actually won in court; the case had dissolved under the weight of negative publicity, fed by post-*Kelo* outrage.

Chen conducted his study and issued his report. He found, lo and behold, that there was a whole lot of eminent domain going on in New Jersey. Many neighborhoods were being designated as "blighted" on the basis of "cursory formalities rather than serious discussion about the validity of the blight designation." Chen made a number of very sensible policy recommendations, such as requiring sworn testimony about blight, recording public hearings about blight, and giving property owners the right to appeal a finding of blight to an impartial third party who does *not* have an interest in the real estate development. He also suggested pay-to-play reforms such as requiring competitive bids on redevelopment contracts. "Government officials and those working on their behalf," wrote the public advocate, "should not be allowed to directly financially benefit from a redevelopment project with which they are involved."[36]

And then nothing happened—because this is New Jersey we're talking about, the most densely populated state in the country, where pay-to-play is a way of life, real estate developers are demigods, and condominiums are being shoehorned into every available square foot of land. But at least Mr. Chen's report was more forthright and useful than the one issued by the federal government in November 2006.

Congress had asked the U.S. Government Accountability Office to study eminent domain in the wake of the *Kelo* case. But GAO bit off more than it could chew, studying all types of eminent domain, including the enormous category of "DOT" takings (Department of Transportation projects, which in most states account for the largest portion of eminent domain work). The GAO report was titled "Eminent Domain: Information about Its Uses and Effect on Property Owners and Communities Is Limited." In other words, it took the GAO fifty-three pages to conclude that it could not conclude anything because states do not compile sufficient data about the number of takings done in any given year, settlements, prices paid, and so forth. Still, it was unusual that eminent domain, largely an issue hashed out in the state courts, was on the federal radar screen at such an intense level of scrutiny.

■ ■ ■

The first anniversary of the *Kelo* decision was noted by a surprisingly large number of pundits. *Kelo* was clearly living on in the popular imagination. But the Private Property Rights Protection Act of 2005 was dead as a doorknob, buried in the Senate Judiciary Committee. All eyes were on the November 2006 election and the many initiatives on state ballots.

The topic of eminent domain had long been the purview of academics and a narrow subspecialty of lawyers. But after June 23, 2005, it found its way into legislative debates and electoral campaigns. Citizens who already were targets of economic development takings suddenly found the vocabulary to express their anger. The *Kelo* case, covered in depth by the media, crystallized the often byzantine form that condemnation proceedings take for the homeowners caught up in them. Armed with a clearer understanding of what has befallen them, they have been hitting the streets in protest.

The post-*Kelo* phoenix rose so high it resulted in eminent domain moratoriums in Ohio and Connecticut, twenty-eight state laws, and eight state constitutional amendments. It also spawned an Arizona law requiring compensation for regulatory takings, as well as attempts at such bills in several other states. It remains to be seen whether this bird has staying power and whether the many laws passed to restrict eminent domain will truly eradicate economic development takings over the long haul. For example, Utah didn't take long before reversing course and amending its strong post-*Kelo* law. It is possible that such takings will continue by way of "blight" loopholes the way eminent domain has traditionally been done since the 1950s.

As for the town that started it all, New London remains fractured and requires gubernatorial supervision. One by one, after considerable hand wringing, the homeowners who participated in the landmark case have settled, with the exception of Susette Kelo and Pasquale Christofaro. In June 2006, Governor Rell sent a letter to the City of New London saying that state funds for settlement would not be available after June 15. With emotions rising around the one-year anniversary of the *Kelo* decision, the state agreed to extend the settlement time for another week, and the parties then came to an agreement.[37] Because of the thunderstorm of publicity that followed the *Kelo* case, the Institute for Justice was able to negotiate an unusual accommodation for Susette Kelo: she may move her house to another location. Kelo said she proposed this solution years ago and was rebuffed by the city. The New London Development Corporation gave her until the summer of 2007 to move her house, because nothing much was happening in Fort Trumbull at the time. The NLDC was still locked in its battle with the city council over that final $4 million. John Brooks, manager of the Fort Trumbull Development Project, insisted it is forthcoming "soon."

CHAPTER 9

DEMOCRACY, FREEPORT STYLE

"I wouldn't mind being put in jail. I've been there a few times before," says Skip Pratt.

"Me too!" says Larry McDonald, breaking into a laugh. Others at the table start nodding and laughing along with him.

Skip proudly shows off a scar on the inside of his wrist that he says he got when he was manhandled by a cop. He is a middle-aged man with a shock of white hair and a mischievous smile. His physique—a wiry frame combined with the start of a potbelly—suggests a lifetime of hard work chased by cold beer.

Skip and Larry are sitting around a small table with six other men and women in the Western Seafood office. Built high up on a system of water-treated wooden supports to safeguard it from floodwaters, the office sits across the road from the big blue packing house on the Old Brazos River in downtown Freeport. The group is assembled for a meeting of the Citizens for Freeport. Wright Gore III has given them access to the office. Strictly speaking, he is not a member of Citizens for Freeport because he now lives in Houston, but he was born and raised in Freeport and has known many of these people for a long time. The Gore family's fate has become intertwined with the political sentiments and the delicate balance of personalities and small-town allegiances of these individuals. Wright III relies upon them, and his gratitude is immeasurable.

In the battle that Wright III has been waging to save Western Seafood, the Citizens have been loyal allies. Wright has come to learn, however, that the Citizens have many reasons for fighting City Hall. Some are doing so out of principle and a dislike for eminent domain, some on the commonsense hunch that if the Gores—who are people of means and own a substantial business—can have their property snatched out from under them, then ordinary folks are all the more ripe for the picking. But the Citizens' ire is also raised by something else: an abiding distrust of the government, especially their own local government, which they know so well.

Wright III says very little during the meeting. When he does speak, the raucous storytelling stops and the room immediately falls silent. In three years of political trench warfare and going toe to toe with the mayor and other officials in countless meetings of the city council and the EDC, this soft-spoken but deliberate young man has earned their respect.

The Citizens begin the meeting with the aim of coming up with a candidate to replace John Smith III on the city council. "We've got to find someone to run against him," says Joaquin Damian, a somber man in his fifties who wears unadorned gray sweatshirts, along with a lifetime of labor and struggle on his face. Joaquin can barely contain his dislike for John Smith III. The Citizens for Freeport agree with him about unseating Smith, whom they see as part of a voting bloc controlled by the mayor, Jim Phillips, a great big bear of a man who is intimidating to many in town. They regard Larry McDonald, one of their group, is the only "good guy" on the city council. He votes his conscience. As Joaquin has pointed out, "Larry isn't in it for the money." Serving on the council pays $100 a month. "Larry donates the council pay to his church," says Joaquin. "He gives it away to poor people."

A few names are bandied about as candidates for Smith's seat. But the talk inevitably drifts toward the marina project and eminent domain and the Gores. The Citizens don't like the way the city is treating the Gores; they don't like eminent domain; and they don't like the priorities of the city council. "If they can do this to the Gores," says Paul Buford, "just imagine what they can do to us."

The Citizens begin reminiscing, like war buddies, about the first time they circulated a petition against the marina project, trying to put it to a vote of the people. It was early summer in 2005 and they were just beginning to gather signatures to get their initiative on the fall ballot. They wanted to ask the voters whether the whole Freeport Economic Development Corporation should be done away with. *They're loaning out $6 million of our money without even asking us how we feel about. Hell, when the question came up about renovating the old Freeport High School, they went and put that to a vote. And that was only $2 million! Dissolve the EDC. Put the damn thing out of its misery.*

It was a bold move, but the strategy had a certain logic to it. The EDC was the only entity in Freeport with powers of eminent domain. It had been created in 1999 by a vote of the people. If it was dissolved, a new vote of the people would be required to create such a monster again.

Early efforts at circulating the petition were difficult. A police officer stopped a volunteer on the ground that a local ordinance prohibited door-to-door peddling without a license. The officer told the volunteer to go to City Hall, presumably to see about getting a license. According to a story in the *Facts,* the chief of police at the time, Henrietta Gonzalez, said that the officer had immediately checked with her supervisor, who told her that citizens of Freeport have a right to circulate petitions door to door. But it is not clear when this First Amendment tutorial took place, or even whether it took place on the same day.[1] The Citizens for Freeport, however, recall that the distribution was interrupted. It is a memory that still rankles because such disruptions in electioneering are no small matter considering how close the final vote was on the EDC ballot. What might have been a minor misunderstanding in another town became the first of many points of contention in a growing litany of complaints between the anti-marina camp and the City of Freeport. Later that day, the city placed leaflets on people's lawns, saying there were "no plans to take any homes through eminent domain."[2]

The Citizens for Freeport were becoming better organized. They went out to circulate the petition again. It was July, mosquito season. This time, they tried not to draw attention to themselves, but the next issue of the *Facts* had a banner headline reading: "Petitioners Adding to Fears, City Says."[3] The harder the city pushed, the more determined the Citizens became. They saw the fight as righting a fundamental wrong. The EDC should never have made this deal in the first place without involving the citizens. Freeport residents, 15 percent of them unemployed, would appreciate it if the city would do basic things for them, like fix the drainage so the streets won't flood into their houses when it rains.

Joyce Adkins, a redheaded lady with a blunt manner of speaking, has made it her business for the last three decades to know where the bodies are buried in Freeport. She has a more visceral take on things. "We don't like *the way they do business*," she says, speaking of the city council and the EDC. "I'm not against the marina. Let them build it. They just shouldn't be loaning city money for it. And we *don't* like eminent domain."

The Citizens for Freeport are motivated in large part by a deep dissatisfaction with the manner in which the city has been run and with how the municipal government controls the life of the Little Man. The marina project and the taking of the Gores' property seem to be one more example of oppression in Freeport. Any stranger who is in town for more than twenty-four hours will soon learn of two major grievances among its citizens: code enforcement and reconnect fees (for water and sewer). These may sound like minor irritants, but when repeated over and over in a poor and working-class city they become like Chinese water torture.

During the last decade, according to the Citizens for Freeport, the city government has stepped up its practice of laying fines on homeowners who have minor exterior code violations under Freeport's Minimum Standards Ordinance. Residents are at the mercy of the MSO, explained Joaquin Damian, a longtime resident who owns several rental properties. The code enforcers can fine you for "a torn screen door, peeling paint, one shingle off the roof. They send a code enforcement officer around." Joyce Adkins said the code means "no clotheslines, no more than two cars in the driveway, [no] peeling paint [or] rotted boards." The fines are small, but enough to pinch a family that is barely getting by. Ignoring a summons can lead to a warrant.

The Freeport budget reveals just how serious the city's code enforcement practice is. The projected budget for 2005–2006 was $13,026,854. That includes $382,350 from "fines and fees"—that is, money collected for all those loose shingles, torn screen doors and bits of peeling paint. The city employs four staffers to do the job, costing a total of $297,376 a year (including benefits, vehicle insurance, laptop computers and so on), a sum projected to increase yearly. While the city certainly needs to demolish unsafe structures and inspect its fast-food joints, the residents are frightened of the code enforcers who poke around their modest neighborhoods, making mountains out of molehills and hitting them up for fines they can't afford.

Then there are the "reconnect" fees. Freeport residents used to get an 8 percent discount if they paid their water bills early. "They did away with that," said Joaquin Damian. Now if you pay your bill late, they hit you with a "$25 disconnect fee and a $25 reconnect fee." There is also a late-pay fee of $10, charged after the 13th of the month, and a cutoff fee of $40 charged after the 21st of the month. Joaquin commented that he used to see disconnect and reconnect fees like that only when tenants vacated apartments or houses changed hands and a water department worker had to actually visit the premises. Now he sees poor people getting hit with fees and losing their service, then having to pay disconnect and reconnect fees for no good reason.

The Freeport budget for 2005–2006 shows the city making $3,400,000 from water sales and sewer charges. On top of that, $150,000 comes from connect and disconnect fees. Freeport is not a transient town; people tend to stay put, either living in their own homes or renting. The population is only 13,500. Why is Freeport collecting disconnect and connect fees adding up to almost 5 percent of its overall water and sewer sales? This burden is bound to fall disproportionately on the poor, and on the landlords who service that population.

"To me, it's taxation without representation," said Joaquin Damian. Policy wonks have another name for it: a regressive tax on the poor and the working class. At the same time the city is imposing this regressive tax, it is embarking on expensive beautification programs and an economic development scheme that promises returns far off in the future, but is funded today with a half-penny sales tax and plans to float a $3 million bond. Those beautification programs are not aimed at the part of town where the poorest people live. "The city is beautifying the part of town near the marina. The white part of town," said Joyce Adkins.

▪ ▪ ▪

Back in the Western Seafood office, the Citizens for Freeport are really grumbling:

The city government, that's what they're really good at, collecting those fines. But ask them to fix the drainage pumps to stop the floods, that's too small a goal for the likes of the EDC and the city council. Now they're all hot on building this private yacht marina. They tell us that way down the line it's going to help the Freeport economy. It's a build-it-and-they-will-come theory. First the marina, and then the hotels and the restaurants will follow. See? At the moment, though, there is absolutely nothing downtown for a yachtsman to take advantage of, should an errant boat wind its way upriver.

And then there's the new marina that feller Marc Grosz is building down at Surfside. They expect to break ground in the summer of 2007. Using his own money, too. Not borrowing a dime. Bought the land outright from Unical—no eminent domain. They're going to have to compete with him and they don't seem to have thought about that. Did you see the look on Mayor Phillips' face when Marc Grosz showed up at the council meeting and started telling everyone about his marina? You could have knocked Phillips over with a feather. All he could do was sit there in shock until finally he couldn't take it no more and then he said —what did he tell Mr. Grosz? Oh yeah! "This is not our concern, Mr. Grosz. You have to go talk to the mayor of Surfside about this." They're loaning $6 million of our money to some millionaire from Dallas, with no guarantee, but it's not our concern that someone is building a marina ten minutes away from here. Lord!

But the money! Hell, our entire annual budget is only $13 million and we're loaning $6 million to Walker. That's H. Walker Royall. You've heard of him. *He's a Blaffer.*

It is particularly galling to the group that the developer, Walker Royall, comes from the famous Blaffer family. To Mr. Royall, the marina project may seem like an ordinary business deal with municipal financing, but to this group of Freeport residents it's as if the decimated East Enders of London had been asked to loan money to the Windsors to reconstruct their city after the Blitz.

And on top of it all, the city was condemning one of the oldest employers in Freeport and wiping out real jobs. Lee Cameron, the director of the EDC, told residents at a town hall meeting that he projected the marina would bring in $60 million in investment for hotels and retail venues "and create 250 to 300 jobs."[4] But people in East Texas know that a marina is seasonal, and even in season the marina itself was expected to employ only about ten or fifteen people. And it wouldn't pay a nickel in taxes to the city for an indefinite period of time.

That's right there in black and white in the development agreement, the Citizens grumble. *The city is promising all manner of pie in the sky. It's just more of the same from the Freeport Council.*

Skip Pratt launches into the story of how he acquired his scars. It was during the campaign against the EDC. The Citizens had gathered enough signatures to get the issue on the ballot. The election was approaching and tensions were running high in town. "I had signs on my front lawn," says Skip. "They urged people to vote in favor of the initiative." One day he went out in the afternoon for an hour and when he came back, "the signs were gone."

Skip called to report the theft and the police department sent a squad car. After he explained what had been stolen to the police officer, according to Skip, "the officer walked over to his police car and got ready to leave."

"You're not gonna write a report or nothing?"

Skip was told, no, there would be no report. If he wanted to see one, he could come down to the police station and request one there, and that was that.

"This is bullshit!" Skip cried.

The next thing Skip knew, he says, he was being slammed up against a wall, then thrown face down onto the concrete slab in front of his house. "My hands were underneath me and the officer wanted me to put my hands behind me, and I was trying to tell him that I couldn't, because he was on top of me. He pulled one of my arms out and put the cuff on it." Skip says he ended up with a busted lip, bruises on the right side of his head and an injured wrist. "My lip still gets numb sometimes." He was arrested for disorderly conduct and resisting arrest. The Freeport Police held him in lockup from 5:00 P.M. that evening until 1:00 P.M. the following afternoon. Skip says the arresting officer did not give him a chance to shut his front door, which remained wide open for eighteen hours, "so anyone in the world could walk right in."

According to Skip, he filed a formal complaint against the arresting officer a few days later. When he asked whether any report had actually been made about the theft of the political signs, he was told that he could not see any police reports; he would need to have a lawyer request them. Skip says the city eventually dropped all criminal charges against him. He says he was never told whether action was taken against the officer, only that such proceedings are confidential. When asked to confirm these events, the chief of police, Jeff Pynes, said, "I'm going to have to read your book, because I don't know what you're talking about." The arrest and Skip's brutality allegations had occurred before Chief Pynes came to Freeport.

I made a formal request to the Freeport City Hall and the Freeport Police Department pursuant to the Texas Open Records Law for copies of Skip Pratt's arrest records and a record of the brutality report he said he filed. This request resulted in a volume of certified mail at my door that had my glum mailman raising his eyebrows in wonder. Although the envelopes were addressed to me, the letters inside were not. I was being "cc'd" on correspondence that one of Freeport's city attorneys, Julian W. Taylor III, was exchanging with Katherine Minter Cary, an attorney in the Open Records Division of the Office of the Attorney General of Texas. Along with these long-winded letters that were not actually written to me, Mr. Taylor had, in stages, thrown in six pages that were from Skip's criminal file, plus an interoffice letter confirming that no "internal investigation" file existed. (Fans of *Law & Order* know this means no cops investigated other cops.)

These papers did not tell the whole story of Skip's arrest and overnight stay at Hotel Freeport. My request had been broad: all documents relating to Skip's arrest and the brutality complaint he told me about, and the disposition of that complaint. Only one of the documents concerned Skip's arrest—on the misdemeanor charge, not the resisting arrest charge. The other documents confirmed that both charges were dismissed. On the resisting arrest charge, a felony, the *state* moved to dismiss on the motion of the chief of police, Richard Miller.

The documents that the city released to me did not confirm or deny Skip's statements concerning his front door, or his physical condition at the time of his arrest. The city says it withheld nine pages from me. Yet the city had no problem letting me see a Disorderly Conduct (Obscene Language) form, on which the arresting officer wrote down verbatim what he alleged Skip said to him that night. Let's just say it was worthy of the rawest, potty-mouthed hip-hop artist. I gleaned from Mr. Taylor's letters that Skip returned to the police station a few days after he was released from custody; Skip remembers that too. The city says he gave a "voluntary statement." Skip came away with the impression that he had filed a brutality complaint.

It's curious to consider that the theft of a couple of political lawn signs worth about $200 could generate nine pages' worth of police investigation, especially if there was no internal investigation of brutality. But the letter to Ms. Cary made clear, you see, that Skip's "complaint" was made as part of a "voluntary statement" in the course of the investigation of the *theft,* and therefore it was handled as part of that investigation. In a separate letter from the police department to the city attorney, the department's record manager confirmed that "there is no evidence showing an internal investigation was ever initiated after receiving the voluntary statement from Mr. Gates [*sic*]." The city attorney argued:

> It is claimed by the City that all of the 9 pages of Exhibit "e" deal with the detection, investigation, and prosecution of a crime only in relation to an investigation that did not result in conviction or deferred adjudication. I note that the "deferred disposition" which Mr. Pratt received in the disorderly conduct case in question is mutually exclusive to the "deferred adjudication" referred to in the preceding sentence, each being governed independently by separate Articles of the Code.[5]

The letter went on in this delightful manner for *three single-spaced pages.* Apparently, the city was willing to stand on its head to make sure I never saw whatever words of "complaint" Skip made about his treatment while in the hands of the law ... after his arrest ... after two signs were stolen ... *from him.*

Of course, none of this certified-letter foreplay to getting screwed by City Hall addresses the fundamentals that really matter for Skip and the greater public of Freeport: After a thorough investigation of the theft, why didn't the police solve the crime? Just who did steal Skip Pratt's signs from his front lawn? It would be nice to think he went through all that hell for some purpose, now wouldn't it?

On February 5, 2007, I received yet another letter not actually written to me. This one was to Mr. Taylor from Ramsey A.

Abarca of the Texas attorney general's office. Mr. Abarca agreed that documents relating to an investigation of a criminal case that ended in a dismissal or deferral of prosecution are exempt from public disclosure. However, he did direct Mr. Taylor to turn over "general information." Nothing further was provided to me.

Well, as Skip likes to say, "Welcome to Freeport!"

■ ■ ■

Around the table at the Citizens for Freeport meeting in the Western Seafood office, no one bats an eye during Skip's story of signs gone missing, a busted lip, a quiet afternoon turned at lightning speed into an overnight stint in the pokey. They all nod their heads in sympathy, waiting their turn to tell their own stories of the EDC petition war.

Cathy Williams pipes up next. She is the quintessential nice neighbor lady, a sweet-looking woman, soft-spoken and modestly dressed, the sort of person anyone would trust to watch their child for an afternoon or to check in on their house while they are away. But she practically spits bullets at the memory of what her former next-door neighbor, Lee Cameron, did during the petition drive.

"We had signs on a commercial building downtown," says Cathy. "The building belonged to Wanda Jones." Cathy takes pains to point out: "We did it with her permission." Wanda Jones is one of the people whose property was condemned as part of the marina project. The Citizens for Freeport had spent about $200 on each of two large plywood signs they put up on Wanda's downtown property. "We *hand-did* every one of them," says Cathy. "We put one up with steel rebars and another between two poles. We worked hard on those signs."

The signs said to vote "Yes" against the EDC. Now, the thing about putting up a sign on Wanda Jones's property is that it happened to be right across from City Hall and the offices of the EDC. That's what made it a choice spot. It also meant that every time Lee Cameron, the director of the EDC, looked out of his window, he was confronted with the signs—posted on one of the properties he was condemning for the marina project—staring him in the face and urging voters in Freeport to put him out of a job. So, this being a democracy and all, Lee Cameron went downstairs, walked across the street, and tore the signs down.

"It's illegal to take away political signs during voting," Cathy says. She had later found the signs in a dumpster not far from City Hall. "He admitted it to me. He told me 'I put it in a dumpster.'" A police report was filed by Wanda Jones's sister, Joyce Adkins, who made a sworn statement that Lee Cameron informed her that he tore down the signs at the behest of the city administration.

Here is where the versions of this story begin to diverge, depending on which side of the marina controversy a person is on. Lee Cameron readily admitted that he tore down the signs, but insisted that Wanda Jones's property at that point "was owned by the EDC." He said the Citizens "did not have permission" from the EDC to put signs there. "They tried to have me arrested," he said with a note of disgust. "The DA refused to charge me. She told me if they put signs there in the future, stack them up and call them to come and get them."

Lee was Cathy's neighbor for fifteen years before he moved up in the world. In Freeport, that means moving to a bigger, nicer house in Lake Jackson, a nearby town that began as a planned community in the 1940s. Lake Jackson is lovely and leafy. The large houses have mature trees in their yards and luxury cars parked on their circular driveways. There are smooth, paved lanes with no sidewalks. It is quiet in Lake Jackson. The cul-de-sacs are nicely tucked away from the main drags and the bustling shopping centers with their national chains. These are the very shopping centers and strip malls that stole away the business from downtown Freeport, draining the lifeblood from that town in the 1960s and 1970s. And the town is a polite distance west of the chemical plants, so people who live in Lake Jackson don't have to be subjected to the belching smoke and the smells. They don't have to confront quite so directly the often unpleasant reality of how so many folks make a living in this part of Brazoria County.

Like many Freeport residents, Cathy can recite chapter and verse how much money Lee Cameron makes on the city payroll and what his perks are. These details are disclosed in the Freeport city budget, and some people make it their business to keep abreast of such things and to measure whether public officials are earning their keep. "He makes about $90,000 a year," Cathy says. She wagers a guess as to how much he collects as a pensioner from Dow, where he was an engineer before he retired and went to work for the city. "He does all right," she figures. Her resentment is palpable. Similar calculations are made about the city manager, Ron Bottoms, but with more bewilderment, even disgust, by people who will never in their lifetimes see incomes creeping up toward the six-figure mark. They cannot fathom how someone can make money in that league and yet set about "saving" their city by fining the poorest among them ten dollars here and five dollars there for torn screens and peeling paint. If he makes that much, he must be smart. So why do their streets still flood when it rains?

The Lake Jackson divide surfaces when people talk about the Gores, too. Both Pappy Gore and Wright Jr. moved to Lake Jackson in the 1980s and built houses just a few doors apart. "It's kind of like *Everybody Loves Raymond,*" joked Wright III. But the truth is, father and son had worked together since Wright Jr. was fourteen, when he started going down to the docks at Western Seafood to unload the boats. When he was old enough, he began driving trucks up to Houston. Wright Jr. has been working at Western Seafood forty-four years, mostly side by side with his father. They were used to being together.

But as hard as the Gores have worked—and it's no secret in town that they work hard—their houses are in Lake Jackson all the same. When the marina controversy hit the papers, there were people in Freeport who regarded the Gores as outsiders who had no right to fight for the land that Western Seafood sits on, right smack in the center of Freeport—not if it was going to hold up the marina project. They say the Gores are standing in the way of progress in Freeport. The way some people see it, the Gores are the only thing between a dying downtown and its revival. *The Gores are putting on airs. They think they're better than us. They don't care about us—they proved that when they moved to Lake Jackson.* One neighbor insinuated that the Gores tolerate Freeport only so they can keep making money there: "Do you think Mr. Gore, who doesn't even live in Freeport, would have his business still in Freeport if Lake Jackson had a harbor?" wrote S. N. "Deke" Deacon in a letter to the editor of the *Facts.*[6] Another letter, sent by Pamela Starnes, expressed anger that the Gores had moved to a fancy suburb:

> Apparently, the people who have not seen fit to take an interest in Freeport only did so after moving from the city 20-plus

> years ago. Not just one of the families, left, but all of them that are now trying to scare the people of Freeport. Now they want to control progress of our city. They took all their new businesses to Lake Jackson. I say take your boats up Oyster Creek [a nearby town] to the City of Enchantment and let us revitalize our city. A city we decided to stick with.... Also, fill [citizens] in on the fair market price value, what the city might have offered and what amount you would be more than happy to let the land go for. That could probably be very interesting. As I see it, the only scandal in Freeport is one created by your organization.[7]

Lake Jackson is about a ten-minute drive from Freeport. It might as well be ten thousand miles.

Nevertheless, Lee crossed the Lake Jackson divide and went to Cathy's house in Freeport to make amends. "He apologized for taking down the signs," says Cathy. "He said he thought that Wanda's building belonged to the city now. I told him, no, it's *still* Wanda's building.

"He told me he didn't know I was involved in the Citizens for Freeport. I said to him, what difference does it make that I'm involved? That shouldn't make any difference at all.

"Lee said to me 'I would have called you before I did it.'" Cathy's voice rises in pitch as she grows more and more agitated at the memory. "I told him, you have no *right* to put those signs in the dumpster. We worked hard to make those signs. We *hand-did* them all. They were expensive."

After that, Cathy stopped speaking to Lee Cameron, except for one time. She was in City Hall and she stopped by his office. "I stuck my head in and said, 'Do you intend to pay us for those signs or not?' And he said 'No, I'm not!'"

Cathy Williams and Joyce Adkins had lived in Freeport long enough to know you have to take a stand. So they went up to the county seat in Angleton to see Jeri Yenne, the district attorney for Brazoria County. They felt this was more than just a matter of $400 worth of signage; this was an attempt to interfere with the efforts of the Citizens for Freeport in the exercise of their First Amendment rights. They wanted Ms. Yenne to prosecute Lee Cameron. Ms. Yenne refused to do so, citing a lack of criminal intent; she told the ladies that this was a community misunderstanding. Now, a misunderstanding about the ownership of the building might excuse the removal of the signs, but it's not clear how it would excuse destroying them and sticking them in a dumpster. Steve Alford, another Freeport resident who is the treasurer of the Citizens and helps with their petitions, went to see Ms. Yenne separately. Handsome and barrel-chested, Steve is a professional diver; he works for a company that gives training support to astronauts at NASA. He is not easily intimidated, nor, given his line of work, is he inclined to waste his breath. But he got nowhere at the district attorney's office. The Citizens group feared that the city government had too much influence at the county level. Whether there was any basis for those feelings, of course, would depend on whom you asked. Maybe people were just blowing things way out of proportion. Or not.

Lee insisted that the building belonged to the EDC. "We have the deed," he said. But there was bad blood between Wanda Jones and the city. Around the time the condemnations began, Wanda was thinking of selling her building. She had it listed for $110,000. The city offered her $90,000. She declined. During the time her building was up for sale, she heard about the marina and figured that perhaps she'd been too hasty in moving to sell; waterfront property would soon be worth a lot more. "She wanted $400,000!" said Lee incredulously, as if Wanda had lost her mind. Actually, Wanda wanted what many property owners in economic development takings want: to share in the bounty that comes with the revitalization. They want the same rewards that would have been theirs if their property had not been yanked away from them. Unfortunately, this would require changes in the statutory compensation laws. The city went through the formal appraisal and commission procedures of Texas law and deposited the amount of $100,000 in escrow. Wanda has been appealing it ever since.

About a month after the district attorney declined to investigate the Lee Cameron sign-destruction misunderstanding, despite the entreaties of three outraged citizens, an odd thing happened to her. A grinch stole the brand-new inflatable Santa from Jeri Yenne's front yard. "Two days is all we had it," her husband, Bill Yenne, lamented to the local paper. Ms. Yenne was so outraged she filed a police report about the theft of the $59 six-feet-tall Santa. She even provided the precise time frame, down to the minute, within which it went missing, the better to catch the thief.

"As District Attorney, Jeri Yenne knows well the consequences the Santa thief could face if caught: it's a Class B misdemeanor, punishable by up to 180 days in jail and up to a $2,000 fine," reported the local paper in ominous tones. "I was so proud of my new pop-up Santa," Yenne said. "The point is, why do you have to damage other people's property?" her husband said. Ms. Yenne turned philosophical: "It's good to be stolen from because it helps you remember how other people feel."[8]

"Jeri Yenne lives in *Lake Jackson,*" said Cathy Williams, believing the statement required no further explanation. "And her husband is the city manager there." Ah, yes, Lake Jackson. Where stealing an inflatable Santa at Christmas is not a prank but a crime punishable by 180 days in jail and a $2,000 fine. Freeport, ten minutes away, is another universe. It's where political signs get thrown in dumpsters. Where the theft of political signs becomes a police incident that lands the *victim* in jail.

▪ ▪ ▪

Nothing in grassroots politics is ever simple. Freeport has a municipal code, a set of laws that govern everything from how elections are conducted to whether or not newspapers can be left on a front lawn. Ordinance 113.03 governs leaflets and handbills. It is described in the code as an advertising ordinance. A person who wants to educate the public or take a position on, say, the war in Iraq, or the coming of the Apocalypse, or eminent domain, can't simply go out there and distribute his handbills declaring his beliefs willy-nilly. He has to bring his handbills to City Hall and have every single word approved by the city manager. The same goes for signs.

And that was what Steve Alford did. His plan was to distribute some color handouts about the marina project, a gummy-candy in the shape of a $100 bill, and bubble gum with a gold wrapper that said, "This is how much money it costs to build the marina." There was also a water bottle with a label stating that the marina project would cut into the levees along the Old Brazos River. The levees were important to residents in the East End, whose houses were close to the river. Finally, Alford had a twenty-minute DVD about the Freeport Economic Development Corporation. The items were all contained in a plastic bag with a hole at the top, so it could be hung on people's doorknobs. Alford presented this package to Ron Bottoms, the city manager, and he approved it.

Then Steve caucused with Wright III. Maybe it was a mistake to rely so much on the DVD. The people in the East End were poor. What if they didn't have DVD players? Steve and Wright made a last-minute change: they printed out hard copies of freeze-frames from the DVD, which was mostly like a PowerPoint presentation anyway. The images explained what the marina deal was all about, how the master plan worked, what it meant for a home to be described as blighted. Then they created a five-minute DVD. If people didn't have a DVD player, they would still get the most important information from the paper handouts. There was nothing in the package that hadn't been approved in a different format. They thought everything would be fine. It wasn't.

On November 8, 2005, Steve Alford set out to distribute the door hangers with members of Citizens for Freeport. They were followed by police cars. An hour or so into the distribution, the police pulled over and ordered Steve to stop what he was doing. The group was told to disburse. The police issued a citation to Steve, charging that he had violated Ordinance 113.03.

"When I got that citation, my elderly aunts were terrified," said Steve. "'He's gonna get hurt,' they said. They remember when things were done that way. This town is still ran by intimidation."

Steve showed up at the police station, only to be told he had appeared at the wrong time. He later learned the citation had been made out incorrectly. Eventually, the charge against him was dropped. The person with discretion over such matters was none other than Wallace Shaw, the city attorney and Mayor Phillips' wing man in city council meetings where Wright III's presence month after month had come to be seen as an act of war. On November 17, Shaw signed the official paper informing the judge that the city declined to prosecute Steve.

But by then it was too late to resume handing out the door hangers. Election day had come and gone. The Citizens for Freeport would have to start all over again seeking permission from the city. And Ron Bottoms was still maintaining that they had not acted properly. Indeed, he would vehemently insist during a city council meeting, packed to the gills with spectators, that the packages distributed by Steve and his group "were not the same thing he showed me for approval," making clear his belief that they had flagrantly disregarded Ordinance 113.03.

Slapping the citation on Steve Alford seemed especially petty given the citywide ground attack the city had waged in the weeks leading up to election day. One day in late October 2005, a curious caravan formed. A truck driven by Mayor Jim Phillips was going around town. Soon the truck was followed by Steve Alford, who wanted to see what Jim was up to, as well as Roy Ross, the husband of Wendi Ross (the publisher of the *Sentinel*). Another man, sitting in the back of the truck driven by the mayor, was throwing copies of the *Sentinel* onto front lawns. The newspapers contained a flier urging people to vote against the dissolution of the EDC. "I drove my truck near where I live," said Mayor Phillips, who lives on Eleventh Street, not far from the City Hall. Other people drove numerous cars and trucks around town that day, he said, tossing what the mayor estimates was around three thousand copies of the *Sentinel* onto the front lawns of "about 90 percent of the homes in Freeport." The fliers had been inserted into the *Sentinel* by a team of people who were against the EDC dissolution ballot, which included the Freeport League and the Main Street Program board and downtown business owners. "There must have been twenty people stuffing those fliers into the *Sentinel*," Mayor Phillips said.

The mayor said he had "no idea how the newspapers were acquired" or how they got delivered to the group that stuffed the fliers into them. A source close to the *Sentinel* said that the publisher did not give permission for the flier to be inserted and that the publisher was not compensated for having the insert in the newspapers. Moreover, the source maintained, the newspapers, which are given away free in stores around Freeport, were taken away from store locations where they had been provided in bulk—without the publisher's permission.

A late-October issue of the *Sentinel* contained a full-page advertisement listing "Lie #1," "Lie #2," Lie #3" and so on, right through "Lie #8."[9] These were lies, the ad declared, told by Wright Gore III. The same advertisement also ran in the *Facts*. In 2005, about 10,000 copies of the *Sentinel* were distributed weekly throughout Brazoria County. The *Facts* is a daily with a county circulation of 23,000. Both papers are read avidly in Freeport.

Below the numbered list of "lies" were the signatures of Mayor Phillips and Councilman James Saccomano. John Smith III signed in his capacity as both councilman and EDC president, along with Norma Garcia, councilwoman and EDC board member, and five additional EDC members. The broadsheet page was illustrated with photocopies of single pages (such as a summons) from complex legal documents that were meaningless when taken out of context, and a hodgepodge of phrases from the thirty-seven-page development agreement. The ad, which was paid for by the mayor according to the disclosure at the bottom of the page, described Wright III as "a man who will stop at nothing to achieve his desired results." The purpose of the ad apparently was to rebut a number of issues that had been raised by Wright III in a letter to Freeport voters sent earlier that fall.

The ad was more brazen than anything the city had attempted on its website or in its glossy newsletter in 2004. This was total warfare. Donald Rumsfeld might have called it Shock and Awe. A better name might have been "schlock and bore," since the authors of this scandal sheet had already trotted out many of these old saws before, though they did throw in some nifty new ones. They offered that tried and true canard about the Gores' staggering "counteroffer" to sell their land for $1,360,000 in "Lie #8." The city knew full well that the Gores did not offer to sell their land, and $1,360,000 was Wright Jr.'s projection of what it would cost to reconfigure his operation if they slapped a bunch of docks upside his packing house. Nonetheless, the city cried foul: "[M]eetings were held with the last resulting in the outrageous offer to sell the property in question for $1,360,000. That translates to $2,700,000.00 per acre. Property on the French Riviera may be worth that much, but in Freeport?"

Under Lie #5, the ad said: "Wright III has consistently and deliberately misrepresented the facts and made false assumptions about the City's contract with Mr. Royall. Contrary to his statement, the loan is secured by Mr. Royall's $1 million and by Mr. Royall's property. (See Figure C.)" Hmmm. Figure C was a box that appeared to contain legalese. It sure looked official. It seemed to be copied directly from the development agreement. Only it wasn't. It contained a sentence that simply didn't appear in the development agreement and didn't accurately sum it up either. This sentence declared that the project developer, the city and the EDC "expressly agree" that the developer will fully "expend" $1 million before any money is taken from the "Construction Fund." In plain English, it said that Walker Royall would spend $1 million of his own money before he would get a penny of the $6 million loan from the city. That would have come as quite a shock to Mr. Royall.

This was the gang that couldn't shoot straight. One year earlier, in the glossy newsletter, they had described that same $1 million as "security" for the marina project. Now, you can't spend money at the start of the project and still use it as security. Moreover, the development agreement actually said the opposite of what that ad in the *Sentinel* would have the citizens of Freeport believe; Walker would have to spend his own money *only* if costs exceeded $6 million, and he got an equity credit for $750,000—the value of the Blaffer land. One million dollars was the cap on what he would ever have to spend—if push came to shove and he actually had to spend his own money.

The rest of the ad was a compendium of confusing blather that smeared Wright III, and by extension his family, by misdirection and hyperbole. Much of it was bound to mislead unsophisticated readers who would not understand, for example, the nuances of legal terms like "mediation" and "arbitration." Such words were tossed about to make the Gores look like obstructionist miscreants. To prove Wright a liar in his statement that the Gores had "proposed mediation" (Lie #7), the ad stated, "The Gore contingent has consistently refused arbitration although we have offered it on numerous occasions." Mediation and arbitration are two different animals. Mediation is not binding. Arbitration, on the other hand, has risks; it cuts off the right to appeal. Lawyers know this but most normal humans don't. The statement was enough to make people think the Gores were litigious bears hungry to tear the city apart in the courtroom.

In any case, the Citizens for Freeport had already gathered the required hundreds of signatures needed to get their "Dissolve the EDC" initiative on the ballot, and had campaigned for the November 2005 election. The easy part was over. Signs had gone missing, lips got busted, door hangers were disqualified, mud had been slung all over town, but election day was yet to come. People still had to vote, and that meant going to the Freeport Police Station.

▪ ▪ ▪

Under the perfect laboratory conditions of a Kennedy School of Government case study or a theoretical law review article, an abusive eminent domain situation can be rectified through the political process. As the old saying goes, "vote the bums out," and by doing so, sweep out their appointed officers who run the economic development corporation. Real life tends to be more complicated. Freeport appears to have come down with a nasty case of voter dilution. It's a particularly insidious type of civil rights violation, hard to spot at first and not easy to cure, but demoralizing all the same. It is a close cousin to injustices of the not-too-distant past such as the poll tax and literacy tests. Today, we are more likely to see tactics like difficult registration procedures, decreasing the number of voting machines in minority areas, purges of registration materials, or abrupt changes of polling places. These actions are legal on their face, but "in fact discourage a group of potential voters from casting a ballot."[10] It adds up to disenfranchisement. No court of law has determined whether the permanent change of polling place in Freeport amounted to disenfranchisement of its minority populations. But one can look at a situation with common sense and apply the lessons of history.

Elections in Freeport used to be at large, or citywide, explained Clan Cameron, a member of Citizens for Freeport. He and some residents of the East End, where many Hispanics live, believed that at-large elections were resulting in lopsided representation on the city council, which was dominated by relatively affluent white men from one area of Freeport. "About five years ago we brought a lawsuit to have the city divided up into wards," Clan said. Their hope was that ward elections would give greater representation to the poor of Freeport.

They won their lawsuit, but they may have lost their war. Soon after the city was divided into wards, the council passed an ordinance changing the polling place for all municipal elections. No longer would they be held in schools or churches, and no longer would they be conveniently held in the same location as county and national elections. Voting in city elections would now be done at the Freeport Police Station. The city maintains that this change was made to save money (by renting fewer voting machines), but it's hard to imagine that the police station was the only suitable public space that was available in all of Freeport.

The Freeport Police Station is a modest, two-story building on the main drag. Police cars are parked out back, and the police headquarters are up a short flight of stairs. Voting takes place in a small room that doubles as the city courtroom and the city council room. It is where police guard city council meetings and where Mayor Phillips admonishes speakers who displease him. During elections, police stroll in and out of the building; there is no way for a citizen to know whether he will bump into a uniformed officer. For the poor who cannot take a day off to fight a code summons and end up with a warrant outstanding, it is a palpable fear. Some citizens may go to the City Hall, a cavernous building with a large lobby, for what is known as "early voting," a courtesy extended to the elderly and the disabled in the weeks before election day. It is not a courtesy extended to those in Freeport who are afraid of men in blue uniforms. Not surprisingly, voter turnout in municipal elections is low. In a ward election for council seats, the turnout can be under 300 votes, according to Mayor Phillips. "In a citywide election, a mayoral election, we can get a turnout of about 1,400," he said.

But getting people to vote on a city ballot when there is a national, state or county election is even more difficult, because the polling places are split; the polling places for these other elections did not change. Voters therefore must go to *both* polling places if they want to vote in the city as well as the state and national elections. Freeport residents are not, for the most part, people with white-collar jobs who can leave work an hour early or arrive late so as to vote at their leisure.

"Most of the people in Freeport work construction jobs," said Joyce Adkins. "That means they don't get off work until 5:30. They can't get to the polling place until at least 6:00. Most of the time they don't even know there's a separate city election going on, or if they do, they don't know they have to go somewhere else to vote. We try to have signs up to tell them. We try to let them know."

Once you get to the police station and go inside to vote, Ms. Adkins said, "They stand real close to you." During the first ballot initiative on the EDC, said Clan Cameron, the people supervising the voting at the police station "made you write what ward you were from" on the slip of paper they handed you when you went in to vote. "That made people real paranoid."

The new polling location has been intimidating to the minority population of Freeport. "We see a few minorities voting at the police station. But not many," said Ms. Adkins. "They're afraid." In a city that is 56 percent Hispanic and 17 percent black, "a few minorities" is not encouraging. The Hispanic voter turnout has been especially hard hit, according to Clan Cameron, who represents Ward A, the East End, which is heavily Hispanic. "The Hispanics in Freeport are 99 percent Mexican," he said. "They have a very deep mistrust and fear of the police. It has been very difficult to get them to go and vote at the police station. During election season, we just go around trying to get out the vote. We just beg people: please go and vote. But they will not go to that police station."

Several members of Citizens for Freeport remember seeing police standing outside the station on election day when the "Dissolve the EDC" initiative was on the ballot. Cathy Williams remembered seeing Mayor Phillips standing outside, confirming Beth Gore's recollection of that night. Cathy recalled being annoyed that she and a group of people were told to move on, not to stand around.

It was a high turnout for Freeport on a day when polling locations were split, with 1,200 people voting. Considering the obstacles and the high-octane opposition waged by the city, the coalition opposed to the marina and eminent domain did pretty well—but not well enough. The initiative to dissolve the EDC lost by twenty-one votes.

"I came home and cried," said Wright III. "I was just standing there in the kitchen, crying. That was the first time I cried since one of my grandparents died. I was so angry."

When he looked up, he saw his parents in the kitchen with him.

"My mother said, 'What's the matter?' I remember I said, 'I'm so sick of this shit!' They both had the most desperate, plaintive looks on their faces. They looked so lost. I realized that if I gave up, that would be it. It would be over. They couldn't fight this thing by themselves."

For Wright III there would be no turning back—no matter how many ballot drives he had to organize, no matter how many times the mayor told him to "sit down and be quiet" at city council meetings or threw him out entirely.

"Wright taught himself how to read when he was two and a half years old," said Beth Gore. "By the time he was three, he was reading the newspaper headlines." She is not bragging. To the contrary, she still is slightly in disbelief over it. Although Wright III has no training as a lawyer, he has helped in the research for most of the briefs written for Western Seafood in the federal court, and hashed over the legal arguments with their attorney, Randy Kocurek, as if he were his co-counsel. The family has had, at various times, a federal court lawyer, a state court condemnation lawyer, and a lawyer on the defamation case; but Wright III oversees all of it, especially the federal case. He and Randy discuss which cases to cite, and the pros and cons of various legal arguments to put forward. Randy says that with most clients he would rather they not be bothering him, but in Wright's case "it was actually helpful having him involved."

Randy is a solo practitioner and the litigation load in the case at times has been crushing; there have been weeks and months when he has "lived and breathed" the case. Eminent domain is typically the bailiwick of a small subset of specialists; this is the first case of its kind that he has handled, and it is a peculiar one, starting off in federal court with such urgency. Nonetheless, he gives as good as he gets, firing back at the city in the grand paper-warrior tradition of large-firm lawyers. He joked with Wright III that the city felt it necessary to put a whole "team" of lawyers up against him.

The case has utterly dominated Wright III's life in a way that is unusual among people who are the subjects of takings. While most people whose homes or businesses are taken in eminent domain experience enormous stress and sadness, most of them view the legal process with bewilderment and leave it to the lawyers. But because the Gore family was unable to secure experienced eminent domain counsel from a large firm in Texas willing to take a case opposing the City of Freeport—or (they suspect) opposing a deal involving the Blaffer family with their many important business interests in Texas—Wright III felt he had to take the laboring oar.

The result is that he was painfully aware of every twist and turn of the legal machinery in all five litigations that were pending in federal and state court (the two state condemnations, the federal right-to-take case, the lease case and the defamation case). But unlike a lawyer working on a client's case, he could not distance himself emotionally from this load of litigation. Even the most dedicated lawyers go home to their families at night, or turn to another case or client for a while and so take a brief respite. But for Wright III it never went away. His family's name—his own name—and the name of his grandfather's business appeared as defendants on the first page of the legal pleadings that he saw day in and day out.

And there were times when the litigation seemed like the least of it. The battle has taken on the nature of a full-time job. Wright III is the one who took calls from the local press in Freeport and Houston. He attended every meeting of the Freeport City Council and the Freeport Economic Development Corporation, week after week, month after month, confronting Mayor Phillips and the EDC, tracking the progress of the marina project and letting the council know that the Gores were still fighting. He navigated the delicate group dynamics of the Citizens for Freeport, an assemblage of spirited, opinionated adults who do not always agree or get along. He helped the group plan the signature-gathering drives and worked with the lawyer to get the language just right to keep the city clerk from rejecting the petitions. He fielded calls from the insurance company, which was haggling over covering the defamation suit.

Wright III is like a patient undergoing open-heart surgery while awake, conscious of every complex step the surgeon is taking, discussing with him where to cut and handing him the scalpel. In the process, his normal life virtually disappeared. He and the young lady he was dating broke up. "She kept asking me, 'Wright, when are you going to give me a ring?' She was in her early thirties. I couldn't blame her for feeling that way," he said. "We'd go out on Saturday night and then Sunday, she'd want to do things, but I'd be back to the case, the petitions. Finally, she just ended it." His business, selling black-box recording devices for cars, has taken a back seat to the litigations. He is thin as a rail. But the passage of time and repeated maneuvering by the city council seem only to have made him more determined—to bring still more appeals, to launch yet another petition.

Wright calls his ailing grandfather several times a week, and Pappy wants to hear the news. Finding it difficult to speak, he gets to the bottom line: "Do we have a judgment yet?" he asks.

Wright III searches for something encouraging to say—some piece of news about the latest petition drive or court hearing, the newest legal tack that he and Randy have come up with, some glimmer of hope on the horizon. He thinks as fast as he can, but often it is not fast enough.

"Aaaw, you waited too long!" says Pappy. "We'll try again tomorrow."

Exhausted from this brief exchange, Pappy hangs up the phone.

This quest for the judgment, the wild ups and downs of the petition drives, the motions lost and re-argued, the injunctions gained and vacated, the process servers, the appeals, the offers that seem to vaporize from meeting to meeting—they are the new roller-coaster ride for grandson and grandfather. Wright III knows that his grandfather will not give up. It is inconceivable that Pappy would tell him: "Just go ahead and walk away from my life's work, just give it away for a song." Once a powerful man who could crush a block of ice and heave a bucket of shrimp, Pappy is frail now; with each passing day it looks more and more like he will die asking for the judgment. It will be left to Wright III to carry on. And so Wright III hangs on for dear life, just like he did back at Fourth Street as a little boy in Pappy's car, wild and gleeful, when Pappy could turn the world into an amusement park, put the pedal to the metal, take a hairpin turn and "don't stop 'til you see the afterlife."

■ ■ ■

A few days later, even with electoral victory in their hands, the group that had signed the full-page ad in the *Sentinel* felt their work wasn't done. The election had been a close one. It couldn't possibly be that the citizens of Freeport were intelligent people with opinions of their own. Heavens, no! They were brainwashed, bamboozled, bewitched by those damnable Gores and their tiny pocket of resistance fighters, the Citizens for Freeport. Fully convinced that Freeport residents were delicate and vulnerable, the mayor, three council members (one of whom was the president of the EDC) and five additional EDC members signed a letter—on official City of Freeport letterhead—to "respond to some of the accusations and misinformation that was put forth during the recent election ... [T]he EDC ***is not taking anybody's home!*** ... We ***are not bulldozing homes*** for developing the marina or any other project! ... The flood levees that protect the city ***will not be compromised!*** We could respond to a number of additional allegations that were made, but our purpose for this letter is to reassure our citizens and to calm any fears that may have been created as a result of any misleading information."[11] The letter was sent in both Spanish and English.

Jeri Yenne, the district attorney, had held her tongue until this point but could hold it no longer. Her office issued letters of admonition to Mayor Phillips, Ron Bottoms, Jim Saccomano, John Smith III and Norma Garcia. These letters warned that "the circumstances of the signing and issuance of [the November 11 group letter] constitute facts that possibly or arguably indicate a violation of Section 551.144 of the Open Meetings Act (regarding impermissible meetings of a governmental body)." The mayor and his allies were told to "refrain" from this sort of thing in the future and advised to take formal training in compliance with the Open Meetings Act.

But it was too little, too late. The mud had been flung and the damage done. The bitterness of the EDC battle would continue to spill over into city council meetings. There would be more petition drives. With the passing months, the Gores and the Citizens for Freeport grew more convinced of the rightness of their cause.

CHAPTER 10

MISERY LOVES COMPANY

In June 2006, Wright Jr., Beth and Wright III traveled to Arlington, Virginia—just outside Washington, D.C.—to attend a conference on economic development takings. For Wright Jr. and Beth it was a mini-vacation. They hadn't taken a real vacation since the whole eminent domain nightmare began. For Wright III, on the other hand, such conferences had become part of his life. He had gotten to know the people at the Institute for Justice, who were hosting the conference. They had even invited him to speak on one of the panels about grassroots organizing. Wright recognized some of the faces from other conferences; this was the small circle of eminent domain resistance fighters in towns and cities across America who were bringing ballot initiatives or organizing grassroots efforts to keep their neighborhoods from becoming footnotes in history books. At least, these were the resisters who could afford to travel, and who still had enough fight left in them to shake, rattle and roll for three days with two hundred others who were as angry as they were.

The conference was also a chance for Wright Jr. and Beth to talk to other people who were going through the same tribulations. There were homemakers, small-business owners, farmers, blue-collar workers and a smattering of white-collar professionals from all over the United States. They had come together to share their stories of what they called "eminent domain abuse." The conference took on the atmosphere of a tent revival meeting, with plenty of standing ovations, tears, people running up the aisles to take pictures of famous speakers and loved ones up on the dais, and spontaneous shout-outs from the audience: "No! My home is *not* blighted!" "That's right, Susette Kelo is *not* moving!"

Some people had come to talk about the homes and businesses they had lost. But most had come because they now stood in the path of the eminent domain wrecking ball and were in search of wisdom. The properties owned by the conference attendees varied: they included farms, seaside homes, urban condominiums, suburban houses. Some of the panels consisted of professionals who could tell how to work the media or lobby legislatures; and the attendees paid attention. But then the veterans appeared, those lucky few whose names had become legendary in eminent domain circles: Scott Mahan of the Save Ardmore Coalition and Julie Wilste of Lakewood, Pennsylvania, and Janice Hundt of Baltimore. When they took the mike, the room fell as silent as the night. The crowd sat at rapt attention, taking copious notes as the war stories were told. The veterans spoke of how they had wrested their homes and businesses from the jaws of the wolf, with rallies and homemade leaflets, bake sales and lobbying, petition drives and phone-call chains, T-shirts and slogans and political buttons, block-by-block lobbying and sleepless nights and strategy huddles that lasted until the break of day. There were stories of local political double-crosses, and of battles that had, in effect, become second jobs.

Wright III's parents would get to see him speak and this was a special treat for them; like any proud parents, they had brought along a camera to snap pictures. If life had proceeded along a normal course, they might have been taking pictures at some happier occasion involving their thirty-three-year-old son. But constant attention to the fight to save Western Seafood had caused Wright III to put aside everything else in his life. When Wright III took his turn during the panel on grassroots activism, he held up a small voice recorder and explained, "I never get within three feet of a public official without one of these!" The packed room erupted in laughter and clapping.

The top-billed stars of the eminent domain circuit appeared as featured speakers. They included Curt Pringle, the mayor of Anaheim, California. Pringle proudly calls his city "property-friendly," and points out that it is the twenty-ninth largest city in the United States. In Anaheim, the administration refuses to use economic development takings, instead fostering growth by reducing regulatory red tape and zoning impediments, and offering creative incentives for new businesses to open. And John Allison, the CEO of BB&T Bank, gave a rousing speech. Mr. Allison had the status of a folk hero in this crowd. His bank has sworn off making loans to developers who will use the money for real estate projects tied to economic development takings. BB&T, a Virginia bank, is a leading small-business lender in the United States, with assets of $110 billion.

In his sweetly rolling southern cadence, Mr. Allison said, "Never again will BB&T provide financial assistance to a developer taking part in any eminent domain project." The bank has "lost some municipal business [as a result of this decision]. On the other hand, we've had thousands of people move checking accounts to our bank." The decision also triggered memories from the community. "I've received many gut-wrenching letters about the effect of eminent domain on some people's lives," said Mr. Allison. But these letters merely confirmed what he already believed, based on his family's experience. He spoke of an elderly great-aunt who was "a victim of urban renewal eminent domain. They bulldozed the homes and built nothing for fifteen years." His great-aunt "was never the same. She could have lived out her life there." The taking was meaningless, cruel and unnecessary. "Why do these pipe dreams need eminent domain and taxpayer subsidies?" he asked, and noted that the "poor, old and minorities make the best targets because they are not politically connected."

Mr. Allison described his youth among poor people in the South. While their homes appeared blighted on the outside, he recalled, the families inside loved and supported one another. In the audience, heads bobbed up and down in understanding. Mr. Allison continued: When he grew older and went out into the world among rich people, he saw many luxurious, beautiful homes—and he was shocked to see the ugliness of the family life within. "*Inside* those homes there was blight!" he said. This remark was met by thunderous applause. For homeowners, the idea that their homes are "blighted" is one of the most difficult aspects of a taking to stomach, since blight carries with it a shameful connotation of slums and degeneracy. But here was a dignified, eloquent man, the CEO of BB&T Bank, telling them that not only were their homes and businesses *not* blighted—which common sense had been telling them all along—but the homes of the richer people who would displace them might well be blighted in a way that matters more.

Mr. Allison came to his position on eminent domain, he told the crowd, as a lifetime reader of Ayn Rand, John Locke and Thomas Aquinas. "There is no such thing as 'the public.' We deal with Suzy Q and John Doe'" at BB&T Bank, he said, instinctively reaching out to every member of the audience as an individual. These were people sick and tired of being told by their local governments that bulldozing their homes and businesses was in the "public interest," and their individual lives were as flies to be swatted. As Mr. Allison spoke of the importance of property rights in the United States, from the time of the Founders until today, you could have heard a pin drop. When he mentioned Cato, Adams, Jefferson and Locke, the assembled farmers, hairdressers, lawyers, shop owners, nurses and teachers hung on his every word. "You have the high moral ground," he assured them. "Yes, sir!" listeners murmured. When he reminded them of the words of the Declaration of Independence, "Life, Liberty and the pursuit of Happiness," the crowd, many with tears in their eyes, jumped to their feet to applaud the man from North Carolina who had come to offer a bit of spiritual healing.

■ ■ ■

Time and again in speeches at the conference in Arlington, the name of John Locke was invoked with almost religious reverence as the inspiration for those who hold property rights dear. In an age when football legends and rock stars are worshipped, it was passing strange to see this wide assortment of Americans, running the gamut from highly educated to old-fashioned street smart, stand and applaud at the mention of a seventeenth-century English Enlightenment philosopher. These were individuals who had been traumatized by the taking or attempted taking of their homes and businesses, and had turned for comfort to the opening passages of the Declaration of Independence, to "Life, Liberty and the pursuit of Happiness."

After *Kelo,* op-ed writers who were outraged by the decision expressed nostalgia for the "Lockean principles cherished by our founders."[1] Scholars debate whether and to what extent John Locke influenced Thomas Jefferson in particular. What matters more for purposes of understanding the history of eminent domain is the general impact that Lockean philosophy and natural law had on the early years of the Republic and the principles of property law. In other words, how did early Americans think about property rights? And how does that thinking influence what we are seeing in today's eminent domain battles?

When we speak of Lockean influence today, we tend to think about the influence John Locke had on America. What is less well known is the impact that *America* had on *Locke*—and all because Locke, unlike most seventeenth-century gentleman scholars, could not afford to quit his day job. For many years he held a position that was a sort of clearinghouse for information on the British colonies. He also nursed a full-time obsession with exotic travel and faraway lands. America in particular lived vividly in Locke's imagination; it was for him a land of fanciful dreams, but also a very real place that presented vexing policy issues. He was fully engaged in finding solutions to problems involving trade, for instance, or the treatment of Indians, or recruitment of settlers.[2] America to John Locke was a source of income and professional pride, and also a source of intellectual inspiration.

It's fair to say that Locke's deep fascination with America helped shape his seminal work on property, *Two Treatises of Government* (1689). Given all the circumstances of his life, one can only wonder if he intended the *Two Treatises* especially for the land he thought most likely to hold the future of mankind upon its shores. For in many ways, Locke was living the life of a subversive. He clearly took risks by associating with radicals, though he was careful to write anonymously. Locke was a man who understood the price of liberty; he very nearly paid for his convictions with his life. It is sobering to consider the boldness with which he wrote about the question of private property, in view of the turbulent times in which he lived.

In Locke's lifetime, England experienced religious strife, conflicts between the Crown and Parliament, civil war, and the brief abolition of the monarchy. England had no king during the 1650s following the sensational execution of Charles I, who had ruled with a heavy hand for eleven years without Parliament. Stability was eventually restored but not for long. King James II was forced to abdicate in 1688, and William of Orange was invited from the Netherlands to take the throne of England, in what became known as the Glorious Revolution. While this was not the first time in English history that a king had been deposed, something new was afoot: the English had peeked through the heavy veils of monarchal rule, and there was a sense abroad in the land that tyranny need no longer be countenanced. A fundamental tipping had occurred in the balance of power between Crown and Parliament.

It was around this time that Locke published his *Two Treatises of Government.* His theory, building on the work of other natural law philosophers such as Grotius and Pufendorf, and in part on the work of Hobbes, was quite radical. In Locke's vision, the state of nature was not such a bad place at all. To begin: all men are created equal. They start out in life in a "State of perfect Freedom to order their Actions … within the Law of Nature."[3] And they all have the same rights of "property." Locke did not mean property only in the narrow sense of real estate or personal objects, as the word is used today. He meant it to encompass all that a man or woman had. In the *Second Treatise,* "property" is a term of art that includes a man's "own Person" as well as material things. It also means "the Labor of his Body and the Work of his Hands."

Most importantly, there was no limit to the potential of a man's property: by working the land, a man could make it his.[4] There is no limit to what he might reap from his hard work, since there is no overriding sovereign in Locke's design who owns all the land, as a descendant of Adam, and parcels it out bit by bit. Locke saw the world as having once been in such singular possession, but he argued that eventually it became common property from which a man, through his labors, could secure his own individual parcel of land, water and food from God's bounty.

Across the Atlantic Ocean, America's untamed wilderness appeared to Locke the perfect setting to explain his theory of the state of nature. "Thus in the beginning all the World was *America,*" he wrote in the *Second Treatise.*[5] Locke didn't bother in his *Two Treatises* to draw comparisons to natives of lands other than America, or to muse about any other terrain as a metaphoric "state of nature." He could easily have done so, being one of the best-informed men in Europe about foreign cultures; through his long association with Oxford and Lord Ashley, he had access to the finest libraries in England. In the introductory essay he wrote for a huge compendium of travel books, he described "A new discovery of a vast country in America extending above 4,000 miles between New France and New Mexico, with a description of rivers, lakes, plants, and animals, manners, customs, and languages of the Indians, etc., [is described by a writer named] L. Hennepin. . . . The promise is very great, but there is little or no proof of such a vast extent of land, which no man has yet seen, and all is framed upon conjectures. . . ."[6] In time, the conjectures would prove true.

Locke became immersed in the administration of the Carolina colony through his association with Lord Ashley (the first Earl of Shaftesbury), one of the eight Lords Proprietors to whom the Crown had deeded the land in 1663. The Lords Proprietors were essentially a joint venture for forward-looking investors.[7] The Charter of Carolina makes clear that ownership of this vast territory, with its rich earth and abundant forests and wildlife, belonged to the Lords Proprietors and their progeny.[8] As secretary to Lord Ashley, Locke was reading and summarizing for the Lords Proprietors every document and letter that came out of the colony, and making suggestions for management. Locke earned his keep; when the population began to dwindle, or too many roughnecks were immigrating, the Lords turned to him to write promotional fliers, seeking out a better ilk of Englishmen to populate the colony. Locke also played an important role in drafting the Carolina Constitution.

The American colonies fed Locke's political imagination, and he had a vested interest in their success. He must have known that America was the most likely place for his theory of the state of nature and property to be played out in the near future. Certainly he understood that his theories of man in a state of nature, with abundant natural resources and virgin land, would never be tested in England or anywhere in Europe.[9] During the second half of the seventeenth century, England was overflowing with landless peasants and working poor who had no place to go and no means to earn a living. They were encouraged to populate the New World, and Locke, in his role as secretary of the Council of Trade, had for many years received reliable intelligence on how settlers were pushing ever westward—away from the reach of feudal tentacles and constricting constitutions, into the beckoning freedom of the American wilderness.

The "vast extent of land" that Locke had speculated about would become the greatest expanse of earth privately owned, by ordinary working people, anywhere in the world in the nineteenth century. The men and women who settled that land felt their ownership rights with a deep and abiding passion. Some of that passion was born from the hardships they had endured to earn that land. But much of it also sprang from the essential promises made to them by the United States government under a Lockean theory of ownership: that the land, once worked up, would be theirs. Through labor, a person comes to own the land.[10]

Locke's description of ownership through labor foreshadows the claims-staking system under which millions of acres of ranch and farmland were settled by pioneers in the American Midwest and West during the nineteenth century. Pioneers staked out designated areas and worked them for a set number of consecutive years, sometimes making a nominal cash payment in addition. It is one thing, however, to say that labor creates ownership and value compared with letting the land remain part of the wilderness (lie "in common"),[11] and quite another to impose a duty on an owner to continue producing value in ever greater amounts in order to justify the right to keep on owning the land. Locke does not say that once in ownership, a man *must continue* to produce increasing levels of value and contribution to the community in order to continue owning his land. In fact, we can be quite certain that Locke believed a man had a right to let his land lie waste, because he did so himself.

Locke was heavily invested in New World companies. By the end of his life, a substantial portion of his income came from these investments, including one in the Bahamas Adventurers. In 1683 he received a letter from Sir Peter Colleton, one of his partners in that company, offering a suggestion:

> I find I am your partner in the Bahama trade which will turne to accompt if you meddle not with planting.... [I]f other men will plant there, I mean the Bahamas, hinder them not, they improve our province, but I would neither have you nor my lord [Ashley] ingadge in it.[12]

Locke took Colleton's advice and allowed the land to lie fallow, while the neighbors worked their land. Colleton's scheme was successful. The land belonging to the partners rose in value along with their neighbors' land, while Locke and Colleton saved on expenses and preserved the richness of their soil. They later sold and made out like bandits.

■ ■ ■

Today in America, we have come to a point where owning private property is seen somehow to imply a duty to produce wealth and value to the community, beyond whatever the tax-assessed value of the property may be in its current use. Under the modern theory of economic development takings, a city council may eye a parcel of land and say, "Why, if we put a shopping mall over there, we could triple our tax revenue." Suddenly, the homeowners on that parcel of land are not doing their civic duty because they are not paying as much as a hypothetical strip-mall developer could pay. This is precisely the rationale used to justify taking away the property of individuals and asking them to make a sacrifice for the community at large. Communities around the country are now saying to their friends and neighbors, with whom they have lived side by side for decades, "You may own your property only so long as you produce enough value for us, only so long as you live up to an ever-changing standard of the needs of the greater community." In other words, if the community wants more tax revenue, it's adios.

"If we look at New London, it's a kind of down-on-its luck, struggling-to-survive city. You say to an electrician, 'We're going to have this great new employment opportunity for you, but this lady won't give up her house.' Well, what right do you have, Mrs. Kelo, from keeping this man from being able to feed his children?" said Georgette Chapman Poindexter, a professor of law and real estate at the University of Pennsylvania, the Wharton School, in an interview with a campus magazine after the *Kelo* decision came down in 2005. Professor Chapman Poindexter concluded that "[t]he sanctity of the individual . . . cannot exist in isolation from the needs of the community."[13] Of course, there are some who would argue that paying a mortgage and property taxes for thirty years gives Susette Kelo the right to tell that electrician—and anyone else, for that matter—that her home is not a legitimate source of social welfare.

Broadly speaking, communities do, and should, try to balance the needs of individuals and the public. But a great deal of suspicion is called for when the people on the lowest rung of the socioeconomic ladder, or the elderly, or those who happen to have the choicest waterfront views, or those who voted against the mayor in the last election, or those who are in a racial or ethnic minority, are singled out, time after time, for the privilege of sacrificing their homes and businesses to the community. It is an especially galling state of affairs when those who take their place on now-prime real estate are richer than those who get the heave-ho.

Nominally, the term "highest and best use" is employed in determining the value of land for purposes of compensating the owner when the land is taken from him. But the words also describe a change in American culture, the tendency of courts and communities to think about property in a different way. The modern approach to eminent domain in the mid-twentieth century essentially evaluates whether owners are deserving or undeserving of their land, based on factors such as tax revenue and the physical appearance of the property. This is now the kernel of the "public purpose" analysis in economic development and blight cases, respectively. The current owner is viewed in comparison with another potential owner and found deficient, because the property is not being put to its "highest and best use." This is wholly different from taking a property, with regrets—no matter what its condition—because it stands in the way of a necessary public project.

In order to justify taking land and giving it to another private party—whether it is for slum clearance, or the building of a marina and condominiums to increase the tax base, or employing a desperate electrician—the municipality and the court first consider whether a new owner will produce more with the land than the current owner does. This inquiry typically begins with a determination that the property is "blighted," "deteriorated," "underdeveloped" or otherwise wasted. The municipality can make the owner out to be a slacker by measuring the current real estate taxes (and, if the land is occupied by a business, payroll taxes and other secondary economic benefits to the community) against the limitless dreams served up on a platter by the white-knight developer or big-box retailer.

In other words, an undeserving "fool" and his land are soon parted.

What many in the land use and development community didn't count on was the vehement reaction that Americans would have, especially working-class and middle-class Americans who have found it easier than the poor people of earlier generations to give voice to their displeasure at getting shoved around this way.

"We *are* good enough," Joe Horney said, softly but insistently. Horney owns an apartment building in Norwood, Ohio, on a triangle of land slated for redevelopment. At the time of the conference in Arlington, Virginia, he and a few others were fighting the taking and had an appeal pending before the Ohio Supreme Court. (One month later, they won that appeal in the first post-*Kelo* decision by a state supreme court.) The Institute for Justice (IJ) has been litigating the case for them.

Joe Horney is a man unaccustomed to public speaking. Like many in the strange world of modern takings, he led an ordinary life until his municipality turned his world upside down by condemning his property. "They took my apartment building so they could build another apartment building," he said, slowly and deliberately, reading from a prepared statement at the conference. There was a note of bewilderment in his voice, even though his legal battle against the taking had been going on for some three years. "They want us to think we're not good enough, but we are." His words evoked a standing ovation by people from around the nation who were themselves the subjects of takings.

Horney's purpose in attending the conference was to thank the Institute for Justice for its ongoing representation of him and his fellow rebels in the Norwood triangle. After he finished his speech at the formal dinner on Saturday night, he unveiled a large granite slab, about two and a half feet square, engraved with the name of the legal case and the names of the individual litigants who had joined in the fight as holdouts. The audience gasped and several people whispered that it looked like a tombstone. Given the grief that Joe Horney expressed, it was no wonder he chose to engrave for posterity on a large slab of stone the name of the case that made him feel like a lesser American.

The City of Norwood went in under a statute that allowed it to take a community deemed to be "deteriorating" and hence in "danger of becoming blighted."[14] And the developer, under compulsion by the city, paid homeowners well in excess of the market value of their homes, in some cases three times the value. The vast majority settled willingly and were happy to get out. But not all of them felt that way, even though the triangular patch of land surrounded by heavy traffic was becoming a difficult, even an unpleasant, place to live. There are always some people for whom money does not tell the whole the story.

Joe Horney internalized a message from the city: that after paying taxes and maintaining a building in Norwood for many years as a decent landlord, he was no longer wanted; the city preferred to have someone else. It may not be the intent of municipalities to make people feel like lesser beings when their land is taken and given to other private owners, but that is often the result. Much of the outrage over economic development takings comes from the idea of replacement. The citizen who was "good enough" for ten, twenty or more years of paying taxes and raising a family, or tending to a business and a community, suddenly is replaced by someone "better." This often leads to a deep sense of betrayal, of the sort one finds in divorce cases.

Bill Giordano, a small, intense man from Long Branch, New Jersey, called the takings in his town "the most *in your face* abuse of eminent domain. The homeowners are World War II vets, senior citizens, families," he said. "They are going to take away their homes to build new homes. We already proved to the city council that Long Branch has an oversupply of condos ... an eighteen-month inventory. The council says it's doing it to remove *urban decay!*" Mr. Giordano was sitting next to Wright III, speaking on the grassroots activism panel at the conference. The motto on his business card was: "Remember ... Us Today ... YOU Tomorrow!!!"

Long Branch is the site of a massive development of high-priced waterfront condominiums on the Jersey shore. Anna DeFaria, an eighty-year-old retired schoolteacher, said that watching the developer tear down a neighbor's house left her shattered; she realized it could well happen to her home also. In a television interview, she said "it would soften the blow" if they needed her home to make way for a hospital or some other public project, but to take her home away simply to build houses for other people was incomprehensible. Mrs. DeFaria is one of numerous elderly residents of Long Branch—including Louis and Lillian Anzalone, 89, Rose LaRosa, 80, Lora Vendetti, 80, and other octogenarians—whose peace of mind and sense of security have been destroyed by the looming redevelopment. Over several months there have been numerous television and print stories covering the Long Branch taking, and none of the homes there even remotely appears to be suffering from urban decay. "It's not urban and there's no decay," said Bill Giordano with disgust.

A sense of how-did-I-get-here shock emanated from many people during the conference. One couple had come from Norborne, Missouri, where they own a farm. The husband, Rodney Cowsert, was handing out cards that said he was the president of Concerned Citizens of Carroll County. He and his wife, dressed very properly in blue suits, were there to transact business. Their farm was being threatened by eminent domain and they were selling it in parcels of one square yard, to people all over the world. For $75 you could buy a ninety-nine-year lease on one of the little parcels and immediately lease it back to Mr. Cowsert so he could keep farming it. The idea was that when the government went to condemn, they would find hundreds or even thousands of these title liens against it, and then just give up because the notice burdens would be so great.

■ ■ ■

After the *Kelo* decision came out, the print and television media were filled with stories about eminent domain. Many of the takings that were reported had begun years earlier, but now it had turned into a regular reporter's beat. The stories ranged from the predictable to the bizarre.

In Oakland, California, a man of Pappy Gore's generation named John Revelli owned a tire shop. Like the Gores, he had been in business for fifty-six years. Then the city council began an economic development taking to revitalize the downtown. The City of Oakland told him he would have to leave. They wanted to put Sears, with its own tire store, in that location instead. Revelli, like the Gores, appealed his case and pinned his hopes on *Kelo*. For its part, the city didn't see what all the fuss was about, since they were offering him "far and away more than what the land value was," according to a FOX News report on November 4, 2005. Revelli thought the compensation was inadequate because his property was fully paid up, and with the increase in values in the area he could no longer afford to buy in that neighborhood. He would have to relocate. He pointed out that no other location was equivalent because most of his customers were women who worked downtown and felt safe dropping off their cars at his shop. "I've worked here full-time since 1959 and I look forward to coming to work every day," Revelli said. "I'm not ready to retire, but the city forced me into this." Sears will also displace another business nearby, called Autohouse. The owner, Tony Fong, told a reporter for the *San Francisco Chronicle,* "I'm an immigrant from China and this has been the fulfillment of my American dream. I worked hard. I played by the rules. But now it's all gone. I've got to start all over."[15]

Economic development takings extended their reach into the generally tony confines of Westchester County, New York, in the town of New Rochelle, when a developer showed interest in finally—blessedly, from the standpoint of city officials—getting rid of a seedy-looking strip along one of the main drags in order to build a retail and residential complex. The storefronts included a Planned Parenthood office, a child care center and something called the Casanova Gentleman's Club. The owners of the child care center and the Casanova Club balked.

In general, the state of New York is no stranger to eminent domain or economic development takings. In New York City, Mayor Michael Bloomberg has bucked the trend of many politicians around the country and declared that he likes eminent domain just fine and plans to use it as much as possible. He believes it is good for the city and good for the economy. One of the nastiest fights over economic development takings has been brewing for several years in Brooklyn, part of Mayor Bloomberg's turf. It concerns the Atlantic Yards development. Some owners of condominiums who bought when the neighborhood was scruffy are fighting tooth and nail with Forest City Ratner Companies, which plans to build an enormous development including a stadium for the New Jersey Nets, as well as thousands of units of housing and retail space. The fight involves complex issues of race and class in the typical maelstrom of New York City politics. So far, eminent domain has been pulled out of the holster, but no one has actually fired a shot. Many people have settled with the Ratner organization and moved. A few are staying put and battling on. A federal suit to stop the project was filed. Dismissed by the district courts, it is now on appeal.

The Saha family in Coatesville, Pennsylvania, fought their city council for six years to save their idyllic horse farm, where they have lived since 1970 and raised their five children. According to the Sahas, the Coatesville city manager and the city solicitor came to their door six years ago and told them their entire farm, some 49 acres, would be needed for the new golf course the town was building as an essential part of a $60 million regional recreation center. The Sahas maintained that the city already had more than enough land to build the golf course—including 110 acres of landfill and 62 acres of undeveloped properties adjacent to their farm; they believed the decision to take their land was arbitrary. The Saha family offered six acres to the city; the city refused. A battle ensued, costing the Sahas $300,000 in legal fees. After a change in management at the Coatesville City Hall and the hiring of a new city manager, the city abandoned its plan to take the Saha farm and settled with the family, agreeing to take the six acres they had offered at the beginning.

CHAPTER 11

TEARING THE TOWN IN TWO

There was a phrase people heard a lot in Freeport during the years of the marina controversy: "sit down and shut up." That is to say, they heard it a lot if they attended city council meetings. They didn't hear it from mothers quieting their children in the back row; a city council meeting was no place to take a child during the marina war, what with all the public shaming of grown people and the general feeling of bad blood. No, folks heard the phrase "sit down and shut up" from their mayor. Now, Mayor Phillips claims he never says "shut up" in so many words. Oh sure, "I tell people be quiet or leave," he says. "We run that council as a *business*. We don't beat any dead horses. We keep people to a time limit." As the mayor talks about how he runs the council meetings, he gets a bit worked up and words tumble out fast. "Everybody wants to say something. Let them appoint a spokesman." And then a moment later: "Anybody has the opportunity to speak. We let *anyone* speak. But we have business to conduct. Everything we do, we have to vote three times on it!"

Before becoming mayor of Freeport in 2005, Jim Phillips was a judge and served on the city council for thirteen years. But more importantly for the social history of this small town, he was the principal of Freeport High School and a teacher there for twenty-three years. "The Gores," Mayor Phillips says, speaking of Wright Jr., Gary and Raymond, "they were all my kids." He speaks to citizens at city council meetings, many of them in their sixties, as if they were still schoolchildren and he were still the principal. As if they were fighting over spitballs, and not speaking out in a public forum about eminent domain and the taking of a family business that employs fifty-six Freeport residents. Mayor Phillips is passionately in favor of the marina project and makes no bones about his dislike for the endless courtroom battles being waged by the Gores, and even more so his dislike for the Citizens for Freeport and their temerity in bringing ballot initiatives aimed at setting aside what the city was trying to do. He sees them as a small group of agitators who don't represent an actual segment of the population in the town.

Being told to sit down and shut up by Mayor Phillips was one of the main things that radicalized Cathy Williams. Before she retired, Cathy had been a sales representative for the electric company and her husband had been on the police force. They were not allowed to voice their political beliefs back then. "It just wasn't done" if you worked for the county government, she explained. But lately she'd been coming to council meetings and speaking up during the "Citizens' Business" part, or "open mike" as it's called. That's when the council gives the citizens a chance to speak their minds. "They're not even supposed to engage in any dialog," said Cathy. "They're supposed to let people talk." Well, when Mayor Phillips, a former Marine, has heard enough or doesn't like the direction things are taking, he just yells at the speaker, "*Set* down and *shud* up!" according to Cathy.

It looks like part of a well-orchestrated affair. Jeff Pynes, chief of the Freeport Police, is on hand during council meetings (which are held in the police building). Chief Pynes stands at the back of the room, about fifteen feet behind the speaker's lectern. Ron Bottoms, the city manager, sits up on the dais but does not vote. He has a microphone, however, and can chime in anytime he wants. "Ron Bottoms will put his finger up in the air and ring it around," Cathy explained. "Then Pynes comes up behind you and that means you have to sit down."

Cathy got fed up with the indignity of it. "I've known these people all my life!" Cathy wasn't the only resident who felt that way. Open mike is important in a small town. Mature people who had grown up and raised children and paid taxes in Freeport for decades felt they had a right to be heard on matters affecting their town. When the marina project came along, a divisive issue to begin with, it rankled all the more to be treated like unruly adolescents. So a group of them—including Cathy Williams, Joyce

Adkins and Skip Pratt—decided they weren't going to take it anymore. They formed Citizens for Freeport, based on the natural affinity of people who were displeased about the course the city was taking.

Freeport is governed under what is known as a council-manager system. This means that the mayor sits on the city council and has one vote, just like any other council member, and is not the head of municipal agencies. He doesn't have the power to hire or fire anyone; he isn't supposed to run things. As a matter of law, he is no more powerful than the other council members. His main official duty is to preside over council meetings, where policies and agendas are set. The city manager, who in theory is supposed to stay out of politics, executes the council's policies and runs the city. He is an unelected, salaried person with a professional background in public administration. This is a system that many smaller cities use, and it is especially popular in the Sun Belt. It is designed to promote efficiency and diminish cronyism.

In the textbook scenario of a council-manager system, the mayor is usually "chosen by the council from among its members." The role of mayor is "largely titular and ceremonial in nature"; in fact, "the mayor in a council-manager city possesses no meaningful administrative, appointive, or veto powers."[1] But the mayor in Freeport is elected at large, rather than chosen by the council. Jim Phillips comes from a ward that is largely white and more affluent than the city's three other wards, and that tends to vote in greater numbers, especially since municipal elections were shifted to the police station. Though Phillips has no official role in the city's administration, he maintains an office at City Hall, the better to keep an eye on things and to hear citizens' grievances. And there is nothing ceremonial about the way he fills the mayoral role. A tall, imposing, older man, he dominates any room he is in. He has a nasty temper, and many people in the town are afraid of him. "He's a bully," said Joyce Adkins in her blunt manner.

One way to look at things in Freeport would be to say that presiding over city council meetings is the one thing that Mayor Phillips is actually allowed to do under Freeport's charter, so he dives into it with gusto. And that would be all well and fine if people didn't feel they have to research the charter, chapter and verse, and then steel their courage before going in to take him on, *mano a mano,* and hope they get to say what they planned to say before being told to sit down and be quiet. Often in the middle of a meeting, Phillips calls upon Wallace Shaw, the city attorney seated next to him, to confirm the legality of his arguments and prove a citizen wrong in front of a chamber packed with spectators.

In contrast, the city manager, Ron Bottoms, has a certain elfin charm, a way of smoothing things over with a smile. Although he has no vote, he sometimes jumps in to defend city policies, and makes plain that he is pushing the council's agenda forward. When things get rough in council meetings, he turns and silently looks at the mayor, as if to say, *this has gone far enough, do something here.* And then the mayor does something, which usually means contradicting the speaker at the lectern, or telling him his time is up; he has been known to put a person out of the room entirely.

When Mayor Phillips presides over meetings, other council members rarely pipe up unless a citizen addresses a question directly to that member, drawing him out, daring him to contradict the mayor. The council takes pains not to cross the mayor—with the lone exception of Clan Cameron, who now occupies the "maverick" seat that Larry McDonald once held. At a meeting in 2005 when Wright III passed around copies of a ballot petition to council members, Mayor Phillips barked at them to pass all the copies to him, before they even had a chance to read the petition. "They all passed it up there like it was their homework," said Larry. "All except me."

Jim Phillips is viewed around town as someone important. He comes from one of a handful of families that own large pieces of ranch land in the area. "This is a feudal town," said Joyce Adkins. Phillips is simultaneously feared and respected. People will complain about him in one breath, and in the next will tell you about acts of generosity he has performed for people in need. All of Freeport is a web of family and social connections that often go back to childhood. When people take sides in the marina debate, these old connections rise up in primordial ways.

Most adults in Freeport remember Jim Phillips, with trepidation, from their school days. "I had him for history in '63," said Skip Pratt. "My mother worked for Phillips as a librarian," said Margaret Ancona, another member of Citizens for Freeport. "He was the principal of my high school," recalled Wright Gore Jr., speaking of the man who now participates in private, off-the-record executive sessions of the city council during which the marina project and the Gores are often discussed. The same man who has told his son, Wright III, to "take a seat" during council meetings, and has even had him tossed out, when Wright III goes down to challenge the council or to demand information. The same man who has signed open letters in the local newspaper, declaring Wright III to be a liar who will "stop at nothing" to get what he wants. Mayor Phillips' wife, Dell, had been Wright III's teacher in the fifth grade.

Wallace Shaw, the city attorney who is at the mayor's beck and call during council meetings, was a deacon at St. Mary Star of the Sea Church, which the Gores attended for decades. Beth Gore takes it as a personal betrayal that Mr. Shaw, now an elderly gentleman, would so clearly take sides against them. "His wife, his whole family, *known them,*" said Beth, counting off the old friends in Freeport who she feels have betrayed her family. "James Saccomano, who's a city councilman, he's at the church. Our children grew up together." Mr. Saccomano is part of the voting bloc on the council that consistently votes with the mayor on marina-related matters.

"And then there's one woman on the council, Norma Garcia—I taught her in second grade. [Beth used to be a teacher.] Yes. And right before all this kinda hit the fan, I called her and I told her I wanted to talk to her," said Beth. "And over the years she's just been a little darling—and 'Miss Gore, Miss Gore' and hug and kiss. I know her family and everything. When all this came up, I said, 'Norma, I'd like to talk to you before the election and the petition and everything.' I guess she was already a city councilwoman at the time. 'But [I said to her] I don't think it's proper for me to talk to you at work.' She works for the judge." (Ms. Garcia works for the justice of the peace in Freeport.) "'Would you mind if I could just speak to you tonight?'" Beth had asked her. "And she said, 'Well, what time do you wanna call? I'm gonna be at some meetings.' And I said, 'What if I call about 8 or 8:30?' And she said, 'That'd be great.' Well, I called her at 8 and it rings and rings. No answer. Call at 8:30 and it rings and rings. No answer. I really . . . It just amazes me."

To be sure, the local paper received many letters in support of the Gores. And the vote on the referendum to dissolve the economic development corporation (EDC) was extremely close. But it was the seats on the city council that ultimately mattered most. And there, a lifetime of social relationships meant nothing. The Gores had a personal or social connection with Jim Phillips (and his wife, Dell), Norma Garcia, James Saccomano, Wallace Shaw (who advised the council)—people who now held the Gores' fate in their hands with an unabashedly pro-marina agenda. "That's been the hardest part," said Beth. "You know, my husband and his family have done so much for the City of Freeport and the community. So many things. You know, they're real modest. I mean, there was nothin' in Freeport but the shrimpin' industry. And they been payin' taxes. Just supporting, *helping* everyone. And all these people are goin' against us now.

"Now, there's still lots of people that support us, and been just wonderful, real good friends. But there's been lot's of people, personal friends of mine that I *thought* were friends, that, I would call them, one on one, unh-unh. They would *not* sign the petition." Beth was referring to the petition calling for a referendum to dissolve the EDC—the first of several initiatives and referenda brought by Citizens for Freeport. That first petition created a political moment reminiscent of the old union organizing song *Which Side Are You On, Man?* Ordinary people unaccustomed to political controversy were asked to take a stand. What surprised Beth and Wright Jr. was that the mayor's promises of municipal riches from the marina project carried such weight with so many people they had known since they were a young couple. "I did a lot of volunteer work for our church, and the PTA, and I had lots of friends, and just loved living there. And then *all this* came about," said Beth, her voice taking on an uncharacteristically hard edge.

It was like an episode of the old television show *This Is Your Life*. There they all were: the deacon of their church, the second-grade student, the high school principal, the fifth-grade teacher, people they had carpooled with, people whose causes they had donated time and money to. These were people with whom the Gores had shared a lifetime in a small town, where the Gores had been good employers and pillars of the community, the kind of neighbor you can rely on. And none of that seemed to mean anything now. At least that was how it looked to a lot of people.

"I really took it very personally and it really hurt. But I told my husband, you know," and here Beth laughed a little, embarrassed to say out loud what she must have thought ruefully to herself a dozen times, "most people go to their graves and they really don't know who their enemies are and who their true friends are, I says, and we know, we found out real quick."

Even if the Gores had never done anything but pay for half of the guillotine gate, that would have been a contribution to the city worth reckoning with. But in quiet ways, the Gores had done much more. For decades, ever since they had established themselves in business, they never turned away anyone looking for help with a charitable or civic cause. They employed off-duty policemen to work security at their dock around the holidays. "It wasn't necessary," said Wright Jr. "It was just a way of our thanking them during the Christmas season when they need extra money." Year after year they supplied shrimp or ice or donated money for the firemen's fundraisers, Main Street promotions, League of United Latin American Citizens (LULAC) festivals, and church fundraisers. They sponsored a yearly civic event called the Blessing of the Fleet, which used to be a major draw attended by thousands of people, even attracting TV personalities to Freeport; these days, the city doesn't do the Blessing of the Fleet anymore. The Gores used to donate ice and shrimp, auction items and gift certificates to local Catholic and Episcopal festivals and fish fries. They sponsored beauty pageant candidates and contributed to the local high school's Project Graduation. They even provided laborers from the Western Seafood packing house when the city needed them for cleanup efforts. The Gores were also financial supporters of the Freeport League, an organization that promoted Freeport in general. Isabel Gore was the president of the league. Now well into her seventies and still going to work every day at Western Seafood, Isabel was named Woman of the Year by the local chapter of the Chamber of Commerce just a few years ago.

"We provided clothing and food for the destitute and donated to more fundraisers for terminally ill Freeport citizens than I can ever remember," wrote Wright Jr. in an email. He added, "In general, there hasn't been (and does not exist) a worthwhile charitable event in Freeport to which we do not agree to contribute." Wright Jr. is a modest man who rarely begins a sentence with the word "I." This information about the Gores' charitable activity was not volunteered, but rather drawn out of him; so his statement—though laced with some well-founded anger—strikes me not as plaintive but merely as factual.

"I know my mother- and father-in-law, it really hurts them," said Beth. "They worked *so* hard, seven days a week. And were really pillars of the community. And still are in many people's eyes. It's really a . . . a . . . ," she stumbled, looking for a word, finally settling for one that hardly seemed strong enough to express her emotion, "a shame. You know, what's happened, and what they've done, what they've done to them."

Many years of good will could be undone with a few vicious rumors, the stroke of an administrative pen on a development agreement, and an economic pipe dream. In the world of economic development takings, there is no past. The past is for suckers; it is the province of sentimentalists. There is only the future. And the future is measured by tax revenues. The current occupant of land is eyeballed for the taxes he pays. If he is found wanting, he is tossed out like yesterday's garbage. And here's what is galling about the tax-revenue comparison in an economic development taking: it is a comparison of a real, live revenue stream against *anticipated* taxes from a phantom. It's easy to be successful on paper. And it's very hard, if not impossible, for home and business owners to box against a shadow.

Does Western Seafood stimulate the economy in Freeport? Certainly. Will the marina? It's hard to say. At the moment, there's nothing concrete to disprove the city council's theory: *Build it and they will come. Hotels! Restaurants! Tourists!* In the meantime, the marina gets an open-ended tax abatement. But hope and prayer laced with financial projections are mighty powerful things; presented in the right way, they can be intoxicating. Hell, many a pioneer went west on the same basis. Who doesn't want a piece of a dream? And so the city council presses forward. It doesn't matter who gets rolled over by those huge wagon wheels in the process. The past be damned. In the meantime, the pressure mounts and the tension in the town worsens. "We had some people go out of business waiting for [the marina] to happen," said Mary Lee Stotler, the head of Freeport's Main Street Program. Two of the businesses were fairly new and had come into the downtown in anticipation of the marina, she said, while the other two were long established. (When pressed for details, Stotler said that one business actually relocated to another area of Freeport, while another business—a restaurant with two locations—closed its downtown location to focus on its second one.) The dustbowl of downtown Freeport was growing larger.

▪ ▪ ▪

Angel Edge-Kant had a bone to pick with Mayor Phillips. The battle over the EDC ballot initiative may have been over, but she was determined to clear the air about what the city did to Steve Alford. That whole incident had left a bad taste in people's mouths, the sense that free speech was being censored by the city manager. To add insult to injury, opponents had monkeyed around with Wendi Ross's paper, the *Sentinel*. Angel believed that a violation of the Freeport Code of Ordinances had occurred.

Look at the way they ticketed Steve Alford for section 113, she thought. *And then Jim Phillips just zips all over town in his truck, and copies of the Sentinel get tossed all over with that insert telling people to vote against the EDC ballot. How are we supposed to fight for what we believe if there are two sets of rules?*

It was time for a showdown. Angel studied section 113 of the code, relating to permits for circulars and newspapers. She went to the city council meeting in early December 2005, loaded for bear.

Angel is a slight woman with a mass of long curly hair. She barely reached above the speaker's lectern at open mike. The council members peered down at her from their high perches. They all had large plaques over their seats with their names inscribed on them, as if everyone in town didn't already know them and the tangle of loyalties and intrigue that each of them brought to the big leather chair from which they now surveyed the room. Mayor Phillips was in the center. Even when seated, he was obviously taller and bolder than the rest of them. To his left sat Wallace Shaw.

Earlier that fall, there had been another confrontation between Angel and the mayor during a council meeting when

Angel tried to raise a matter not on the agenda and insisted on getting answers to her questions. Afterward, Shaw sent Angel an email:

> Ms. Kant,
> Take a look at Section 7.02(a)(2), Texas Penal Code.
> Wallace Shaw

Section 7.02 is called "Criminal Responsibility for Conduct of Another." Part (a)(2) of the statute applies to acting with "the intent to promote or assist the commission" of a crime by another person. Under the Texas Open Meetings Act, council members are not supposed to engage in dialog during the "Citizens' Business" part of the meeting. The implication here is that Angel, by egging on the council to have a dialog during open mike, was promoting the commission of a crime by council members. Angel wrote back:

> Dear Mr. Shaw:
> ... My first question is how did an open meeting question become the subject of criminal law, as opposed to civil law? In the Penal code that you gave me I cannot figure out if you are saying that the Mayor committed an offence by his own conduct, or are you saying that the Mayor is responsible for me because you think I am a criminal? Or are you saying that I am responsible for the Mayor because he is an innocent or a non-responsible person. Or are you trying to say that I am conspiring to commit a felony. Mr. Shaw I really do not understand which of these you believe applies to me but I am asking for you to explain it to me. Thank you in advance for answering my question.
> Kind Regards,
> Angel Kant

The city attorney wrote back:

> Ms. Edge:
> My agreement with the City only allows me to answer questions put to me by the Mayor, a majority of the City Council or the City Manager or his designee. Therefore, I cannot answer the questions you have raised in your last e-mail. However, I consider it my obligation to "warn" anyone at a public meeting of the applicable law. That was what I was trying to do for you at

the meeting and my limited response to your first e-mail was a follow up to that by pointing out to you (by specific reference to it) Section 7.02(a)(2) of the Penal Code for you to read and arrive at your own conclusions....
Sincerely yours,
Wallace Shaw

Now Angel Kant, having recently been warned of her criminal tendencies by Wallace Shaw, stood ready at the lectern. There was only one friendly face up there: Larry McDonald. Angel's voice shook a little, but she plunged in.

"Why is it that Mr. Bottoms has to approve everything that gets distributed in this city?"

"You don't expect us to answer that, do you?" asked the mayor. "We'll send you written answers."

"What is the guidelines for Mr. Bottoms to approve or deny such materials, or is that in his sole discretion? And what is the procedure for bypassing Mr. Bottoms if he denies the permit?"

Angel wanted the city to justify the permit procedure under Section 113 of the Freeport Code of Ordinances, which had been used to ticket Steve Alford and disrupt the campaigning during the Dissolve the EDC election. It seemed like a law intended for advertising, not political speech.

"I can answer that last one," said Mayor Phillips. "If you are not satisfied with his decision, you can contact me or you can appeal directly to this council. Correct, Mr. Shaw?"

Angel took a moment. *Might as well move on.* This was an obvious dead end.

"The problem I am having is with this last election," she said. "There was a flier out by Real Citizens of Freeport [a group opposing Citizens for Freeport]. Was there a permit pulled by Real Citizens of Freeport?"

"Yes."

"A permit pulled by a Mr. Jones. But Mr. Jones didn't have a permit to fold the circular into the *Sentinel* newspaper? Why not?"

"Because I purchased the paper," said Mayor Phillips. "Hundreds of papers."

Now it was clear to Phillips what was happening. Angel was at the council that evening to lay bare the details of the *Sentinel* escapade. This would be precisely the sort of verbal fisticuffs that Phillips reveled in.

Phillips said to Angel that the *Sentinel* did not charge him for stuffing the flier or carrying the flier in the newspaper, because he purchased only the newspapers, *before* the flier went in them. (This differed from his recollection of the events two years later, when he spoke with me and said he had nothing to do with obtaining the papers. "I did not spearhead that effort," he said to me.)

"Did you assist in distributing the papers?" Angel asked. The Freeport Code has a very strict rule about throwing or distributing unsolicited newspapers and circulars. This is what led to Steve Alford's ticket and the disruption of the EDC ballot campaign.

Phillips leaned forward in his seat and said very slowly, pausing between each word, "I ... drove ... the ... truck."

"The police stopped *other* citizens distributing materials they had a permit for!"

"The city issued a citation to Mr. Alford for distributing extra materials that *Mr. Bottoms* did not approve. Mr. Shaw since then has dismissed this ticket," said the mayor.

This was Ron Bottoms' cue. All of a sudden, his face took on an uncharacteristically dark look, as if this were the gravest of matters. "The materials distributed by Mr. Jones *was* what was distributed," said Ron. "The permit that Mr. Alford applied for, uh, the material that was represented to me, that was gonna be distributed, was nowhere to what was actually distributed. Therefore, the two weren't, I feel it was misrepresented to me what was gonna be distributed."

"So it is legal to put a circular inside a newspaper and distribute that way?" Angel asked.

"The ordinance says nothing about newspapers," said Ron.

Angel pointed her index finger up in the air and started reciting from the Freeport Code: "you must have a permit ... to cast or throw a newspaper that is UN-SO-LI-CI-TED."

Phillips started rolling a pencil between the palms of his hands, a sign he is truly angry. He locked his eyes on her.

"Any newspapers can be thrown. It is excluded by law," the mayor said. "And by the way, before you go any further, yes, we did check with the district attorney's office. And yes ma'am, we did check with the Texas attorney general before we did it. I'm not dumb, nor am I stupid."

A little chuckle broke out in the room.

"And *I* have checked with them *after the fact,*" said Angel.

"What's that?"

"I have checked with them after the fact," Angel repeated.

Phillips leaned forward slowly before answering, as if considering something. Then he said in a low, steady voice, "That's correct. I *was* aware of that."

The suffocating "Big Brother Is Watching You" reality of small-town life fell over the room like a cloud of dust. Angel took a moment to recover herself. She shuffled some papers around on the lectern.

"So the owner of the *Sentinel* was paid for the insertion of the fliers?"

"No. She was paid for the newspapers themselves."

"Miss Ross told me she presented you with a bill for the inserts—"

"I didn't have to. It was my newspaper. I'd already purchased it. Thank you."

"As a citizen of Freeport," said Angel, "I am really upset."

"Well—"

"There are certain people in this town—"

"Look, I'm gonna tell you very quickly, we're not going anywhere with this argument. If you have a problem with this being in violation of the law, you need to take it to the *law.* We're not gonna sit here, and go over this, and you know, your word, his word, our word, their word.... If you have some concerns about the ordinance itself, share it with us ..."

"May I speak now?"

"Yes ... I'm telling you now, if you have something that you wish to discuss relating to the ordinance and the way it is written, that you'd like for us to discuss, get on with it, if you don't, then please have a seat."

"As a citizen of Freeport I am very upset that certain people are allowed to break the law, or get what they want done—"

"That's *it*!" Mayor Phillips shouted and banged the gavel. "You may have a seat, Miss Angel."

Angel did not sit down. She continued speaking.

"Either have a seat, or *outside,*" he said, pointing his finger at the door.

"Yes, sir. Thank you," Angel said.

She turned and walked toward the back of the room, where a small commotion was taking place. Joyce Adkins was standing up.

"Mrs. Adkins," said the mayor, "you may be excused also."

"Oh, I'm waaaalkin' out the door right now, Your Honor," said Joyce. "Your Godship!"

Councilman Larry McDonald was so appalled at what had just transpired that he got up and left the dais in protest. All the others on the dais remained seated.

■ ■ ■

Despite the heavy voter dilution in Ward A and other parts of Freeport, the ward system was having an effect. In 2006 there was a black man and a Hispanic woman on the council. But ethnic diversity on a city council does not necessarily mean very much if a single political center of power remains in control. The new council members voted with Mayor Phillips, endorsing the marina and other projects aimed at beautifying the city and reviving the downtown area. Larry McDonald, who represented Ward A and whose mother is Hispanic, was the lone dissenter throughout 2005 and into 2006. Later in the spring of 2006, Larry's term was up. The Citizens for Freeport hatched a plan for Larry to give up his council seat in order to run for mayor against Jim Phillips in the spring of 2007. In the meantime, they ran Clan Cameron, another outspoken member of Citizens for Freeport, for Larry's council seat. The first leg of the plan succeeded. Clan gained the council seat and became the lone holdout on all votes concerning beautification projects, overturning ballot initiatives, and anything that furthered the case against the Gores. Although the balance of the voting did not change, the tenor of council meetings did, because Clan lacked Larry's kindly demeanor.

Clan is living proof of the old adage that still waters run deep. Tall and lanky, usually dressed in jeans and a hooded sweatshirt, he is a Desert Storm veteran and works at a nonprofit organization where he helps people with disabilities in nearby Angleton. Clan is so taciturn and speaks in such a slow, measured way that one might be tempted to underestimate him. That would be a mistake. Clan Cameron has a slow burn that builds to a boil over many months. Clan's anger tends to rise up as he sloshes through the floodwaters on Fourth Street, which he said had flooded so badly that "twice during the last three years during storms, you could run a boat down my street." He has seen this kind of neglect going on for years in Freeport neighborhoods. "I don't know if I am a nice man," he said during a 2005 bid for mayor, "but I believe I am a good man." Clan is the moralist on the city council, a man with a deep sense of justice and a keen instinct for sniffing out a rat.

"What ya'll doing is *evil*!" Clan thundered at the council during one meeting.

That certainly woke people up in the peanut gallery. But the Citizens for Freeport who sat among them knew that something controversial was on the agenda that night. On its face, it appeared to be a rather ordinary bit of business. The city was considering demolishing an unsafe structure: a single-family home. Things like that tend to come up at council, but this house was different. Unoccupied and owned by an estate, it sat very close to some city-owned land that was going to be bulldozed for the marina project. Tongues had been wagging that the city wanted to bulldoze this house too.

From the beginning of the marina controversy, the promise never to take a single home had been the great line drawn in the sand by the city itself. It was the sweetener to sell the marina project to the citizens of Freeport. The mantra "Your homes are safe!" was repeated over and over by city officials in a public relations campaign to counter the one being waged by Wright Gore III. The city was sticking to this mantra as late as 2006—as if taking away family businesses were not problematic either morally or socially, despite the deep rift it was creating in the town. When I appeared with pad and pencil at a city council meeting, Mayor Phillips made a beeline for me, grasped my hand in his large paw, pumped it up and down and said, by way of introduction, "We don't condemn homes in this town." Only after he gave that a chance to sink in did he say, "My name is Jim Phillips. Who are you?"

The city had framed the marina project as one in which a smattering of businesses along the Old Brazos River would be sacrificed for the economic good of all the homeowners in the entire city, while no homeowners would ever have to sacrifice their homes. Only those Gores (*who live in Lake Jackson, anyway*) and two or three other businessmen would lose; everyone else would benefit. From the perspective of voter support, that's a stroke of political genius. But it holds up only as long as the promise not to take homes holds out. When Wright III did the first door-hanger campaign in the summer of 2004 to alert residents that their homes had been designated as blighted in the master plan, the paranoia set in.

Now the city council was discussing the demolition of a home that was right by the marina project. Clan Cameron was the only member of the council willing to take on the mayor when he crossed over the so-called sacred line of taking homes. He called the plans "evil." But it was only *after* the meeting, in a conversation with the mayor, that he learned the nitty-gritty details of how the house was actually to be acquired. The city had come up with a clever way of doing it without using eminent domain. The method the city had in mind was to inform the owner that the structure was worth nothing. However, the city in its magnanimity would offer to demolish the building and the city would then accept the land on which the building sat as compensation for the demolition. Ain't that grand? Since it happened to be near the marina property, well, perhaps the city could turn over the land that the house sat on to the Walker partnership. The Citizens for Freeport feared this was a ruse. Could this be the first of many homes to topple one day in the name of economic development in Freeport?

In the theater-of-the-absurd that Freeport politics had become, Wright III was standing nearby with a tape recorder when Mayor Phillips revealed the demolition plan to Clan Cameron. He taped the conversation and later copied it onto CD-ROMs, which he popped into plastic cases along with a written transcript and a rather unflattering photo of Mayor Phillips haranguing some poor soul during a council meeting. Wright III then distributed a few hundred of the plastic box sets to residents of Freeport as part of his PR guerilla warfare. Mayor Phillips threatened to sue him. Given the number of lawsuits then pending against Wright III and his family, he responded casually, "Get in line."

■ ■ ■

"People have been talking about a marina in Freeport for forty years," said Ron Bottoms. He was bubbling over with excitement. "There was a non-binding referendum in the 1980s about a marina," he said. "We went to *him,*" added Norma Garcia, a member of the city council, referring to Walker Royall. They were rebutting the position of the Gore family that the whole marina idea was dreamed up by Walker. To the contrary, they insisted it was the city's idea and believed the city should get the credit for it. From the city council's point of view, the marina is part of a larger plan to spruce up Freeport, which has been looking tired for a long time. Ron Bottoms wants "to make Freeport a destination."

It had been four years since the city asked the Maritime Trust Company to create a master plan for Freeport. The resulting plan was never formally adopted by the city, and the city was not obligated to follow it. Yet having started down that path, the city seemed determined not to change course no matter what obstacles arose. The master plan suggested a marina, among many other things, so a marina there shall be. And Freeport is not a city where the council will butt heads with the economic development corporation; to the contrary, the council controls its EDC, unlike the situation in New London. It's no surprise that the EDC, too, has shown little flexibility in working with the Gores. Two council members, Norma Garcia and John Smith III, also serve on the EDC; Smith is its president. Surely they carry their political allegiances and their obligations as council members in the door with them to EDC meetings. When the mayor signed the public advertisement excoriating Wright III, five EDC members joined him.

So the EDC forges ahead with its vision. Visit the Freeport City Hall and you'll see a series of lovely watercolors in the lobby. It is Freeport's dreams on display. Each picture has a caption worthy of a Currier & Ives print: Nature Center at Bryan Beach; Hike & Bike Trail Along the Scenic Old Brazos River; Riverplace Plaza at the Head of the Old River; Fishing Pier at Bryan Beach on the Brazos River; Brazosport Boulevard Improvements; Scenic Overlook Along the Old Brazos River. These are ambitious plans for a small town that is no stranger to HUD grants. At the moment they are dreams, except for the Riverplace Plaza, a plain, squat building now used for events. Beautification still awaits this city, surrounded like a prisoner of war by chemical plants, but there is a beginning.

When you drive into Freeport along the main drag where Highway 288 intersects with the Dow Canal, you come up along a row of palm trees that are illuminated at night with fiber optic lighting. The palm trees are part of the makeover of a long, desolate patch of grass, which is now perked up with brick pavers and stainless steel columns. There is also a sign that welcomes you to Freeport. It's a pretty sight if you look quickly enough to catch it. And it should be pretty. That "gateway to the city," as it's officially called, cost $1.56 million.[2] Lest you think for a moment you are entering a tropical paradise, however, there is soon a large street sign that says "Chlorine Road." That's an important landmark, and one that many visitors to the town are searching for, because it marks the main entrance to the Dow Chemical plant, where thousands of people work in blue-collar jobs. Chlorine is very significant in Freeport. The mere mention of it makes people grow misty with nostalgia. "Oh, our eyes used to run from it during the daytime," said Wright Gore Jr. He grew up during Dow's bad old days, before the federal government knocked some environmental sense into the chemical industry.

Life in Freeport is not without many kinds of ironies. The city and its corporate ally, the Dow Chemical Company, were willing to fight for the right to keep on making chlorine—lots of it. In 2005, the U.S. Department of Energy went sniffing around a place called Stratton Ridge, part of the Dow complex, and got a notion to use eminent domain to take some land there for a new strategic petroleum reserve. The City of Freeport and Dow started lobbying vigorously against it. The infrastructure for the petroleum reserve would have shortened the life span of the salt mines that Dow uses to make chlorine, and eventually that would have meant the loss of thousands of jobs. Mayor Phillips came out vocally against the DOE project. "'Eminent' and 'domain' are fighting words in Texas," said Nate Ellis, a DOE official, to the *Houston Chronicle* in August 2006. The city and Dow supplied information to the DOE about how the new reserve would negatively impact the county in terms of lost jobs and tax revenue. They hoped it wouldn't fall on deaf ears. It didn't. The Department of Energy ultimately decided not to place the new petroleum reserve at Stratton Ridge. Western Seafood did not receive the same consideration.

Wright Jr. looks back with fondness on the days when Freeport smelled of chlorine because it reminds him of the time he spent working with his father down at the loading docks. Most men his age in Freeport earned their living outdoors and came to know the smell of chlorine, just as the generation or two before them knew the smell of sulfur. But you can't blame a town for wanting to move up in the world. And so the palm trees went in, with the pretty spotlights trained on them at night. But it wasn't without some political blood being shed.

The beautification program, according to a story in the *Houston Business Journal,* was aimed at shaking off a "faded" and "blighted environmental image."[3] Some in Freeport think it was outrageous to spend money on beautification when essential infrastructure needs to be improved. There were pumping stations that had broken down, and heavy rains brought flooding. Joyce Adkins recalled, "A little old lady got up during the open mike portion of a city council meeting and said, 'Just two of those palm trees could have saved my house from flooding.' This is all part of why we don't like *the way they do business.*"

As in many big, dysfunctional families, the fight over money in Freeport is not really about money but about something else: about values, priorities, promises and disappointments, jealousies and justice. The controversy over the marina has brought many long-simmering fights to a head. The infrastructure issue is directly related to the question of the marina because the city is divided over whether to fix the infrastructure first and beautify the city later, or do the reverse. Clan Cameron and the Citizens for Freeport believe that the way to attract business is to improve basic infrastructure and services, not prettify the city in superficial ways. Larry McDonald, former Ward A councilman, is well aware of the problems faced by the poorest residents of Freeport. In a 2004 *Facts* interview about an election that year, he said that he believed the priority was improving infrastructure in Freeport because his family recently had been flooded out of its home. "During the last hurricane, I had to evacuate some of my in-laws who never received water in their house and get them out at 3 o'clock in the morning," he said. "We need to find a means of getting water out of here."[4]

The marina development plan called for the repositioning of certain levees if the engineers required it. The levees in Freeport are high mounds of earth that run the length of the south bank of the Old Brazos River. They are sacred ground to the residents of the East End. Clan raised the issue of the levees again and again during 2005 and 2006. Throughout the marina controversy, the occupants of City Hall assured Clan and the East End residents that the levees would not be cut. But in November 2006, when the city decided to move forward and get ready to break ground, suddenly people were talking about cutting the levees and building flood-retaining walls. Clan protested: this is the type of thing they had in New Orleans, and look what happened there. Lee Cameron, director of the EDC, replied that the Old Brazos River hadn't been out of its banks in all the thirty-eight years he had lived in the area. Then someone reminded him about Hurricane Carla, when a breach did happen.[5] If the levees are breached, it will be mostly the East End that pays the price, and the residents there are overwhelmingly poor.

■ ■ ■

The marina project had taken center stage in the mayoral election in May 2005, a month before the *Kelo* decision came down. Jim Phillips had won in a four-way election, while two candidates split the anti-marina vote. "We realized then that it was a mistake not to band together," said Clan Cameron, who had run as one of the anti-marina candidates.

"There's an old guard that has controlled the city for years," said Clan. "We are chipping into it. It's a generational change. It's going to take some time." The city council was shaken by what had happened with the Dissolve the EDC petition in November 2005, when Freeport came within twenty-one votes of having its economic development corporation dismantled before its very eyes. Executive sessions were scheduled regularly for council meeting nights; behind closed doors, according to official agendas, the council discussed matters such as "attorney conflict of interest" and other sensitive issues that justify closed sessions under the Texas Open Meetings Act. The common suspicion in town was: they're talking about the Gores, the petitions, the whole damn mess.

The narrow defeat of Dissolve the EDC did not deter Wright III or the Citizens for Freeport. They brought five more petitions for ballot initiatives and referenda. But the voters of Freeport never got to have their say in the voting booth on any of them, even though the Citizens for Freeport gathered hundreds upon hundreds of signatures, sticking to Freeport Code procedures as meticulously as they could.

There was a petition to prohibit the use of eminent domain for private business—a *Kelo*-backlash type of petition like those appearing around the country—that was rejected by City Hall on a hypertechnicality. The rejected petition arrived in a FedEx box at the offices of Western Seafood, just down the block from the City Hall. The package was addressed to Wright III, even though he was not a circulator of the petition and had not submitted it to City Hall, and even though Western Seafood, as a corporation, could not be a circulator. The petition was rejected on the grounds that the affidavit form for the circulators was improper—even though the group had been careful to use exactly the same form they had used before on the Dissolve the EDC petition, which City Hall had accepted. Frustrated, Wright consulted election law specialists—more legal fees.

As they were deciding what to do next, an odd blip appeared on the political radar screen in Freeport. The city council passed a resolution approving the loan of $6 million from the city to the EDC, and then passed another resolution approving the loan from the EDC to Freeport Marina LP, Walker Royall's partnership. If this were a film, this would be the point where everyone in the room would do a fast-action double-take. Hadn't the council approved those loans years ago, when the city signed the development agreement in 2003?

It's a funny thing about those loan resolutions. You see, the city council had never gotten around to passing resolutions to approve the loan back in 2003 when it entered into the development agreement. Maybe they figured they would just wait until it was time to actually transfer the funds. Clearly, they never imagined so much opposition. Under the Freeport Code, citizens have thirty days from the time of a resolution to bring a petition and put it to a vote of the people in a referendum. The city took the position that the thirty-day clock on social protest started ticking the moment they signed the development agreement. Ah, yes. People are supposed to bring a referendum to repeal a loan *referred to* in (not actually attached to) a document you have to make a formal Open Records request just to get your hands on.

The Citizens for Freeport went out into the streets in June 2006 and circulated twin petitions to repeal the loan resolutions. They obtained the necessary number of signatures and gave them to the council. This put the council in a difficult position. Now the referenda were supposed to be put to a vote of the people. The whole damn marina could go down the tubes.

The city council was getting fed up with all this incessant democracy, so they brought a lawsuit to stop it. The city sued Western Seafood in state court, asking the court for a declaration that when the city council votes to loan millions of dollars to the economic development corporation and then in turn to a private developer, that is an administrative action, not a legislative one. Sure, an administrative decision, like hiring someone or putting up a traffic light or ordering paper clips—not something the people have a say in. "A bond issue requires a vote of the public, of your citizens, that's why it's two totally different things," Mayor Phillips said, explaining why he believed the city council should be able to approve the $6 million loan without citizen input.[6] Of course, the city was going to float a bond to pay for half of the marina loan, and the loan would be made to a borrower who was giving no guarantees, but why quibble?

This was turning into an old-fashioned Texas dogfight. The Citizens for Freeport were not intimidated, nor had they forgotten the rebuff of a few months ago when the "no eminent domain for private business" petition had been bounced because someone at City Hall didn't like the circulator affidavits. They hit the streets again in July, the height of mosquito season, once again with a petition to prohibit eminent domain for private use, but this time with the circulator affidavit amended so as to avoid even the slightest election-law peccadillo before City Hall.

In the never-ending Ping-Pong game, the city immediately amended the new lawsuit against Western Seafood, asking the state court to put the kibosh on the July petition, too. Basically, the argument was that the city just wouldn't be able to run the joint if the initiative passed; such an ordinance could cover "street signs" or who knows what. The city described it as amending a zoning ordinance. It's hard to figure how the court justified keeping Western Seafood in the case as the party defendant. Legally, a corporation can't bring a petition. The only justification for suing them, as the city put it (in legalese), was that Western Seafood was the instigator here.

The Gores said in for a dime, in for a dollar; they defended the case. Odd as the case was, the judge was determined to resolve it then and there with the cast of characters before him. Judge May ruled at the end of August 2006. He ruled against the city on the matter of the petitions to repeal the loan resolutions. When a city council sits down to vote on a loan of millions of dollars, he said, that is actually a legislative decision, not an administrative one. He ruled for the city, however, on the question of the petition against eminent domain, saying that state law did not permit amending a zoning ordinance by petition. The city appealed the entire decision.

Soon, a new petition was flying around town. The Citizens for Freeport brought out a petition to prohibit the city from loaning public funds to private businesses. It was accepted by the city clerk, creating an ordinance under the Freeport charter (although it was vulnerable to repeal by the city council). Then it was sent to the city council, which voted to *adopt* it. Now, why would a pro-marina council adopt an ordinance that prohibited the city from making the very sort of loan that was contemplated in the downtown development plans? Because if the council had voted against it, then the proposed ordinance, under law, would have to be put to a vote of the people—and that meant some intense public debate. Well, we can't have that, now can we? So the council voted in favor of an ordinance that was anathema to everything it had been working toward for the past several years. But that wasn't the end of the story. Not by a long shot.

Another petition was brought by the pro-marina lobby: members of planning commissions and other city-affiliated organizations, as well as some downtown businesses. The purpose of this petition was to repeal the ordinance that had just gone on the books, prohibiting the city from making loans to private parties. The city hosted a biker party (as in motorcycle riders), called Summertime Blues, and passed around the petition, which soon garnered 250 signatures.

According to a statement Wallace Shaw made to the local paper, the city council had the power to repeal the ordinance because it conflicted with the Texas Government Code. Cathy

Williams said, "They knew that they could vote at council to either adopt it or repeal it. It wasn't necessary for them to bring their petition. They were just proving they could do it." Reflecting on how she felt about it all, she said, "I wasn't destroyed by it. We'll go out again."

If it wasn't necessary for the city council to bring a counter-petition, then why gather hundreds of sweaty bikers to get their signatures?

Because the town had *lost it.* Stepped over the edge beyond clear thinking and reason and crossed the border into that land called spite. An economic development taking had driven them there. The question was: how were they going to get themselves out?

▪ ▪ ▪

During the spring of 2006, the Gores' appeal to the U.S. Court of Appeals for the Fifth Circuit was argued. Randy Kocurek was primed and ready. He had an intensive "moot court" session—a sort of practice drill—over the phone with Dana Berliner, a senior counsel from the Institute for Justice. Dana had represented the homeowners in the *Kelo* case and was well versed in eminent domain law. She had also been handling similar cases around the country, including the *Norwood* case in Ohio, which was shaping up to be the first post-*Kelo* case to be decided by a state supreme court. Just as importantly, Dana had been a law clerk to the chief judge of the Fifth Circuit. Law clerks work closely with their judges. They get to know how they think and what types of questions they are likely to ask. Dana pressed Randy to answer the most difficult questions that she thought the judge would put to him during the argument.

The Gores asked the Court of Appeals to do a number of things. They wanted the court to reverse Judge Kent and say that he was wrong about the Texas Development Corporation Act. In addition, an important thing had happened since Judge Kent ruled: in response to *Kelo,* the Texas legislature had enacted a statute to restrict eminent domain. The statute, having no grandfather clause, was ambiguous as to whether it covered pending cases. This was an important issue of state law, the Gores argued, and therefore it should be decided by the Texas Supreme Court. They asked that the question be sent to the state court. (Federal courts will sometimes do this when a new question of state law pops up.)

Meanwhile, another wrinkle of Texas law emerged. Like other states, Texas has urban renewal statutes among its municipalities. Under those statutes, municipalities in Texas can take homes and businesses if there is a finding of blight or a finding that the neighborhood is "deteriorat*ing*." The same kind of statute was being litigated in Ohio in the *Norwood* case.

On October 25, 2006, Wright III returned to Austin with his cousin Patrick to testify at a hearing by the Joint Interim Committee to Study the Power of Eminent Domain. Wright was there to offer up to them his family's experience as they pondered the wisdom of Texas Chapter 374, which allows blight takings. This part of Texas law, he told them, allows "virtually any private-to-private transfer of property that last year's Senate Bill 7 sought to repeal." He gave them a copy of a magazine article about his family, and asked them to think about the plight of people far poorer than the Gores. Listening to Wright that day and hearing the weariness in his voice, one couldn't help but wonder if he was beginning to run out of steam.

▪ ▪ ▪

"How much more do you think we can spend on frivolous, so-called beautification before we are taxed out of our own homes?" asked Cathy Williams during open mike at the city council meeting on October 2, 2006. "I'm just a retired housewife, but capable of understanding that if evaluations go up and you did not lower the tax rate, you definitely got an increase [in real estate taxes]. You took away the discount on early payment of water, now you want to increase the garbage rates. What can we expect next before things are changed? I am waiting for a marina tax."

Cathy Williams is a smart lady. People keeping a close eye on the marina project in Freeport know that the marina won't be paying a penny in taxes for a very long time. In fact, the development agreement leaves the tax abatement open-ended, not an unusual feature in municipal economic development takings. A similar provision existed in the deal between General Motors and Detroit in the infamous Poletown taking. The only limitation on tax abatements in such a situation becomes the applicable statutes;

that is, the abatement continues as long as the law allows. In Poletown, the weight of GM was enough to ram a special law through the Detroit City Council allowing for a twelve-year tax abatement. In the Freeport marina project, moreover, the developer won't be paying a penny in interest on its loan for five years or until the project "breaks even," whichever comes sooner.

As it stands now, Western Seafood pays over $77,000 in taxes every year, a large part of which goes directly to the city, and the remainder of which benefits the city indirectly through payments to the county and surrounding district. If Western Seafood goes out of business, it will probably mean the end of Trico, a shrimp boat operator and Western Seafood's major supplier. Scott Glick, who used to own 1,333 linear feet along the Old Brazos, settled with the city and moved his company, J&S Marine, to a much smaller location inland. (He needs only a small launch site to run his business). Owning a far smaller property now, he will pay much less in taxes to the city.

As Cathy Williams figured out, someone is going to have to replace all that tax revenue while the marina is being built and the abatement is in effect. What will tide the city over until those hotels and restaurants that the EDC keeps promising start banging down Freeport's door to get part of all that marina action? If indeed that ever happens. Freeport residents have seen other business ventures come and go. Downriver on the Old Brazos sits a rusting metal heap into which the city had ploughed tons of dough: the Gladny Ice Plant. The thought of ice being produced from this enormous tin box in the blazing Texas sun put me in mind of the Paul Theroux novel *Mosquito Coast,* in which a man takes a sudden notion to move his family to the jungles of Central America and bring ice to the natives, and slowly but surely goes completely berserk. Of course, a private citizen can do any damn thing he wants with his money. But when the government goes into business and starts condemning land, that's another story entirely. Judging from that giant-sized rusting tin, Freeport doesn't have much of a track record.

There were "heated repercussions" to what the city did on that petition to repeal the loan resolutions, said Cathy Williams. It was the last straw. It was the end of civility in council meetings. Wright III tangled with the mayor and was angrily told to take a seat. At first, he did so. But he was sick of being told to sit down by the mayor in a city where his father's business, Pappy's business, was being run of town. He jumped up again and stood at the lectern. "No," he said, "I will not be seated." Mayor Phillips motioned for Chief Pynes to remove him. Wright III told his cousin Patrick, "Film me!" Then he dropped his arms limply to his sides, "civil rights style," as he later called it. Chief Pynes came up behind him and rather gingerly grasped the back of his shirt collar and escorted him down the aisle, past all the spectators. Joaquin Damian stood near the door with his arms held out in front of him, wrists together.

"Take me too," he said to Chief Pynes.

Chief Pynes ignored him and led Wright III into the hallway, with the members of Citizens for Freeport filing out after him.

One by one, the avenues for redress were shutting down. It was over for Wright III in the city council. The petition situation, it seemed, was a dead end. It was up to the courts to speak.

And then they did.

■ ■ ■

Since 2004, the Gores had been trying to hold off the Texas condemnation process in state court, fearing disaster. But life is full of surprises. Their state court lawyer, an old-fashioned Texan straight shooter named Margaret Pollard, was arguing the same issue that had been argued in federal court, concerning the Texas Development Corporation Act. Basically, the argument was that a flaw in the Freeport EDC charter made it unlawful for the EDC to condemn land for tourism and recreation. Ms. Pollard found that she was getting a warm reception on this issue in state court. Judge Blackstock seemed to be concerned about it. The issue kept coming up in conferences. There were actually two different state court cases pending: one case for the 330 feet, and another—before Judge Holder—for the 100 feet owned by Western Shellfish. Judge Holder mentioned to the lawyers that he was aware of Judge Blackstock's concern about the Texas Development Corporation Act.

In the federal court, Judge Kent had not been very worried about this point. But in the state courts, judges were more familiar with the history of the statute. This law was no mere technicality. It had begun as a taxing statute. "It was supposed to help small cities bring industry in," said Margaret Pollard. Later on, larger cities figured out they could use it as a way to raise money for big projects like sports arenas, and the law was amended. But when the Freeport EDC was created in 1999, its charter contained the old language, from before the law was changed. With that type of language, Ms. Pollard explained, you could argue that unless the EDC were to amend its charter, it was not supposed to be taxing its citizens for this sort of tourism project.

The city made a motion for summary judgment on the 330 feet of Western Seafood land. To everyone's shock, Judge Blackstock ruled *against* the city in a one-sentence decision. He did not state his reasons.

That was it. Three years, $450,000 in legal fees. Six citizen petitions. Fifty or more council and EDC meetings. Thousands of hours of work. One sentence from Judge Blackstock and it was over.

Or was it? The city had a right to appeal. But appealing from a one-sentence decision in Texas is like walking through a minefield. By rendering such a cryptic decision, Judge Blackstock had handed the Gores a tremendous gift. In Texas, Ms. Pollard, said, the burden is on the appealing party to show why the decision is wrong. If no reason is given, then the appealing party has to address every reason "the judge must have based it on and why all of them are wrong." But that would be a risky move. After all, the EDC had already condemned Wanda Jones's property, threatened eminent domain against Scott Glick, and commenced a case against Dennis Henderson. By appealing, they risked creating a judicial record that the EDC didn't have the power under the Freeport charter to do any of those things in the first place.

And there was still a decision pending on the federal appeal.

■ ■ ■

On October 11, 2006, the U.S. Court of Appeals for the Fifth Circuit ruled on the Gores' appeal. In essence, they split the baby. The Court of Appeals considered the Gores' case in light of the *Kelo* decision, which had happened while their appeal was pending. The Gores argued that their case fell within the exception described by Justice Kennedy in his concurring opinion: that a higher level of judicial scrutiny should be applied where there is impermissible favoritism of a particular private party. The Fifth Circuit wrote that the facts in the Gores' case did not warrant a higher level of scrutiny. "[T]he Blaffer estate heirs own acres of property along the river where the marina is to be built, [and] the City's interest in their cooperation is logical."[7] However, the appeals court did send the case back to Judge Kent in the district court, in light of the new law regarding eminent domain that had been passed by the Texas legislature.

Suddenly everyone was in limbo. What was going to happen next? The city could appeal from Judge Blackstock's decision. The parties could keep fighting in front of Judge Kent. They could do one, or both. For a brief moment it seemed, blessedly, that they would do neither. A settlement hovered in the air; documents were faxed back and forth; people breathed a little easier; the dream of Freeport as a destination was so close Ron Bottoms could taste it.

Then one day Mayor Phillips went out to mow some tall grass on a tractor and had an accident of biblical proportions. And the brief peace in Freeport went to hell in a handcart.

EPILOGUE

Pappy Gore died on July 23, 2006, at his home in Lake Jackson. "One of the nurses came and told my grandmother that he just stopped breathing," said Wright III. The *Facts* ran a banner headline announcing that the founder of Western Seafood had died, and featured a story chronicling his many accomplishments as a businessman and civic leader. The boy who started life with two pairs of overalls and went on to build a business with the sweat of his back and his native intelligence, the lifelong prankster and fan of *Webster's Unabridged Dictionary,* was gone at the age of eighty-six. He died without a judgment.

If he had been able to hang on just a few months longer, he would have seen the city pull the biggest Roseanne Roseannadanna move of all time. After insisting for three years that all 330 feet—oh, excuse me, the city always said it was *only 300* feet—were desperately needed, that the marina could not be built without it; after subjecting the Gores to three years of untold stress, grief and fear, and nearly half a million dollars in legal fees; and after casting a dark shadow over the end of the otherwise miraculous life of Pappy Gore, the City of Freeport said, in essence, "Never mind."

The city announced it would build *around* the Gores. Not only that, it would build a *public* marina. And never mind that nasty $6 million loan that had everyone so riled up. Now who could possibly object to all this? For a brief, golden moment, the Gores and the city had what looked like a deal to settle the lawsuits. Things simmered down in Freeport—for a while.

The city had to do something because it found itself in a conundrum. Judge May ruled that, gee whiz, a decision to loan

$6 million of taxpayer money is a legislative act that the citizens of Freeport get to have a say in. The city council was faced with a choice: put the loan referenda to a vote of the people or appeal from Judge May's decision. A vote was risky; after all, the Dissolve the EDC ballot had lost by only twenty-one votes. And what about future million-dollar loans the council might want to make without citizen meddling? A precedent was at stake. Yet there was the risk that the marina contract could expire while the matter was appealed. The last time it had expired, the city council voted to renew the contract three months before its expiration date. The council took care of that bit of business nice and early because a fall election was looming—in which the marina was a major controversy. The council members had wanted to be sure to lock in the marina contract in case any of them lost their seats.

Now things were more complicated. The city had taken a beating in state court and Walker Royall had been kept waiting mighty long. It was time for some creative thinking.

The legal artillery was called in. There was a stroke of pure genius: the city would appeal Judge May's decision *and* build the marina—it would just take some tweaking. A new development agreement surfaced: another monster of legalese not to be easily understood by Freeport's lay public (assuming they could get hold it). But it contained a few gems worth noting. The city, having insisted on the wisdom of a private marina since 2002, would now build a public marina and bear the startup risks. Walker would only be involved in operating it. At least that's how things would begin.

The city had already played the eminent domain Monopoly game, moving everyone around, spending more than a million dollars in the process. It had condemned the land of Wanda Jones, started an eminent domain case and then settled with Dennis Henderson, and held the eminent domain cudgel over the head of Scott Glick. It moved Glick's business (J&S Marine) to the old Gladny Ice Plant property outside the guillotine gate, and moved Henderson's business (Trico) to the tail end of what used to be Glick's property. Moving Trico to that spot cost the city $300,000. Now the city can lease all that great waterfront land to Walker. Plus, of course, Walker keeps the Blaffer land. (Now he doesn't need to give the city a mortgage on this land.) The city can loan *itself* the money—that is, loan $6 million to its own economic development corporation—to build the marina. Under the new development agreement, the EDC will build the marina. So the EDC goes into the construction business! They already built some palm trees with pavers for $1.56 million, so building an entire marina with a dry-dock storage building for $6 million should be a snap.

Under the draft agreement, Walker's limited partnership, Freeport Marina LP, then operates the marina, paying a monthly fee to the city. According to Lee Cameron, Walker will run the marina as a "joint venture with Sun Resorts." It's a forty-year lease with an option to renew. It also contains an "early buy-out provision at an amortized price," said Lee. This means that all of the lease payments made by Walker and his partners will count toward the purchase price if they decide to buy it. The purchase option "can be exercised at any time within the forty years of the lease," Lee explained. Even as soon as one year after the marina opens.

So Walker may come to own the marina after all. Under the draft agreement that was being circulated, he could buy it for $6 million (minus the lease payments he's made)—no matter how much it ultimately costs the city to build. In press reports, the city has referred to the marina repeatedly as a $7 or $8 million project. Walker may buy it at the end of year one, or if he prefers, in year 3 or 10 or 32 . . . whenever. Let's say the marina is a fabulous success and is worth hundreds of millions of dollars; the deal doesn't change. Those who come to have rights in Walker's limited partnership in the future could still buy the marina for $6 million as late as 80 years from now if the option to renew were exercised. Walker also has another option, good for the first 36 months of the marina's operation, to buy the Glick riverfront property for $1,000 a linear foot, which is roughly what the city paid for it. This 1,333 linear feet of riverfront will be the heart of the marina. After 20 years of paying fees on the lease (ranging from $24,000 to $39,000 a month, all amortizable), Walker's partnership then pays only $100 a month in rent to the city for the next 20 to 60 years, as the case may be.

The EDC doesn't expect much public resistance to the new plan for a public marina. "I think we'll still have some opposition," says Lee Cameron. What occurred before was "little in number, but heavily financed. So it looks like a big operation but it's really not." The Citizens for Freeport are used to being regarded as so much dirt beneath Freeport's welcome mat. Yet the marina controversy made Freeport a different kind of place. Perhaps the biggest surprise in the three-year battle was the capacity of small-town grudges and loyalties to take on new dimensions when people who have known one another for a lifetime hold the power to take each other's property away and give it to someone else. Slights and jealousies, class differences, rumors and gossip that may have seemed petty in the past suddenly take on life-or-death proportions. An election becomes a consuming citywide melodrama. It remains to be seen whether Lee is right about resistance to the new plan.

Lee Cameron said the city lost $2 million because of the delay in building the marina. Asked what he based his $2 million estimate on, he replied that the "publicity" surrounding the new permit application with the Army Corps of Engineers had generated interest from "a combination of commercial and residential potential investors and they have bought property." He declined to name them. He would only say that the property they bought is vacant, undeveloped land. It must be a pretty big secret, since the president of the EDC, John Smith III, told the *Facts* in February 2007 that some hotels and restaurants were showing an interest and gathering information; there was "nothing concrete at this moment but they are definitely interested."[1] Of course, nothing was stopping the city from going ahead with its marina plans downriver from Western Seafood all these years—which is what the city eventually ended up doing.

Mary Stotler says some progress has been made. The sunken boats have been pulled from the river and the waterfront land under city control has been cleared. Nearly four years into the marina battle there is finally a long, skinny stretch of land along the Old Brazos that is flat and construction-ready. There is room for about 250 boat slips and a large dry dock. This is being accomplished without taking an inch from Western Seafood. Lee Cameron is optimistic about the marina; he says it will be up and running by the summer of 2007. (Perhaps those unidentified investors will have broken ground by then too.) Yet in April, the Army Corps of Engineers had not yet finished its work. The Gores intend to object to the new marina plan that the city is filing; they believe it poses an even worse navigation hazard than the old one. It's déjà vu all over again.

And what of the Gores, now that the city is going to build around them? In the fall of 2006, a banner headline ran in the local paper: *Gores and City Have a Deal!* When I spoke with the parties around that time, it seemed that they had a deal in principle. Margaret Pollard, the Gores' lawyer, thought they had a deal, as did Lee Cameron. It was to work like this: The city agreed to drop its appeal in the state court eminent domain case against the 330 feet and not to pursue the 100-feet state court case. The Gores would get to keep the entire 330 feet of land adjacent to Western Seafood. In return, the Gores agreed to drop their federal lawsuit and sell to the city the 100 linear feet they owned downriver (the Western Shellfish land). In addition, the Gores agreed that if they ever decided to sell their Western Seafood riverfront property, they would give the city a "right of first refusal" (first dibs, so to speak) on buying it. The city agreed to pay the Gores $368,000—the amount of money they had spent on legal fees relating to eminent domain. For legal reasons, this would be "papered" as payment for the 100 feet of Western Shellfish land. (The city's legal fees were mostly covered by municipal insurance. Its out-of-pocket legal fees came to about $50,000.) The city would not reimburse the Gores for legal fees relating to election law.

Under this deal, the Gores would have gone uncompensated for about $130,000 of legal fees (in addition to travel costs and time away from business), as well as going through the worst three years of their lives. All for the privilege of giving up their Western Shellfish land and keeping their Western Seafood land. Ironically, from the beginning they had been willing to negotiate with the city to give up the 100 feet and hand over *part* of the 330 feet. If everything hadn't erupted like Krakatoa, if the city had earned the Gores' trust, the city might have ended up with some of that land. Instead, *the city* got a rare Texas ruling saying they could *not* take land in eminent domain. But Wright III, reviewing how the proposed deal was structured, explained the onerous tax consequences to his father.

"That's when I asked the city if we could do the same deal but lease the land to them instead," said Wright III. "That would be the only way to get this moving quickly, and also to compensate us fairly. As it is, the $368,000 wasn't the full amount we had paid out in legal fees."

According to Wright III, this seemed to push the city over the edge. He says the Gores were given an ultimatum to accept the original deal—plus take down his website—on the eve of a key hearing in the 100-feet Western Shellfish case. He and his father refused. The city was fed up. Everyone went back to legal fisticuffs. To make matters worse, they soon found themselves fighting without parental supervision when Freeport's *über* father figure got into a bizarre accident.

■ ■ ■

Freeport is no better and no worse than any other town. Just under the surface in every town and city lies a complex web of relationships, often more complicated than anyone imagines. This became evident in Freeport in December 2006. "Jim Phillips' life flight was called," Angel Kant wrote to me in an email. "He got ran over by his own tractor." The seventy-three-year-old mayor stepped off his tractor while the motor was on and it ran over him—twice. He survived and spent a week in intensive care.

The town rallied. Phillips may have been a domineering mayor, but he was *their* domineering mayor. Angel Kant was outraged that the *Houston Chronicle* and the *Facts* weren't taking the accident seriously enough. "I called the *Chronicle* and I spoke to an editor up there and I said, 'our mayor down here has got ran over by a tractor! Are you gonna write about that? What's *wrong* with you?'" Clan Cameron, who had locked horns with Mayor Phillips since the day he took a seat on the city council, went to visit him at the rehabilitation facility where he had been transferred. The Gores sent flowers to him; Dell Phillips called to thank them. The old civility that people had known in Freeport was starting to return, at least on the surface.

Jim Phillips' "life flight" may have been called, but only his boarding pass was collected. He is a tough old bird. By the time spring rolled around, Phillips was back in City Hall most afternoons. Time was healing the mayor's wounds. It would take more to heal the deeper wounds in Freeport.

Mayor Phillips said the city council voted on the settlement deal and approved it and the offer is "still on the table." Wright III says there is no official record of such a vote and suggests that the discussion must have taken place in a private executive session. In any event, the Gores want a universal settlement that includes Walker's suits. Walker has not backed off from either of his lawsuits against the Gores and Western Seafood. The website is still up. The $36,000 lease case is headed to trial. Mayor Phillips says the city has no control over what Walker does. Trust between the parties is in short supply. And so the Gores and the city whip round and round like Dante's Paolo and Francesca in their eminent domain circle of hell, locked in their peculiar embrace of shared history, jealousy, righteousness, fraternity, ambition and the American lust for land.

■ ■ ■

When June 23 of 2006 rolled around, columnists and news reporters noted the one-year anniversary of the *Kelo* decision the way anniversaries of *Roe v. Wade* and other major Supreme Court cases are often noted. The post-*Kelo* phoenix rose again during the midterm elections of November 2006, when voters in nine states passed various kinds of *Kelo*-backlash measures. In Florida, Georgia, Louisiana, Michigan, Nevada, New Hampshire, North Dakota and South Carolina, voters approved constitutional amendments that forbid the use of eminent domain in which land is transferred from one private party to another private party for economic development purposes. (Nevadans will vote again in 2008 to reaffirm the amendment.) Oregon passed a statute reforming its eminent domain laws.

But the backlash was also taking a more aggressive turn in the referenda that became known as "*Kelo*-Plus." These were combination ballot measures intended to radically change longstanding zoning laws. The measures were wrapped in the language of eminent domain reform, described as eliminating "regulatory takings" as well as ending a pernicious form of eminent domain abuse. *Kelo*-Plus measures were part of what advocates described as a "property rights movement," which picked up considerable steam, with the post-*Kelo* momentum enabling activists to get traction for the unsexy subject of "regulatory takings."

A regulatory taking is when a city or state passes a zoning law that diminishes the value of property you own. Let's say you own some vacant land that you plan to farm or build on. Then someone spots a rare species of toad near your land, and the state passes new environmental rules that make development impossible. But the state refuses to compensate you even a single penny. Or your city passes ordinances on how you may or may not develop the land you own in town, but will not compensate you for the zoning restrictions they are imposing.

After *Kelo*, regulatory takings reform was suddenly being covered in national newspapers such as the *Wall Street Journal*. Howard Rich, a real estate investor and chairman of the libertarian Americans for Limited Government, was pouring an undisclosed amount of money into citizen-initiated ballot measures in multiple states around the country. The *Washington Times* reported that the "liberal Ballot Initiative Strategy Center—a critic of Mr. Rich—said this week the total spending by his affiliated groups on 2006 ballot measures exceeded $13.2 million."[2] In November 2006, *Kelo*-Plus measures were on the ballots in Arizona (Proposition 207), California (Proposition 90), Idaho (Proposition 2) and Washington (Proposition 933).

The warm, fuzzy feeling that had brought everyone together over *Kelo* was no longer evident when it came to the *Kelo*-Plus measures. Long ago, Rodgers and Hammerstein wondered what the world would be like if the farmer and the cowboy could be friends. For a brief political moment, they were friends in *Kelo*. Who had ever seen a case in which the Cato Institute, the NAACP, the Goldwater Institute, the American Farm Bureau Federation, the Southern Christian Leadership Conference and AARP were all on the same side? But the old, predictable political lines could be drawn again over regulatory takings: conservatives are for strengthened property rights and liberals are against them because they interfere with the environment and other priorities such as containing urban sprawl.

Meanwhile, the Ohio Supreme Court had given a big victory to the homeowners in *Norwood v. Horney*. Since this was the first time a state's highest court had considered economic development takings since *Kelo*, it would show which way the judicial winds were blowing. Those expecting a shocker were not disappointed.

In July 2006, a unanimous court ruled that economic development could not be used in that state as a stand-alone basis for a taking. A city would have to do more than say a neighborhood was "deteriorat*ing*" in order to take it under an urban renewal or economic development plan. As the court put it, "deteriorating" was a "standardless standard." But the court stopped there. It did not rule that economic development takings are impermissible under the Ohio Constitution.

The decision was immediately hailed in the conservative press as a necessary course correction after the abomination of *Kelo*. The *Weekly Standard* shot off a quick piece the next day breathlessly praising the decision as a "smashing victory for property owners."[3] The lawyers from the Institute for Justice, bone-weary after their stinging loss at the U.S. Supreme Court and after slugging this one out all the way to Ohio's top court, were ecstatic, as were their clients, an elderly couple named Carl and Joy Gamble along with Joe Horney, the man who had given that slab of granite in homage to his lawyers at the Institute for Justice.

It seems the only people in Ohio who thought the taking had been a good idea—other than the real estate developer, Rookwood Partners, Ltd., and the City of Norwood—were the sixty-eight families who had voluntarily settled with Rookwood, many of them for more than double the fair market value of their homes. Most of them agreed and were glad to get out of a neighborhood hemmed in by an interstate highway and commercial zoning. Norwood did not succumb to the ugly duckling syndrome, but made clear to the developer that homeowners were to be well compensated. In this regard, Norwood could serve as a reform paradigm.

While the case was ongoing, the Ohio legislature convened a task force on eminent domain, which issued its recommendations right after the *Norwood* decision came out. The task force recommended making it tougher to do eminent domain under a "blight" standard in Ohio—but not *too* tough. If the legislature adopts the report's majority draft, economic development takings can be done in neighborhoods that are only 50 percent blighted. In short, the overall effect of the *Norwood* decision and the task force was to train the eyes of cities and developers upon Ohio's poorest neighborhoods. Pick a neighborhood in which you can prove that half of it is blighted. The task force recommends that a blighted community may be taken and turned over to a "another private use . . . so long as the entity taking the property demonstrate[s] how the taking will clearly *benefit the community as a whole* more than the private entity to whom it is given." (Emphasis added.)[4] This kind of justification can be made whenever tax revenues and jobs are projected. It's the same old razzmatazz of economic development takings that states and municipalities have been riffing and bee-bopping to since the days of Poletown. Only now the vocabulary of public meetings and filings will be very carefully changed, since the task force also recommended that government revenues not be used as a "basis" for a finding of blight. "Ohio should go *on record* as forbidding the use of eminent domain *solely* for government revenue generation purposes." (Emphasis in the original.)[5] Ah, yes. *Go on record.* That should mean a lot to the poor people whose homes are snatched out from under them so a mall can be built.

What transpired in Ohio is an example of the *Kelo* backlash in full throttle. The Ohio Supreme Court made clear that it was aware the country was watching and waiting for its decision. This resulted in a cautious ruling that safeguarded middle-class and working-class neighborhoods from economic development takings, while leaving the poorest populations—those least likely to advocate for a fair deal—vulnerable to them. What of Riviera Beach, the largest taking that was pending at the time of *Kelo?* The *Kelo*-backlash wave and support from Governor Jeb Bush helped the residents oust their pro–eminent domain mayor and his council, killing the development deal. It remains to be seen whether Florida will stay a reform state or take the path of Utah and repeal its radical reform law.

Many of the *Kelo*-backlash statutes passed around the country have contained exceptions for blight. Time will tell what the consequences of these loopholes will be. We may see cities turning their lust for land upon the poorest neighborhoods again, in a twenty-first-century version of the urban renewal bulldozing of the past.

ACKNOWLEDGMENTS

There are many people who helped with this book. My sincere thanks to my "*Kelo*-watchers" who scanned the news and sent me clippings of developments around the country: Joseph Cooper, Donna Cornachio, Margaret Daisley, Gary Skoning and Elizabeth Ann Tursi. Many thanks to Tod Lindberg for publishing "How Eminent Domain Ran Amok" in *Policy Review* (2005) and to Rachel Abrams for her editorial help with it. *Bulldozed* grew out of that article and I very much appreciate the support of the Hoover Institution, which made it possible for me to attend the Supreme Court argument in the *Kelo* case. I am grateful to Kate Moran, an intrepid reporter formerly of the New London *Day,* for her generous help in understanding that city's politics. Thank you, Mario Rosado, for your kindness in digging up information about Chavez Ravine; it didn't make it into this book, but perhaps the next project!

A special thanks to Professor Richard Epstein for his friendship and encouragement. I am grateful to my agents Lynn Chu and Glen Hartley, to the team at Encounter Books and Carol Staswick, my editor. I extend my heartfelt thanks to the Gore family for letting me into their lives and spending many hours with me and patiently answering what must have been very tedious questions. I most especially thank them for the privilege of allowing me to meet and interview Wright Winston (Pappy) Gore Sr. when he was ailing. Finally, I thank my men, grown up and young: Tom, Henry and Joshua Main, for putting up with a distracted wife and mommy while this book got written.

NOTES

Chapter 1—The Fish House

[1] Gary Cartwright, *Galveston: A History of the Island* (New York: Atheneum, 1991), p. 249.

[2] Hugh Best, *Debrett's Texas Peerage* (New York: Coward-McCann Inc., 1983), p. 91.

[3] Ibid., p. 94.

[4] "Milestones in MFAH History," available at the website of the Museum of Fines Arts, Houston, at http://www.mfah.org/main.asp?target=info. See entry for 1947.

[5] Best, *Debrett's Texas Peerage,* p. 176.

[6] Ibid., p. 176.

[7] "Milestones in MFAH History," entries for 1952 and 1953.

[8] Best, *Debrett's Texas Peerage,* pp. 97–98.

[9] Richard Kay, "King Basil! Gong for Caribbean Barman Who Romanced Viscountess," *Daily Mail* (London), September 28, 2006, available at http://www.mailonsunday.co.uk/pages/live/articles/columnists/columnists.html?in_page_id+1772&in_article_id+350660&in_author_id+230.

[10] Michael Baker, "Freeport Puts up $6 million for Marina," *The Facts* (Brazoria County), August 27, 2003, p. 1.

Chapter 2—The Mystery Fax

[1] Kelly Hawes, "Opinions: Marina Gamble Might Well Pay Off," *The Facts* (Brazoria County), September 10, 2003.

[2] Ibid.

[3] *Western Seafood Company v. City of Freeport, Texas, and Freeport Economic Development Corporation,* No. CIV. A. G-03-811, U.S. District Court for the Southern District of Texas, Galveston Division, Request for Additional Time and Preliminary Comments

in Opposition to the Application, regarding Permit Application No. 23112, submitted by Randall A. Kocurek, dated September 11, 2003, and addressed to Chris Wrbas, attached as an exhibit to Motion for Preliminary Injunction, filed September 25, 2003, p. 5.

[4] Ibid. (Emphasis in original.)

[5] *Western Seafood Company v. City of Freeport,* No. CIV. A. G-03-811, City's Rule 12(b) Motion to Dismiss and Response to Motion for Preliminary Injunction, filed October 15, 2003.

[6] Dan Tarver, "Exclusive Interview with H. Walker Royall, General Partner—Freeport Waterfront Properties, LP," *Freeport Sentinel,* May 6, 2005, p. 1.

[7] Ibid.

[8] Ibid.

[9] Geoffrey Gagnon, "A Property Owner's Nightmare," *Best Life,* November 2006, p. 84.

Chapter 3—April Fools

[1] Jenna Colley, "Dallas Developers in Middle of Marina Fight: Eminent Domain Challenge Emanates from Freeport," *Dallas Business Journal,* June 23, 2006.

[2] *Western Seafood Company v. City of Freeport, Texas, and Freeport Economic Development Corporation,* No. CIV. A. G-03-811, U.S. District Court for the Southern District of Texas, Galveston Division, Order Granting Defendants' Motion for Summary Judgment, August 5, 2004, p. 1.

[3] *Western Seafood Company v. City of Freeport, Texas, and Freeport Economic Development Corporation,* No. CIV. A. G-04-242, U.S. District Court for the Southern District of Texas, Galveston Division, Deposition of Ron Bottoms, April 29, 2004, p. 8.

[4] *H. Walker Royall v. Wright W. Gore, Jr. et al.,* District Court of Brazoria County, Cause No. 29996, Plaintiff's Second Amended Petition, Exhibit D, Letter of Walter Herring dated April 8, 2004.

[5] Master Plan for the Downtown Study Core Area for the City of Freeport, Texas, submitted by Maritime Trust Company with Morris Architects, David Evans & Associates, Goldston Engineering Inc., CDS Research, October 2002, pp. 18–19 and passim.

[6] Michael Baker, "Freeport Says Fliers Intended as Scare," *The Facts* (Brazoria County), April 8, 2004.

[7] Available at http://www.freeport.tx.us/Marina_News.htm. (Emphasis added.)

[8] Baker, "Freeport Says Fliers Intended as Scare."

Chapter 4—On the River

[1] *Housing Authority of Dallas v. Higginbotham,* 135 Tex. 158, 165 (Tex. 1959).

[2] *Davis v. City of Lubbock,* 326 S.W. 2d 699 (Tex. 1959); and *Atwood v. Willacy County Navigation District,* 271 S.W. 2d 137 (Tex. Civ. App. 1954).

[3] *Western Seafood Company v. City of Freeport, Texas, and Freeport Economic Development Corporation,* No. CIV. A. G-04-242, U.S. District Court for the Southern District of Texas, Galveston Division, Transcript of Hearing before the Honorable Samuel B. Kent, April 13, 2004.

[4] *Western Seafood Company v. City of Freeport, Texas, and Freeport Economic Development Corporation,* No. CIV. A. G-03-811, U.S. District Court for the Southern District of Texas, Galveston Division, Order Granting Defendants' Motion for Summary Judgment, August 5, 2004, p. 10.

[5] Ibid., p. 14.

[6] Ibid., p. 15.

[7] Ibid., pp. 16–17.

[8] *H. Walker Royall v. Wright W. Gore, Jr., Dennis Henderson, Wright W. Gore, III, and Western Seafood Company,* Cause No. 29996, District Court of Brazoria County, Texas, 238th [*sic*] District, Plaintiff's Second Amended Complaint, p. 3.

[9] *Freeport Waterfront Properties LP v. Western Seafood Company,* Cause No. 29997, District Court of Brazoria County, 239th District. Oral Deposition of Wright W. Gore, Jr., May 17, 2005.

[10] Chunhua Zen Zheng, "Freeport Sets Regulations for On-Premise Signs," *Houston Chronicle,* September 28, 2004.

[11] Michael Baker, "Freeport, Publisher Spar over Ordinance," *The Facts* (Brazoria County), September 24, 2004.

[12] Ibid.

[13] Ibid.

[14] Ibid.

[15] Zheng, "Freeport Sets Regulations for On-Premise Signs."

[16] *City of Opportunity Newsletter 2004,* ed. Mary Lee Stotler, City of Freeport, published by Em-Print Company.

Chapter 5—Madison's Beef, Webster's Showdown

[1] Madison "was ahead of his time in arguing that the dominant danger in America came from a possibly overweening majority rather than from self-interested government agents," wrote Akil Amar. Madison managed to "slip the takings clause through"

by cleverly "bundl[ing]" it into what became the Fifth Amendment, which largely deals with criminal procedure. See Akil Amar, "The Bill of Rights as Constitution," *Yale Law Journal,* Centennial Issue, vol. 100, no. 5 (March 1991), p. 1159.

[2] Allan Nevins, *The American States During and After the Revolution* (New York: MacMillan, 1924), p. 268.

[3] Ibid., p. 507.

[4] Ibid., p. 268.

[5] Jackson Turner Main, *The Antifederalists: Critics of the Constitution, 1781–1788* (Chapel Hill: University of North Carolina Press, 1961), pp. 163–64.

[6] Robert Allen Rutland, *The Birth of the Bill of Rights* (Chapel Hill: University of North Carolina Press, 1955), p. 204, citing letter of Fisher Ames to Thomas Dwight, June 11, 1789, in *The Works of Fisher Ames,* ed. Seth Ames (Boston, 1854), vol. 1, pp. 52–53.

[7] William Michael Treanor, "The Origins and Original Significance of the Just Compensation Clause of the Fifth Amendment," *Yale Law Journal,* vol. 94, no. 3 (January 1985), pp. 694, 709.

[8] James Madison, "Notes in Preparation for Paper Money Speech," circa November 1786, in *The Papers of James Madison,* ed. William Hutchison (Chicago: University of Chicago Press, 1962), vol. 9, p. 158.

[9] Drew R. McCoy, *The Last of the Fathers: James Madison and the Republican Legacy* (Cambridge, U.K.: Cambridge University Press, 1989), p. 204.

[10] Ibid., p. 206.

[11] James W. Ely Jr., "That Due Satisfaction May Be Made: The Fifth Amendment and the Origins of the Compensation Principle," *American Journal of Legal History,* vol. 36, no. 1 (January 1992), p. 14 and nn. 69 and 70.

[12] Alexander Keyssar, *The Right to Vote: The Contested History of Democracy in the United States* (New York: Basic Books, 2000), pp. 15–21. See also "Table A.1, Suffrage Requirements: 1776–1790" and "Table A.2, Property and Taxpaying Requirements for Suffrage: 1790–1855."

[13] James Madison, "Notes on Suffrage," in *Letters and Other Writings of James Madison, 4th President of the United States* (New York: R. Worthington, 1884), vol. 4 (1829–1836), p. 22. According to this edition, Madison's "Notes on Suffrage," a collection of essays on voting, were written "at different periods after his retirement from public life." In the "Notes," Madison mentions his speeches

at the Constitutional Convention of 1787 and, referring to himself in the third person, comments that "These observations (in the speech of James Madison . . .) do not convey the speaker's more full and mature view of the subject, which is subjoined. He felt too much at the time the example of Virginia."

[14] Ibid., p. 23.

[15] Ibid., p. 24.

[16] Letter from James Madison to N. P. Trist, Montpellier, April 1827, in *Letters and Other Writings of James Madison,* vol. 3 (1816–1828), pp. 575–76. The letter concerns recent issues of the *Harmony Gazette* and Madison's opinion of columns written by Owen with respect to economic distress in Great Britain.

[17] *The Papers of Daniel Webster: Legal Papers,* vol. 3, *The Federal Practice,* Part II, ed. Andrew J. King (Hanover, N.H.: Published for Dartmouth College by the University Press of New England, 1989), p. 716.

[18] *The Oxford Companion to the Supreme Court of the United States,* ed. Kermit L. Hall, et al. (New York: Oxford University Press, 1992), p. 858.

[19] Ibid., p. 858.

[20] *Proprietors of the Charles River Bridge v. Proprietors of the Warren Bridge,* 36 U.S. 420, 506 (1837), argument of Senator John Davis of Massachusetts.

[21] See Robert V. Remini, *Daniel Webster: The Man and His Time* (W. W. Norton & Co., 1997), p. 458.

[22] Letter from D. W. to Jeremiah Mason, February 13, 1837, Washington, in *The Papers of Daniel Webster: Correspondence,* vol. 4 (1835–1839), ed. Charles Wiltse and Harold D. Moser (Hanover, N.H.: Published for Dartmouth College by the University Press of New England, 1980).

[23] *Proprietors of the Charles River Bridge v. Proprietors of the Warren Bridge,* 36 U.S. 420, 547 (1837).

[24] Letter from D. W. to Jeremiah Mason, February 13, 1837.

[25] See Remini, *Daniel Webster: The Man and His Time,* p. 461.

[26] Letter from D. W. to Franklin Haver, Friday, January 29 [1847], in *The Papers of Daniel Webster: Correspondence*, vol. 6 (1844–1849), ed. Charles Wiltse and Wendy B. Tilghman (Hanover, N.H.: Published for Dartmouth College by the University Press of New England, 1984), p. 206.

[27] Letter of D. W. to Fletcher Webster, Washington, February 7, 1847, in *The Papers of Daniel Webster: Legal Papers,* vol. 3, *The Federal Practice,* Part II, p. 709.

[28] *West River Bridge Co. v. Dix,* 47 U.S. 507, 510, 513 (1848).
[29] *West River Bridge Co. v. Dix,* 47 U.S. 507, 520 (1848)
[30] "U.S. Supreme Court," *Weekly Eagle,* vol. 1, no. 45, p. 2 (published as the *Semi-Weekly Eagle,* January 14, 1848).
[31] *West River Bridge Co. v. Dix,* 47 U.S. 507, 521 (1848), brief of Mr. Webster and Mr. Collmer, for the plaintiffs.

Chapter 6: Blight, Beauty, Bounty

[1] Henry J. Munneke, "Eminent Domain: Lessons from the Past," ORER Letter, Spring 1991 (Published by the Office of Real Estate Research at the University of Illinois at Urbana-Champaign); available at www. business.uiuc.edu/orer.V5-2-1.pdf.
[2] Ibid.
[3] *Scudder v. Trenton Del. Falls Co.,* 1 N.J. Eq. 694 (1832).
[4] Harry N. Schieber, "Property Law, Expropriation, and Resource Allocation by Government: The United States, 1789–1910," *Journal of Economic History,* vol. 33, no. 1 (March 1973), p. 240.
[5] Ibid., p. 241.
[6] "State Constitutional Limitations on the Power of Eminent Domain," *Harvard Law Review,* vol. 77, no. 4 (February 1964), p. 717.
[7] A. James Heins, *Constitutional Restrictions against State Debt* (Madison: University of Wisconsin Press, 1963), p. vi.
[8] Ibid., pp. vi, 16 and 19.
[9] Benjamin Ginsberg, "Berman v. Parker: Congress, the Court, and the Public Purpose," *Polity,* vol. 4, no. 1 (Autumn 1971), p. 53.
[10] Ibid.
[11] Ibid., p. 55.
[12] Ibid., p. 56.
[13] President's Advisory Committee on Government Housing and Programs, Albert M. Cole, Chairman, "Recommendations on Government Housing Policies and Programs," Report of the Subcommittee on Urban Redevelopment, Rehabilitation and Conservation (Washington: U.S. Government Printing Office, December 1953). Emphasis (capitalization) in the original.
[14] Martin Anderson, *The Federal Bulldozer: A Critical Analysis of Urban Renewal 1949–1962* (Cambridge, Mass.: MIT Press, 1964).
[15] See also Ginsberg, "Berman v. Parker, Congress, the Court, and the Public Purpose," p. 79. *Berman* became "the crucial legal precedent in the use of eminent domain" in federal redevelopment programs.

[16] Charlotte Allen, "A Wreck of a Plan: Look at How Renewal Ruined SW," *Washingtonpost.com,* July 17, 2005, p. B01.

[17] *Berman v. Parker,* 348 U.S. 26, 31 (1954).

[18] Jon C. Teaford, "Urban Renewal and Its Aftermath," *Housing Policy Debate,* vol. 11, no. 2, Fannie Mae Foundation, 2000. See www.fanniemae.org/programs.

[19] See Anderson, *The Federal Bulldozer,* p. 64; also Raúl Homero Villa, "Ghosts in the Growth Machine: Critical Spatial Consciousness in Los Angeles Chicano Writing," *Social Text,* vol. 17, no. 1 (Spring 1999), p. 120.

[20] Though *Berman* started out under the 1945 Redevelopment Act, by the time the Planning Commission got rolling, the project was eligible for and received funding under the Federal Housing Act of 1949. See Ginsberg, "Berman v. Parker: Congress, the Court, and the Public Purpose," p. 57.

[21] Ibid., pp. 65–66.

[22] Jane Jacobs, Brief submitted in *Kelo v. City of New London,* Supreme Court of the United States, No. 04-108, December 2004, p. 12, citing to Howard Gillette Jr., *Between Justice and Beauty: Race, Planning, and the Failure of Urban Policy in Washington, D.C.* (1995), pp. 163–64. As *amici curiae* in *Kelo,* the NAACP argued that eminent domain, through urban renewal projects, often was used as a tool for the strategic removal of minority communities. NAACP, Brief submitted in *Kelo,* p. 8. See also Wilbur C. Rich, *Coleman Young and Detroit Politics: From Social Activist to Power Broker* (Detroit: Wayne State University Press, 1989), p. 191.

[23] *Berman v. Parker,* 348 U.S. 26, 33 (1954).

[24] According to Jane Jacobs, 60 percent of all families displaced by urban renewal condemnations between 1949 and 1963 were nonwhite. See Jacobs, Brief submitted in *Kelo,* pp. 11–12, citing to Bernard J. Frieden and Lynne B. Sagalyn, *Downtown Inc.: How America Rebuilds Cities* (Cambridge, Mass.: MIT Press, 1989); Anderson, *The Federal Bulldozer;* and Wendell E. Pritchett, "The 'Public Menace' of Blight: Urban Renewal and the Private Uses of Eminent Domain," *Yale Law & Policy Review,* vol. 21, no. 1 (2003). See also NAACP Brief submitted in *Kelo,* p. 7.

[25] Teaford, "Urban Renewal and Its Aftermath," *Housing Policy Debate,* vol. 11, no. 2, Fannie Mae Foundation, 2000, p. 459.

[26] Ibid., p. 460.

[27] Ibid., citing to Frieden and Sagalyn, *Downtown, Inc.: How America Rebuilds Cities.*

[28] Ibid., p. 460.

[29] Estimates differ as to the number of residents and business owners displaced by the massive condemnation of the Poletown neighborhood. Jane Jacobs estimated the number at 4,200 people. See Jacobs, Brief submitted in *Kelo.*

[30] Rich, *Coleman Young and Detroit Politics,* p. 72.

[31] Ibid., p. 182.

[32] David Fasenfast, "Community Politics and Urban Redevelopment: Poletown, Detroit, and General Motors," *Urban Affairs Quarterly,* vol. 22, no. 1 (September 1986), p. 114.

[33] Rich, *Coleman Young and Detroit Politics,* p. 191.

[34] *Poletown Neighborhood Council v. Detroit,* 410 Mich. 616, 655 (1981).

[35] Samuel R. Staley and John P. Blair, *Eminent Domain, Private Property, and Redevelopment: An Economic Development Analysis,* Reason Foundation Policy Study 331 (February 2005), p. 2.

[36] John E. Mogk, "Restricting Condemnation Power Overturns Precedent, Empowers Speculators and Hurts Detroit," *Detroit News,* August 8, 2004.

Chapter 7—*Kelo*

[1] Kate Moran, "A Question of Leadership: New London Debates How It Does Business," *The Day* (New London), October 17, 2004.

[2] *Susette Kelo et al., Petitioners, v. City of New London, Connecticut, et al.,* Supreme Court of the United States, No. 04108, Transcript of Oral Argument, Tuesday, February 22, 2005, p. 43.

[3] *Kelo v. City of New London,* 545 U.S. 469, 475 (June 23, 2005) (Stevens, J.).

[4] Terri Cullen, "What's 'Just' in Cases of Eminent Domain," Wall Street Journal Guide to Property, WSJ.com: RealEstateJournal.com, July 1, 2005.

[5] "NLJ Roundtable: Life after Poletown: What Is the Future of Takings in America?" *National Law Journal,* December 6, 2004, p. 12.

[6] *Kelo v. City of New London,* 545 U.S. 469, 473 (June 23, 2005) (Stevens, J.).

[7] "Eminent Domain Chronology," *The Day* (New London), Region News, July 1, 2006.

[8] Kate Moran, "With Vacant Lots and Cash Needs, NLDC Reaches a Crucial Juncture," *The Day* (New London), January 18, 2004.

[9] Moran, "A Question of Leadership."

[10] Kate Moran, "New London Councilors Balk at NLDC Funding Request," *The Day* (New London), July 7, 2003.

[11] "Eminent Domain Chronology," *The Day.*

[12] Kate Moran, "NLDC Head Chastises City Officials for a 'Lack of Vision,'" *The Day* (New London), April 30, 2004.

[13] Ibid.

[14] Moran, "New London Councilors Balk at NLDC Funding Request:"

[15] *Hawaii Housing Authority v. Midkiff,* 467 U.S. 229 (1984).

[16] Kathleen M. Sullivan, "The Supreme Court, 1991–Forward: The Justices of Rules and Standards," *Harvard Law Review* 106 (1992), pp. 22–123.

[17] Ibid.

[18] *Kelo v. City of New London,* 545 U.S. 469, 489 (2005), Stevens majority opinion at p. 19.

[19] *Kelo v. City of New London,* 545 U.S. 469, 503 (2005), O'Connor dissent at p. 10.

[20] *Kelo v. City of New London,* 545 U.S. 469, 505 (2005), O'Connor dissent at pp. 12–13.

Chapter 8—The *Kelo* Backlash

[1] Thayer Evans, "Freeport Moves to Seize 3 Properties," *Houston Chronicle,* June 23, 2005.

[2] Jeff Murrah, Letter to the Editor, "Freeport Taking Advantage of Private-Property Owners," *The Facts* (Brazoria County), June 30, 2005.

[3] William R. Levesque, "A Shell of Its Former Self," *St. Petersburg Times, Online,* June 26, 2006, available at http://www.sptimes.com/2006/ 06/26/Business/A_shell_of_its_former.shtml.

[4] Ibid. There are shrimpers who suspect that some countries are getting around the tariff altogether by shipping their shrimp through countries that are not subject to it.

[5] Adam Karlin, "Property Seizure Backlash," *Christian Science Monitor,* www.csmonitor.com, July 6, 2005. See also, Julia Vitullo-Martin, "Eminent Domain: The Good, the Bad, and the Ugly," Center for Rethinking Development, Manhattan Institute, May 2006, www.manhattan-institute.org (citing MSNBC poll).

[6] House Resolution 340, 109th Congress, 1st Session, June 24, 2005.

[7] "Eminent Mistake," Editorial, *St. Petersburg Times,* June 24, 2005, p. A16.

[8] Robert J. Caldwell, "Property Wrongs: A Supreme Blunder," *San Diego Union Tribune,* July 3, 2005, p. G1.

[9] Daniel Weintraub, "Court: OK to Take from the Poor, Give to the Rich," *Sacramento Bee,* June 28, 2005, p. B7.

[10] Carrie Johnson, "Rush Is On to Calm Homeowners," *St. Petersburg Times,* July 7, 2005, p. A1.

[11] T. R. Fehrenbach, "High Court Rules on the Side of State Socialism," *San Antonio Express-News,* July 17, 2005, p. H3.

[12] Mike Salinero, "Court Expands Power to Seize Land," *Tampa Tribune,* June 24, 2005, p. 1.

[13] Patrick McIlheran, "When 'Public Purpose' Means You Don't Count," *Milwaukee Journal Sentinel,* July 17, 2005, p. 4.

[14] Barbara O'Brien, "Neighborhood Shudders at Eminent Domain's Reach," *Buffalo News,* July 1, 2005, p. A1.

[15] Rev. J. David Trawick, "High Court's Property Ruling Should Spur Christians to Action," *San Antonio Express-News,* July 2, 2005, p. B7.

[16] Abdon M. Pallasch, David Roeder, Eric Herman, "Court Shows Homeowners Door: Development Trumps Property Rights," *Chicago Sun-Times,* June 24, 2004, p. 65.

[17] Avi Salzman, Laura Mansnerus, "For Homeowners, Frustration and Anger at Ruling," *New York Times,* June 24, 2005, p. A20.

[18] "Eminent Domain Ruling Has Dire Implications," Editorial & Comment, *Columbus Dispatch,* July 3, 2005, p. D4.

[19] Carrie Johnson, "Official Power to Seize Land Expands," *St. Petersburg Times,* June 24, 2005, p. A1.

[20] George Will, "The U.S. Supreme Court Ruling Drains the Phrase 'Public Use' of Its Clearly Intended Function," *Chicago Sun-Times,* June 24, 2005, p. 51.

[21] Howard Troxler, "High Court Takes Fifth, Proceeds to Ruin It," *St. Petersburg Times,* June 28, 2005, p. B1.

[22] Townsend A. "Van" Van Fleet, "Supreme Court Is All Wrong About...," *Washington Post,* June 30, 2005, p. T2.

[23] Bruce C. Kaufman, "Taking of Land Might Shock Madison," *Kentucky Post,* July 18, 2005.

[24] John Hart and Gary Hart, "Life, Liberty and the Pursuit of Your Land," *Denver Post,* July 10, 2005, Perspective, p. E4.

[25] Kenneth R. Harney, "Eminent Domain Ruling Has Strong Response," *Washington Post,* July 23, 2005, p. F1.

[26] Carolyn Lochhead, "Foes in Congress Unite in Defense of Property," *San Francisco Chronicle,* July 1, 2005, p. A1.

[27] Tresa Baldas, "States Ride Post-'Kelo' Wave of Legislation," *National Law Journal,* vol. 27, no. 47 (August 1, 2005), p. 1.

[28] "Don't *Kelo* My House," *Wall Street Journal,* February, 28, 2006, Review & Outlook, p. A16.

29 Timothy Sandefur, "The Pain of Eminent Domain," Cato Institute, June 8, 2006, www.cato.org/pub_display.php?pub_id=6420.

30 Harney, "Eminent Domain Ruling Has Strong Response."

31 David W. Chen, "Candidates in New Jersey Agree on Eminent Domain," *New York Times,* July 15, 2005, p. B7.

32 Ibid.

33 Ibid.

34 Robert A. George, "Eminently Odd," *New York Post,* August 30, 2005, p. 29.

35 Mike Ward, "Eminent Domain Bill Headed to Perry," *Austin American-Statesman,* August 17, 2005.

36 "Reforming the Use of Eminent Domain for Private Redevelopment in New Jersey," Department of the Public Advocate, May 18, 2006, pp. 7 and 3.

37 "Eminent Domain Chronology," *The Day* (New London), Region News, July 1, 2006.

Chapter 9—Democracy, Freeport Style

1 Lucretia Fernandez, "Gores Take Marina Fight Door to Door," *The Facts* (Brazoria County), June 25, 2005.

2 Lucretia Fernandez, "Petitioners Adding to Fears, City Says," *The Facts,* July 3, 2005.

3 Ibid.

4 Zen T. C. Zheng, "Freeport Marina Project Draws Mixed Reactions," *Houston Chronicle,* May 4, 2005.

5 Letter from Julian W. Taylor III to Ms. Katherine Minter Cary, December 12, 2006, copied to Carla T. Main.

6 S. N. "Deke" Deacon, Letter to the Editor, "City Should Be Smart about Backing New Business," *The Facts,* June 30, 2005.

7 Pamela Starnes, Letter to the Editor, "Organization Created Scandal in Freeport," *The Facts,* April 29, 2004.

8 Jen Sansbury, "Thieves Steal from Officials," *The Facts,* November 24, 2005.

9 It is unclear whether the anti-dissolution advertisement in the *Sentinel* appeared in the same issue that the flier was stuffed into. The advertisement ran in an October 2005 issue, either midway or late in the month, judging by ads that appear near it. A source familiar with the incident stated that the distribution of the flier-stuffed *Sentinel* occurred in late October, and a story about it appeared on the front page of the *Sentinel* during the first week of November 2005.

[10] "Minority Vote Dilution: An Overview," in *Minority Vote Dilution,* ed. Chandler Davidson, under the auspices of the Joint Center for Political Studies (Washington, D.C.: Howard University Press, 1989), p. 3.

[11] Letter to the Citizens of Freeport, dated November 11, 2005, from James W. Phillips, John Smith III, Jim Saccomano, Norma Moreno Garcia, Jacque Cundieff, Ronald Theriot, Hank Lippold, Carlos Martinez and Louie Jones.

Chapter 10—Misery Loves Company

[1] For example, Donald L. Boudreaux, "Recalling Kelo: 'Progressives' Are Regressive," *Investor's Business Daily,* June 20, 2006.

[2] Barbara Arneil, *John Locke and America: The Defence of English Colonialism* (Oxford, U.K.: Clarendon Press, 1996), p. 118.

[3] John Locke, *Two Treatises of Government,* A Critical Edition with an Introduction and Notes by Peter Laslett (Cambridge, U.K.: Cambridge University Press, 1960, repr. 1963), *The Second Treatise,* ch. 2, "Of the State of Nature," § 4, p. 309.

[4] Ibid., ch. 5, "Of Property," § 27, pp. 328–29.

[5] Ibid., ch. 5, "Of Property," § 49, p. 343. (Emphasis in the original.)

[6] Although this "General Preface" is unsigned (like all of Locke's writing), it has generally been attributed to Locke with a fair degree of certainty. In it, he reviews hundreds of travel memoirs and adventure books that had been published in English, Latin, French and Spanish. His essay includes commentary on books about dozens of exotic lands such as China, Peru, Arabia, Persia, Jerusalem, Siam, Mexico, Iceland, Africa, Egypt and Japan. But time and again Locke returns to explorations of America, its cultures and its geography. John Locke, "The Catalog and Character of Most Books of Travel," General Preface to *A Collection of Voyages and Travels: some now first printed from original manuscripts, others now first published in English: in six volumes: with a general preface, giving an account of the progress of navigation, from its first beginning: illustrated with a great number of useful maps and cuts, curiously engraved,* compiled by Awnsham and John Churchill (London: Printed by assignment from Messrs Churchill for John Walthoe, 1732) (bound in 12 volumes), Lenox Collection of the New York Public Library.

[7] Herman Lebovics, "The Uses of America in Locke's Second Treatise of Government," *Journal of the History of Ideas,* vol. 47, no. 4 (October–December 1986), p. 576.

[8] *See* The First Charter Granted by King Charles II to the Lords Proprietors of Carolina, London: Printed, and are to be sold by Richard Parker, at the Unicorn under the Piazza Exchange (printed 1704). The language of the Carolina Charter of 1662 is in the form of a deed, describing the Carolina Territory by metes and bounds and its northern (Virginian) and southern (Floridian) borders, made for the purpose "to transport and make an ample colony." (In the collection of the New York Public Library.)

[9] Lebovics, "The Uses of America in Locke's Second Treatise of Government," pp. 574–75.

[10] Locke, *The Second Treatise,* ch. 5, "Of Property," § 30, p. 331.

[11] Ibid., ch. 5, "Of Property," § 37, p. 336. "[H]e who appropriates land to himself by his labour, does not lessen but increase the common stock of mankind. For the provisions serving to the support of humane life, produced by one acre of inclosed land, are . . . ten times more, than those which are yielded by an acre of land, of an equal richnesse, lyeing wast in common."

[12] Barbara Arneil, *John Locke and America: The Defence of English Colonialism* (Oxford: Clarendon Press, 1996), pp. 68–69.

[13] Ritu Kalra, "Property Rights and Wrongs," *Wharton Alumni Magazine,* Fall 2005, p. 25.

[14] *City of Norwood v. Horney et al.,* Court of Appeals, First Appellate District of Ohio, Hamilton County, Ohio, Decision of Judge Mark P. Painter.

[15] Jim Herron Zamora, "City Forces out 2 Downtown Businesses," *San Francisco Chronicle,* July 2, 2005.

Chapter 11—Tearing the Town in Two

[1] Bernard H. Ross and Myron A. Levine, *Urban Politics: Power in Metropolitan America,* 7th ed. (Belmont, Calif.: Thomson Wadsworth, 2006), p. 147.

[2] Nancy Sarnoff, "Freeport Shakes Shadow of Dow: Faded Image Leads Town to Launch Multiple Projects," *Houston Business Journal,* February 24, 2003, www.houston.bizjournals.com.

[3] Ibid.

[4] Michael Baker, "Marina Center of Freeport Election," *The Facts* (Brazoria County), April 21, 2004.

[5] Velda Hunter, "Freeport Wants to Rebuild Levee for Marina," *The Facts,* November 21, 2006.

[6] Chris Robinson, "Petitions Call for Marina Loan Vote," *The Facts,* July 5, 2006.

[7] *Western Seafood Company, Plaintiff-Appellant, v. United States, et al., Defendants, and City of Freeport, Texas, and Freeport Economic Development Corporation, Defendants-Appellees,* U.S. Court of Appeals for the Fifth Circuit, No. 04-41196, October 11, 2006.

Epilogue

[1] Terry Hagerty, "City, Businesses See Potential Downtown," *The Facts* (Brazoria County), February 5, 2007.

[2] Associated Press, "Libertarian Bankrolls Many Ballot Measures," *Washington Times,* October 27, 2006, www.washingtontimes.com.

[3] Duncan Currie, "When Eminent Domain Loses: The Ohio Supreme Court Strikes a Major Blow for Property Rights," *Weekly Standard,* July 27, 2006.

[4] Final Report of the Task Force to Study Eminent Domain, August 1, 2006, submitted pursuant to SB 167, 126th Ohio General Assembly. See p. 13, Farmland, Majority Task Force Recommendation, and p. 11, Blighted Parcels, Majority Task Force Recommendation.

[5] Ibid. See p. 11, Use of Eminent Domain Solely for Revenue Generation Purposes, Majority Task Force Recommendation.

INDEX